chicano revolt in a texas town

chicano revolt
in a texas town

john staples shockley

UNIVERSITY   OF   NOTRE   DAME   PRESS
NOTRE DAME   LONDON

Library of Congress Cataloging in Publication Data

Shockley, John Staples, 1944-
  Chicano revolt in a Texas town.

  Bibliography: p.
  1. Crystal City, Tex.—Politics and government.
  2. Mexican Americans—Crystal City, Tex. I. Title.
F394.C83S56 1974   320.9'764'43706   73-11565
ISBN 0-268-00502-8
ISBN 0-268-00500-1 (pbk.)

The University of Notre Dame Press is grateful to the Ford Foundation for
funds received through the U.S.-Mexico Border Studies Project at the
University of Notre Dame toward the manufacture of this book. The
opinions expressed in the book do not necessarily represent the views of
the Ford Foundation.

Manufactured in the United States of America

contents

preface

On two occasions, in 1963 and again in 1969, the dusty South Texas town of Crystal City made the headlines. Both times Mexican Americans of the community gained control of the local government, ousting Anglos from their rule. Why did these revolts occur? How were they carried out? Why did the first revolt fail? Does the second seem more permanent? These were questions I had in mind in doing the research for this book, and this is basically what this book is about.

The primary research was done during the fall and winter of 1970-1971 in Texas. Although headquartered in Austin, I made three trips to Crystal City—in November and December of 1970, and in February of 1971. Altogether I interviewed and sometimes reinterviewed around three dozen residents.[1] In between visits to Crystal City I interviewed people outside the town who had at one time or another been connected with events there. These interviews took me to Dallas, San Antonio, Denton, College Station, Fort Worth, Georgetown, Blanco, as well as to Austin. These people outside Crystal City, who were often ex-residents, were at times invaluable for providing me with facts and with contacts. In some ways it seemed easier for them to discuss events in Crystal City since they were no longer in the community. At the same time I was able to locate several students who had at one time or another done work on Crystal City, and all of them proved to be helpful.[2] Mike Miller, a student in rural sociology at Texas A & M University who was writing his master's thesis on Crystal City, proved particularly helpful.

Conducting research in a situation of conflict, polarization, and great fluidity is, however, difficult. I made efforts to talk to as many people as possible, to maintain neutrality, and to be as accurate as possible with facts, but these efforts were only partially successful. My effort to write a comprehensive and balanced treatment of events in the community was hindered by many factors, including the fact that four of the most prominent and knowledgeable Anglos in the community refused to see me at all. I also found myself reluctant to ask people who were kind enough to see me certain questions which I felt would be extremely painful for them to answer, or which could very easily be interpreted as "unfair" or "loaded" questions. Although careful reading of local newspapers over the last fifteen years, examination of other state papers, and a search for all written accounts on the subject partially overcame this problem, the information I was able to obtain about the political history and conflict in the community and the recent changes has still been slanted in a number of ways.

My attempt to maintain neutrality in the community unquestionably limited the kind of scholarly activity I could engage in. And I have often wondered how my research would have been different had I been a participant observer making no attempt to be neutral. Different it certainly would have been, because I would then have been able to do things and observe things which were not possible without aligning myself with one side or another. In fact, in writing this work I have felt increasingly that full "objectivity" and full "impartiality" are impossible to achieve. Not only have my interests directed my questions (and thus my data) into certain areas; I have also been amazed at how the order and juxtaposition of certain well-known and indisputable facts can make these facts appear very different.

Conducting the study by myself meant further that I was severely constrained in the type of methods I could employ. I did not engage in random sampling, nor did I use structured questionnaires. Neither did I try to develop a sophisticated technique for determining which particular individuals were most "powerful" in the community. My concern was more basic. It was to try to find out what had happened in the community, what had changed and what had not changed, how people felt about this, and then from all this to try to determine tentatively why these events had taken place.

All this has meant that I have at times had to generalize about groups of people in ways that are both frustrating and perhaps misleading. It has meant that I have often had to protect the identity and sources of my statements. But given my resources and the obvious tensions in the community, I did not know how to overcome these problems. In addition to these serious limitations upon the study, I should also mention that space limitations and ethical considerations have required me to leave out some material I might have included. And I have also been unable to obtain some important information that I sought.

All these limitations on my attempt to do a serious, scholarly study of the community have increased my eagerness to have others—both scholars and local people, Anglos and Mexicans— also write about the community. There is a wealth of facts and of experiences, of anguish and of happiness, relating to the changes and the attempted changes. Those people who have lived through it can write about it in ways no one else can. Thus I hope that all sides will one day write of their experiences.

Through my attempt at explaining events in Crystal City, I also became interested in the general area of South Texas. Although I did no work on other communities in this area, many of the factors which have made Crystal City so explosive are present, in different proportions, in these other communities. How these towns have been able to avoid, or suppress, political catharsis is complementary to the study of Crystal City. The impact of Crystal City on the region has been and will continue to be profound, but how these other communities have and will react to these possible changes has yet to be studied. Nevertheless this study may give us a better comprehension of the Chicano movement, of race relations, and of conflict and political change in general. Crystal City is clearly unique, but through the rage and struggle that has occurred in this community in the last decade, we may find certain clues to the premises of American government. We may also discover a part of the reality of power and resources in America. Those elsewhere who are attempting a basic reordering of the role of government toward greater concern for people at the bottom may be encountering similar problems that will give us a basis for comparison. These other communities and struggles may all have something in common with Crystal City, even if the mesquite, the roadrunners, and La Raza are missing. Thus my work, as it relates to Crystal City, to the Chicano movement, and to more basic questions of political change in America, is clearly not meant to be definitive. It is meant to stimulate others to look at the things I have tried to examine.

Because I think that the upheavals in Crystal City cannot be understood without attention to the historical processes which have shaped and constrained the people of the community— both Mexican and Anglo—I have tried to devote part of the study to a historical examination of the area. The chapters throughout are thus organized chronologically rather than by subject matter. This has at times led to a certain awkwardness in presentation, but where changes of content within the chapters have been either major or abrupt, I have tried to signal this by use of subheadings. Since this is a case study which rests to a large extent upon descriptive analysis, I have tried to wait until the last chapter to engage in systematic discussion of the implications of the study for the future of the Chicano movement and the practice of American politics generally. Certain theoretical concepts as they relate to Crystal City—particularly those dealing with democratic theory and pluralism, colonialism, and what seems to be the reciprocal relationship of political events to citizen attitudes—I hope to deal with in forthcoming articles.

acknowledgments

This study would have been impossible without the help of a number of people. As an outsider coming into a community to ask questions about subjects that were often controversial or painful, I was very much dependent upon the cooperation and trust of people in the community on all sides. To all those I interviewed, both in Crystal City and around the state, I express my deep gratitude. Most of their names appear in the bibliography at the end of the work.

Several of these people went way beyond the normal limits of help, and to these especially am I grateful. Because the subject matter of this work is controversial and because these people represent various sides in the political conflict there, I think it best not to list here these people to whom I am most indebted. But they may rest assured that I have not forgotten their lives, their work, and their help.

To students Carl Earl-Leufvin, Rick Appleton, and John Ziller of the University of Texas and Mike Miller of Texas A & M University, I owe thanks for their willingness to share with me papers and research they had done on Crystal City. And to my old friend Roger Speegle I express my thanks for his putting me in touch with several people who were able to assist me.

Professors Robert Booth Fowler, Murray Edelman, Joel

xi

Grossman and Joan Moore, at one time all at the University of Wisconsin, carefully and critically read the manuscript and offered many valuable suggestions, not all of which I have been able to follow. Professor Lyle Brown of Baylor University was also most helpful.

The editors of the University of Notre Dame Press have been most helpful and cooperative, and to them and to Professors Art Rubel and Julian Samora I also offer my thanks.

Lastly, I want to thank my wife. Not only did she read and offer suggestions on the entire manuscript, but through her renditions of the Brahms Opus 119 she helped place the book in proper perspective.

Although this work was made possible only through the help of these people, I alone bear responsibility for its contents, and for any possible errors of fact or judgment.

1 the setting

A six-foot statue of Popeye in the center of town reminds all that Crystal City is no ordinary community. It is "the Spinach Capital of the World." As such it is the center of the Winter Garden Area of Texas, rich not only in spinach but in a number of other winter vegetables that can be grown in the area and marketed throughout the country. But Popeye is only one aspect of the town's uniqueness—a uniqueness which is the reason for this study. It was in this town of slightly less than 10,000 people, overwhelmingly composed of Mexican Americans, that a group of five undereducated and poor Mexican Americans were swept into office as city councilmen in 1963. Backed by the Teamsters who had organized the Del Monte spinach plant on the outskirts of town, and supported further by the San Antonio-based Political Association of Spanish-Speaking Organizations, the all-Latin slate defeated the old Anglo establishment which had run the town since its inception in 1907. At the time this happened, Crystal City was the only community in Texas, and perhaps in the Southwest, where Anglos had been ousted from decades of rule.

Although this first revolt ended in failure two years later, it was in this same community in 1969 that a successful school strike led to a second political revolt, more radical and more

1

successful than the first. This second revolt saw the birth of the
Raza Unida Party, and Crystal City became the first community
to experience a takeover of the city government and school
system by an independent Chicano political party. The transfor-
mations that have occurred in the community are producing
reverberations in Chicano-Anglo relations throughout the
Southwest. The leader of this Chicano revolt, José Angel Gutiérrez, is becoming one of the primary forces of the Chicano
movement in the country. The town thus occupies a unique
position in the Chicano struggle and can in a real sense be
viewed as the cradle of the Chicano movement.

This study will attempt to examine and understand the
history of Crystal City and the two revolts, in the process
hoping to understand what has happened and why, what has
changed and what has not changed, and why revolts of this sort
have been so unusual. In trying to answer questions such as
these, and to determine what factors seem to have been most
crucial in leading to the explosive situation in Crystal City, a
look into the economic, social, and political history of the area
and the background of the community is essential.[1] The town is
located slightly over one hundred miles southwest of San Antonio, about forty miles from the Mexican border at Piedras
Negras. This places the community in an area of Texas which
was, until only shortly before the turn of the century, a disputed territory. The Mexican government, the newly-established
state of Texas, and Comanche and Lipan Indians were all laying
claims to the area. Although the Texas revolt against Mexico in
1836 ended successfully, the area around Crystal City was part
of the territory between the Nueces River and the Rio Grande
which was still being fought over. Even after American intervention and conquest of the area in the Mexican War of 1846-1848,
the area continued in turmoil. This resulted from Texan (and
American) claims to the area being weak indeed.[2] Since Americans were more interested in Manifest Destiny than in legality
of claims, pacification and control of the area did not come
quickly, easily, or without leaving a history of distrust and
bitterness on all sides. The Indians were finally all driven from
the area or killed. The relationship between the Anglos and the
Mexicans was more complicated, with a good deal of killing
occurring between these two groups as well.

Writing about this area of Texas, Paul S. Taylor has said that

the "idea of 'lost territory' was part of the emotional background of Mexicans who personally clashed with Texans,"[3] and
that

> among the traditions still whispered among Mexicans and
> Americans in the entire region between the Nueces and the
> lower Rio Grande are the stories that in one way or another—
> by chicane, by creating alarm for their personal safety, or by
> even stronger measures, many of the Mexican property own-
> ers were "run out" of the country and their lands obtained
> cheaply.[4]

The area where Crystal City was to be located shared in this
early history of turmoil. Accounts by Crystal City historians are
instructive. In his history of Zavala County, of which Crystal
City was to become the county seat in 1928, R. C. Tate has
noted that the days before the turn of the century "were hard
days for the pioneers as the country furnished hiding places for
desperate men—men who were fugitives from justice and who
were ready to shoot first and then ask questions, and who shot
Mexicans for the fun of it."[5] Under such conditions the area
developed a number of notorious personalities.[6]

For the Anglo settlers moving into the area to establish the
first permanent settlements, dealing with Indians, Mexicans, and
outlaws was only part of the problem. The land itself was
semi-arid, and prone to periodic droughts and floods. The
region was covered with a thick brush of mesquite, cactus, and
grasses. Problems of grazing rights, water holes, and fencing-in
of the range drove many ranchers to impoverishment, and kept
relations among Anglos from stabilizing. In the absence of an
established, legitimate government, all people, whether they
were belligerent or not, had to be prepared to defend themselves.

Gradually, with the increase in American settlers into South
Texas, and with the rise of Porfirio Díaz in Mexico, conditions
began to stabilize. Both sides started to contribute to the
pacification of the border area. On the side recognized as
American territory, Anglos consolidated their dominant position over Mexicans. But the long tradition of political violence
in South Texas, encompassing such battles as the Alamo, San
Jacinto, the Mexican War, and the numerous border skirmishes
which followed led to social, economic, and political relations
between the two groups which were not that different from

colonialism.[7] The Anglos tended to think of Mexicans as conquered, subordinate people, and Mexicans tended to think of
Anglos as villains who had stolen their land and deprived them
of their livelihood.[8] If Mexicans chose to stay in the area
conquered by the Anglos, or to come over in search of work,
they were expected to be subservient and deferential.

With this stabilization in relations along the border, Anglo
economic development of the area increased. More large ranches
were established, with Longhorn cattle, sheep, and horses grazing the range. With the discovery of the first artesian well in the
area in 1884, the problem of water scarcity seemed solved and
the possibility of farming opened up. At the turn of the century
large-scale agricultural farming was tried with the Bermuda
onion, and the results produced phenomenal profits. As these
few ventures became known,

> Land speculators and men of vision saw that all the ingredi-
> ents necessary for a successful irrigated farming area were
> present. The region was becoming known for its fertile soil,
> mild climate, and abundance of pure water. Add to this a
> proven crop with a potential for enormous profits, and the
> stage was set for the beginnings of a series of some of the
> greatest land colonization schemes in South Texas history.[9]

In 1907 the owners of one of the largest ranches in the area,
the Cross-S Ranch, decided to take advantage of the economic
opportunities. They began to break up the ranch into ten-acre
plots to be sold to cultivators and to develop a town at the same
time. Because of the clear artesian water in the area, the
developers decided to name the town Crystal City. With the
help of advertising, people from all over the country and from a
number of foreign countries came to settle in Crystal City and
farm their ten-acre plots.

The introduction of farming into this "Winter Garden" area,
so-called because farming took place in the winter months,
produced profound economic and social changes. The movement from ranching to farming required much labor. Although
the Anglos had earlier driven Mexicans from the area and had
usually looked upon them as more of a menace than a value,
they began to change their attitude. Mexicans now became an
indispensable source of cheap labor. In fact, the Mexican was
essential to the rise of farming not only in the Winter Garden

Area, but in all of South Texas. Paul Taylor noted that "the American whites have become the farmers. The Mexicans as laborers have cleared the land of brush and tended the cotton and vegetable crops. The roles of the two races in this development have been sharply distinguished."[10] Corroborating the importance of the Mexican to the development of agriculture has been the finding by Sheldon C. Menefee of the Works Progress Administration. Menefee found that a reservoir of low-paid Mexican labor just across the border was from the beginning an important factor in the development of large-scale agriculture in South Texas. In his study done in 1938, Menefee further noted that Crystal City Mexicans provided

> a striking example of the relationship between low-paid labor and the development of certain types of agriculture. Spinach and onion farming reached their present proportions in south Texas largely because of the presence of thousands of Mexicans who have customarily worked for wages of a dollar a day or less.[11]

Although inadequate marketing procedures hampered the early growth of farming in the area, by the 1920's better transportation, better packing procedures, and the introduction of spinach led to a tremendous boom in the area. With a twenty-fold increase in the number of acres being farmed between 1919 and 1929 in Zavala County, Crystal City's population grew rapidly, and thousands of Mexicans poured into the community to find work.[12]

The overthrow of Díaz in Mexico and the coming of the Mexican Revolution in 1910 coincided with the Anglos' desire to have Mexican farm labor. Although fear of raids from across the border put stress upon Anglo-Mexican relations, the thousands of refugees in search of work provided growers with an inexhaustible supply of cheap labor. Gradually some Anglos began to react to the large influx of Mexicans with skepticism or anxiety, but the large landowners were always powerful enough to prevent any serious tampering with the importation of Mexicans, regardless of the federal laws on immigration.[13]
The results of the economic transformation of the area around Crystal City were such that by 1930 Crystal City was overwhelmingly composed of Mexicans.[14]

Although the success of spinach and the growth of farming of a number of winter vegetables produced a boom for the area, few of Crystal City's Mexicans were year-round residents of the town. Because these cool-season vegetables were planted only in the winter months, Crystal City's Mexican population had to become migrants in order to find work during the late spring, summer, and early autumn months. But because of the certainty of work during winter with the spinach crop, the overwhelming majority of migrants always returned to Crystal City in the autumn and considered it their home base.

The spinach boom, however, lasted only a decade. With the coming of the depression, demand for the crop fell off drastically. At the same time technological improvements began to bring mechanization to the fields and an increased demand for processed and then frozen, rather than fresh, vegetables. These developments meant that in the 1930's the switch from ranching to farming was halted, and the need for stoop labor gradually began to decline. Although many of Crystal City's Mexicans tried to leave the migrant trail to settle in other parts of the country, most continued to think of the town as their home, even as employment opportunities slackened.

In 1938 when the Works Progress Administration did a study of migrant workers in Crystal City, the agency concluded that the future seemed to be for continuing displacement and consequent unemployment of the migrant worker.[15] The study showed that Crystal City migrants seemed to be better off than other migrants, because of their ability to dovetail their work in various crops and thus reduce periods of unemployment to a minimum. In spite of this ability to find work most of the year, however, the agency reported that

> The average cash income of the 300 Mexican families studied in Crystal City totaled $506 in 1938. The figure was increased to $561 per family when prerequisites such as housing, wood, and water received by the migratory farm workers were included. Since the families averaged 5.5 persons, the average yearly income among the Mexican migrants was approximately $100 per person in 1938.[16]

The overwhelming uniformity of the Crystal City Mexican population was revealed by the report's finding that of the 300 families interviewed by random sample, over ninety percent were engaged in migrant labor, and over ninety percent worked

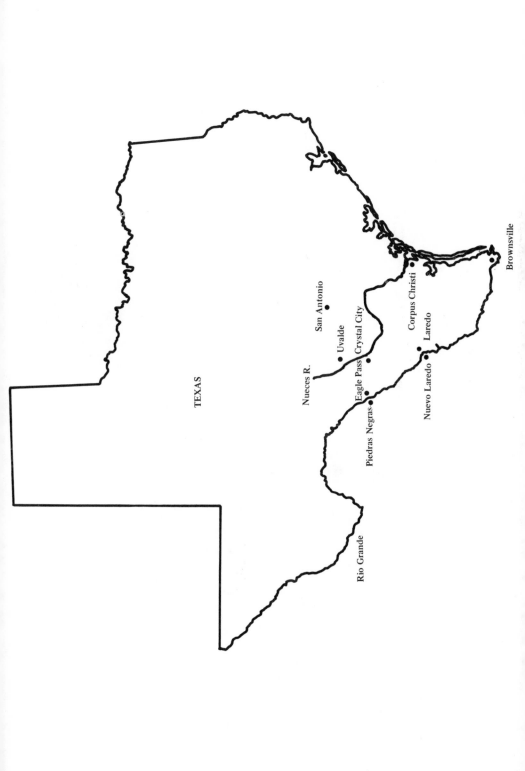

TEXAS

San Antonio

Uvalde

Nueces R.

Crystal City

Eagle Pass

Corpus Christi

Laredo

Piedras Negras

Nuevo Laredo

Brownsville

Rio Grande

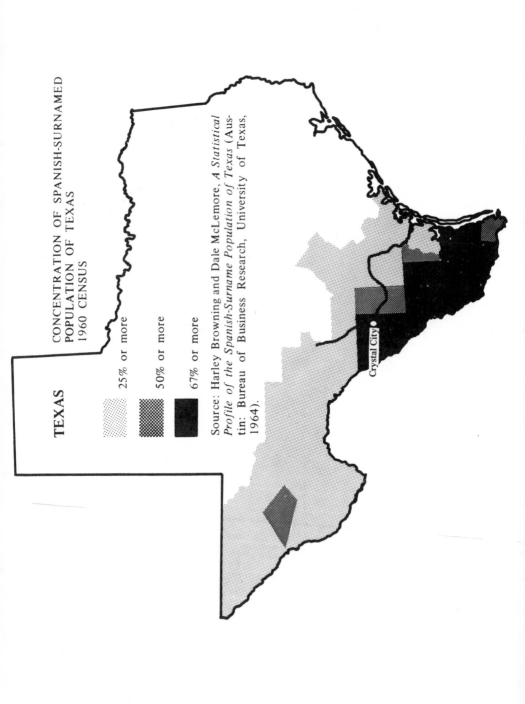

TEXAS

CONCENTRATION OF SPANISH-SURNAMED
POPULATION OF TEXAS
1960 CENSUS

25% or more

50% or more

67% or more

Crystal City

Source: Harley Browning and Dale McLemore, *A Statistical Profile of the Spanish-Surname Population of Texas* (Austin: Bureau of Business Research, University of Texas, 1964).

in the spinach harvest at some time during the year.[17] This basic socio-economic homogeneity of the Mexican population, even though it declined in later years, was to have an important impact upon the town's development.

As might be expected, given these economic conditions, the life of Crystal City Mexicans was not easy, and their living conditions were less than adequate. Menefee reported that

> The Mexican sections of Crystal City form a large semi-rural slum. More than half of the Mexicans own their houses or shacks, but most of the dwellings in the Mexican quarter are crudely built and in very bad repair. Few have electricity or plumbing. The houses are badly overcrowded; there was an average of 2.6 persons per room at the time of the survey.[18]

With the coming of World War II and a concomitant increase in demand for vegetables, the Crystal City area enjoyed a return to more prosperous conditions.[19] Greater acreage was planted, and more money returned to the area. Shortly after the war the large California Packing Corporation, later to be renamed Del Monte, decided to move into the area. In buying 3,200 acres of choice fields north of the city, and in establishing a canning plant, the company instantly became the most important producer in the area. It also provided many permanent and seasonal jobs in its cannery and in the fields.

Even with the establishment of Del Monte and the capital it brought into the community, conditions since the war have never equalled the rapid growth and boom period which occurred in the decade before the depression. The amount of acreage under cultivation in 1964 was only slightly greater than in 1929. Although this acreage was yielding greater profits, profits were reaching fewer people, owing to continued mechanization and to the decline of the small farmer. By the 1967-1968 season, the 13,320 acres of planted cool-season vegetables in Zavala County belonged to only thirty-four farms.[20] Their increased use of machines for the planting and harvesting of crops meant that fewer and fewer jobs were available for Crystal City Mexicans. Unemployment and an increasing search for jobs elsewhere have been the result of this mechanization.

The earlier years of cultivation were also taking their toll upon the land. Lack of control over the use of artesian wells resulted in a serious depletion of underground water. This,

SUMMARY OF MEDIAN EARNINGS AND HOURS IN VARIOUS TYPES
OF WORK OF CRYSTAL CITY MEXICANS, 1938

Type of Work	No. Of Families	Average Family Cash Earnings	Average Individual Weekly Earnings	Average Hours Per Week	Hourly Wage*	Average Duration of Job (days)
Total	300	$506	$4.53	43	10¢	86
Spinach	277	$124	$3.13	40	8¢	79
Beets	188	$400	$6.33	49	13¢	196
Cotton	100	$200	$4.22	47	9¢	85
Onions	89	$ 43				
Other farm	35	$ 71				
Nonfarm:						
Private Employment	49	$ 97	$3.75	49	8¢	90
Emergency Government Employment	13	$208	$6.00**	30	20¢	132

*Computed by the author from other data given in the table.
**Allows for time lost.
Source: Seldon C. Menefee, *Mexican Migratory Workers of South Texas*, prepared by the Federal Works Agency, Works Progress Administration (Washington, D.C.: U.S. Government Printing Office, 1941), Table 5, p. 56.

along with poor marketing practices and the increased cost of labor, meant that the economic foundations for growing winter vegetables profitably were seriously weakened. In his 1969 study of the economy of vegetable production in the Winter Garden Area, James Tiller concluded by arguing that "a continuation of present farming practices and marketing policies will inevitably result in the dissolution of the area's fresh market vegetable industry," which might mean that the area's towns would also die.[21] Although this is most likely too drastic and pessimistic a forecast for the economic future of Crystal City, it does seem clear that the days of economic boom and growth are over.[22]

While these economic developments were taking place and were working severe hardship on many in the community, a number of Mexican Americans were gradually upgrading themselves.[23] Since the end of the economic boom meant that Mexicans were no longer moving in great numbers into the community in search of work, the Mexican-American population of the community stabilized. Particularly for those who were able to find semipermanent work in Crystal City and thus were year-round citizens of the community, conditions improved. A few in the Mexican-American community began opening up small shops, such as groceries, barber shops, bakeries, gas stations, fruit stands, and taverns. Thus the community gradually began to develop a small middle class.

This general social upgrading can perhaps best be measured by changes in the school system. In the early days there was no school at all for Mexicans. After 1925, however, a series of small Mexican elementary schools were set up around the community. Those Mexicans who were able to continue on beyond elementary school were then able to enter the Anglo schools. Migrant children, however, had to leave the community in the early spring with their families and did not return until the late fall. It was thus extremely difficult for them to get credit for a year's work in school. The setting up of small Mexican elementary schools, therefore, did not mean that all Mexicans were attending school. In his survey of the Crystal City schools in the late 1930's, William McKinley Pridgen noted that "only about fifty percent of the entire white scholastic population of Zavala County . . . were enrolled in any public secondary school during the year 1938-1939."[24] Pridgen further noted that average daily attendance was only sixty percent of those enrolled. To be precise, this meant that only thirty-two percent of the scholastic population was attending classes in the school year of 1938-1939.[25] But considering that less than thirty-two percent of the population of the county was Anglo by 1930, this meant that a number of Mexicans, although a distinct minority, were going to school regularly.[26]

Improvement in the education of Mexican children was hampered by the fact that it was often not in the economic interest of the Anglo community to educate Mexican children. As Paul Taylor observed in his examination of Dimmit County, which is immediately to the south of Crystal City:

> ... the schools for Americans are operated on revenues derived because of Mexicans listed on the scholastic census. The state aid, usually amounting to about $15 per child per annum, is apportioned to school districts on the basis of the number of children shown by the school census. The result is that the Mexicans are diligently enrolled on the census; but the revenues are applied principally to the education of the American children. . . . The practice is justified, when any justification is offered, mainly by the fact that the Americans are the principal taxpayers.[27]

Taylor concluded that this was not the only reason, however, for Mexican education being distinctly inferior:

> The main reasons for wishing the Mexican to remain uneducated, then, is belief in the desirability of cheap laborers who will remain laborers. Besides, so long as the present method of apportioning state financial aid continues, there is an immediate financial advantage to the dominant group in discouraging others from attending school.[28]

Given these conditions, facilities in the Mexican schools were something less than "separate but equal." Pridgen recorded that as of 1938, the Crystal City school system had ten elementary schools: one for Anglos, eight for Mexicans, and one for Negroes. He further noted that the proliferation of small, understaffed, overcrowded, and ill-equipped Mexican schools meant that Mexicans were not getting an equal education.

By 1942—when R. C. Tate did his study—there had been notable improvement and consolidation. There were now only three Mexican elementaries. But valuation of these schools, compared with the number of teachers employed, still produced serious inequalities:[29]

School	Valuation	No. of Teachers	Teacher/Valuation Ratio
Mexican Elementary	$ 6,000	4	1,500
Mexican Elementary	$24,000	11	2,180
Mexican Elementary	$ 3,000	5	600
Anglo Elementary	$35,000	9	3,880
Negro School	$ 250	1	250
High School	$93,000	?	?

Even if it assumed that teachers at the Mexican schools did not have larger classes than Anglo teachers had, inequalities are obvious. Teachers at the Anglo elementary had equipment and facilities averaging over double that for Mexican schools, and more than ten times that for the Negro school. Further, the high school, which was overwhelmingly Anglo, had a greater value than all the other schools in the district combined.

The school system, then, as with the economic system noted earlier, seems to have been run by and for the Anglos. But no matter how slow improvement in Mexican education may have been, the fact remains that there was definite improvement. This betterment in Mexican education can perhaps best be measured by examining high-school graduates. Whereas in 1931, the first year of the new high school, there were no Mexican graduates, by 1940 there were three out of the graduating class of thirty-one. By 1950 there were nine Mexican-American graduates, and by the late 1950's, a majority of those graduating from high school were Mexican Americans.

The Supreme Court's decision in *Brown v. Board of Education* in 1954 seems to have accelerated the process of improvement. After the famous decision, the Anglo elementary school was integrated with the admission of a few Mexicans who could pass language proficiency exams and with the tiny handful of Negro children in the community.[30]

While this gradual improvement in the educational system was occurring in Crystal City, and a small middle class was developing in the Mexican community, the Mexicans were also making improvements on the political front. Zavala County and Crystal City, like the rest of the Winter Garden Area, had been, since the beginning of Anglo settlement, completely dominated politically by the Anglos. Bearing this in mind, however, it does appear that Crystal City was not as extreme in political subordination as Dimmit County, located immediately to the south of Zavala County. There Paul Taylor noted the introduction of the white primary to prevent Mexicans from voting at all. In Zavala County this did not occur. Mexicans voted, although it may not have been a regular practice, and they were almost assuredly so carefully controlled that it would be more accurate to say that they were voted, as the following account suggests. R. C. Tate has written of the struggle to determine whether Crystal City would become the new county seat:

> In 1926 an election was held to decide this issue. Since a large part of Crystal City's citizens were Mexicans, the Anglo-American citizens decided to have a big celebration in the Mexicans' honor and obtain their votes in the coming election. Some of the men wore their guns as trouble was expected from the other parts of the county because it was at this time of year—after the onion harvest—that the Mexicans left Crystal City to work in harvests elsewhere. Crystal City people naturally expected efforts to be made to try and get these many voters moved out before time to cast a ballot. During the celebration a car loaded with voters who were opposed to [moving the county seat to Crystal City] drove up and, as prearranged, was immediately surrounded by grim-faced, determined men who spoke . . . to the effect that they were to leave at once. . . . Crystal City voted its Mexicans but lost the election, anyway. It was not until 1928 that the right was won to move the courthouse to Crystal City.[31]

In "voting its Mexicans" Crystal City was following a practice common to South Texas.[32] Although the great majority of Mexican Americans in Crystal City did not vote during the years of Anglo rule, a few *jefes* (small-time political bosses) arose among those Mexicans who did vote. These leaders would maintain small followings and would develop a brokerage mentality toward the various Anglo politicians who would deal with them.

The Mexican-American community, then, was not completely shut out of the political process, although all elected officials—for the county, city, and schools—were Anglos. Although
Mexicans may have voted, their votes were mainly used by one
Anglo faction against another, and it was acknowledged by all
that the Anglos ran things in the area. Through the years this
brokerage attitude on the part of Mexican-American *jefes* continued, even though Mexicans constituted the overwhelming
numerical majority of the community.

This brief overview of the economic, social, and political
history of Crystal City from its foundation to the 1950's
indicates that Crystal City has been very much a product of the
economic resources of the area and the social and political
relationships which thereby resulted. The town's history has
been closely connected to the movement from ranching to
farming, and the prospects and problems that have followed
from this movement. At the same time, the town has been very
much influenced by the political, social, and economic thought
of South Texas. In these three aspects of life in the community,
Mexican Americans were unquestionably subordinate to Anglo
Americans. The ranch and farm land was owned by Anglos and
the riches off the land went overwhelmingly to the Anglos.
Social discrimination was common, and the school system was
run by Anglo teachers and Anglo administrators, basically for
Anglo children, even as the Mexican-American children increasingly began going to school and continuing in school.[33] Politically as well the Anglos were unquestionably in control of the
situation. But racial lines were not a taut as they might have
been, or were in some other areas of Texas. And there were
certainly fewer barriers than experienced between Anglos and
Negroes. Calvin Trillin has commented on the situation:

> Although Crystal City has always had a certain number of
> open, straight-forward bigots, it has not been the kind of
> place in which Anglo control is maintained by violence or
> even by denying Mexican-Americans the right to vote. The
> Anglos own everything. They like to tell visitors about the
> decent, hard-working Mexicans they grew up with—
> Mexicans who would have been appalled at people who
> wanted something for nothing or at people who tried to
> create friction between the races. [They have] taken polit-
> ical as well as economic control more or less for
> granted. . . .[34]

In being situated in South Texas, then, Crystal City, Zavala County, and the Winter Garden Area as a whole have been influenced by the social, economic, and political thought and practices of this area of Texas. But on closer examination of these aspects of the history of Crystal City, its similarities with the rest of South Texas give way to important differences. Crystal City has taken fairly general elements of the region and produced a compound which is more nearly unique than general. And it is this uniqueness which seems to have made the community much more ripe for revolt than most other communities in South Texas.

unusual features of crystal city

In the first place, the community has been overwhelmingly Mexican American to an extent that is not common even for South Texas. Although the revolution in Mexico and the economic transformation of southern and western Texas produced a wide strip along the Rio Grande where Mexican Americans form either a significant minority or a majority of the population, Crystal City and Zavala County are disproportionately Mexican American. According to the 1960 census, thirty-eight counties in South and West Texas are more than thirty-five percent Mexican American. Of these thirty-eight counties, seventeen are more than fifty percent Mexican American. But for Zavala County, the 1960 census showed that 74.4 percent of its inhabitants were Spanish-surnamed. This ranked the county as seventh in the state of Texas in terms of percentage of Spanish surnames.[35] The town of Crystal City, however, has been even more heavily Mexican American than the rest of Zavala County. The most common estimates placed the percentage during the 1960's at slightly over eighty percent.[36] This heavy proportion of Mexican Americans resulted from the town's economic foundation—its being a base for farm labor in the area. As one Anglo official expressed it to me: "All this town was ever intended to be was a labor camp!" Mexicans were encouraged to come into the area, the more the better, because it tended to depress wages and also insure that the farms would have plenty of people to perform stoop labor.

The movement from ranching to farming produced a second

important element which has shaped the character of the town. Crystal City is a new town, a twentieth-century town. There have been a few other moderate-sized communities in South Texas where such a high concentration of Mexican Americans could be found, such as Laredo, Eagle Pass, and Brownsville. But these towns have tended to be older communities, generally situated on the border, with well-established Mexican-American families who have always played an important role in community affairs.[37] Crystal City is more similar to certain towns in the Rio Grande Valley—such as Harlingen, McAllen, Edinburg, Pharr, and Weslaco—where the movement to farming likewise brought the creation of new towns which were heavily populated by farm laborers from Mexico.[38] Crystal City was not founded by Spanish explorers or by later Mexican settlers; it is not even one of the older, smaller settlements that grew up in Zavala County and the surrounding area after the Civil War. It was instead the deliberate creation of a group of Anglo speculators. The decision to break up the Cross-S Ranch and the selling and buying of plots of land were all carried out by Anglos. Because of this the town was dominated from the very beginning by Anglos who had no need to compromise with older, established Mexican-American families.[39]

These two characteristics of the community have in turn shaped a third aspect of great importance to the town. The Mexicans who came to Crystal City came almost exclusively to perform stoop labor for the Anglo farmers. They were not of established families along the border. Tending to be more Indian than Spanish, tending to be newcomers to the northern side of the Rio Grande, and often having come to Texas by less than legal means, these Mexicans were much easier to control than the established families of the border. As one Anglo commented in noting the difference between Crystal City's Mexican population and those of the established families along the border, "They look different, these Mexicans." Desperately in search of work of any kind and hoping not to be deported, "these Mexicans" were not in a position to think of themselves or to act as fullfledged citizens of Crystal City. Indeed, they were not supposed to be real citizens of the community. They were recruited to perform the tasks the Anglos told them to do, and if they didn't like it, they could always "go back to Mexico."

As Paul Taylor has noted, "The Americans here have always held the idea that the Mexicans are here just to work."[40]

With the influx of these Mexicans, race lines became class lines. Mexicans did the manual labor, Anglos owned the land and made the money. Although this practice is not unusual for South Texas, the degree to which class lines were the same as race lines made the town again somewhat unusual. In being forced to migrate because of their dependence upon stoop labor, the Mexicans reinforced the Anglos attitude towards them as being "here just to work." At the same time, being migrants, they began to encounter different experiences and different ways of being treated from those they had encountered in South Texas. In particular, they tended to earn higher wages and meet with less racial discrimination when they worked in the north.[41] They were set apart in the community not only as Mexicans but as migrants. Being gone from Crystal City during much of the year and earning wages elsewhere, they were less susceptible to Anglo pressure upon their return. It was more difficult for the Anglos to attempt to acculturate or control them.

These factors made Crystal City different from most other communities in South Texas. The situation was not explosive, however, so long as the Mexicans did not think of themselves as people able to challenge the Anglos over issues, run for office, and in general partake in the running of a democratic society. But this attitude of noninvolvement in the community's decision-making was gradually being eroded, and the erosion process was furthered by the establishment after the Second World War of the large California Packing Plant, later renamed Del Monte. The plant, which by its very magnitude centralized much of the vegetable growing in the area, employed hundreds of Mexican-American workers, most of them seasonally, but some of them for the entire year. In addition to providing much needed employment for the area, the plant was California-owned, and thus was subject to some ideas uncommon to South Texas. The most surprising of these was the plant's decision to allow unionization, as all their other plants were unionized. By 1956 a small Teamsters union was established at the plant and was recognized without any friction by the company.[42]

The decision by Del Monte to move into Crystal City and establish a large plant, although it was welcomed by many in the city's agricultural and business establishment, ultimately weakened these local Anglos' ability to control the situation. [43] Having a large-scale plant employing hundreds of workers, paying wages which were not common for the area, and then allowing the workers the opportunity to unionize set Crystal City off even further from other South Texas communities.

Even with these potentially explosive ingredients—an overwhelming majority of Mexican Americans in the process of improving themselves relative to the Anglos, an Anglo-run community, and a Teamsters union—the situation in the community hardly changed for nearly a decade. The community continued to be run by the same Anglo leadership, many of whom were from the original families who had governed the community since 1907. As in most small communities in America, its younger citizens often left the community to seek better opportunities elsewhere, and thus the old leadership had never been seriously challenged. Because of the form of government—a weak mayor and council with a strong city manager—the offices of mayor and councilmen were not very appealing and went formally unpaid. The mayor, Bruce Holsomback, had been in office since the twenties.[44] The town government was run by the city manager, L. L. Williams, who had been in office for three decades.

No doubt many Anglos felt that younger, more innovative leaders were needed, just as many Anglos realized that their complete dominance could not continue forever. But it was difficult for farsighted Anglos to take the initiative to alter the status quo, since this would mean hurting Anglo friends. The city manager was one of those who recognized that the situation would eventually change, and he set about in several ways to bring a few Mexicans into the government, if only to protect the Anglos from a more massive engulfment. A Mexican was appointed to the city council, and one was hired to work with the city secretarial help in the city hall.[45] By the early 1960's a small but growing Mexican-American middle class had developed and had a few organizations of its own, such as a Mexican Chamber of Commerce. This group was beginning to be consulted on some matters. But the Mexican middle class was small, and owing to the history of the community, it was still quite fragile. Neither the Anglos nor the great majority of Mexican Americans themselves looked to this group for leadership.

developments in the decade before the revolt

Aside from the gradual incorporation of a few token Mexican Americans in the city government, two developments seem to have occurred which had real impact upon the town's government in the decade before the revolt. The first was the veterans land scandal, which was a statewide scandal involving several people high in the Shivers administration. A program intended to help veterans obtain land had instead been used by interested land speculators to buy land that the state thought was going to veterans.[46] Through the bribing of state appraisers the program had also been used to get the state to buy land for veterans from the realtors at grossly inflated land values. Anglo land speculators would get veterans to apply for land, which the state would then buy for the veterans from the speculators at inflated prices. Through long-term low-interest loans, the veterans were then supposed to reimburse the state for the purchased land. But since the veterans used by the speculators often did not even know they were supposed to be buying land, the veterans would default on their payments. The state was then left holding land which it had paid high prices to purchase for veterans. In Crystal City the scandal turned out to be a rather blatant case of Anglo land speculators (who seem to have been connected to some officials in both the city and county governments) using Mexican veterans to obtain more land or money for themselves by "buying off" the confused and unsuspecting veterans.[47]

More than one Mexican in the community mentioned that this scandal and resultant trials of those involved in the speculation was the first time the Mexicans in the community had followed local government or had realized that some local leaders were engaging in activities which other Anglos considered to be illegal. The immediate results of the scandal were rather small however. It was rather something for the Mexican community to remember and to act upon when a situation presented itself at a later date.

The second development in the community in the decade preceding the revolt was the city government's decision to apply for and use urban renewal funds for a renovation of the city. The town had long been one of the poorest in the state, with almost no paved streets in the Mexican sections and with considerably less than half the town having sewage connections.[48] In 1950 the average Mexican American twenty-five years of age or older had received slightly over one and one-half years of education, and the average family income was considerably less than $2,000 a year.[49] The decision to apply for urban renewal and to float bonds was not prompted so much by these statistics but rather by city statistics in the mid-1950's showing that the city was not dying but was growing at a pace it had not known since before the depression. With these indicators of growth, the city government was willing to embark on city improvements.[50] The decision to adopt an urban renewal program was made in 1957-1958, but the program was proceeding at a snail's pace and was having only limited impact on the community by 1963. The reaction of many in the Mexican community to urban renewal was one of hostility toward the condemning of their homes and the relocations that might be forced on them.[51] Most important of all, the city government was now making itself more conspicuous to the people, Mexican American as well as Anglo, migrant as well as permanent resident.

Cautious moves toward racial accommodation, the land scandal, and the urban renewal program were the major developments in Crystal City in the decade before the revolt. All three seem to have worked toward partially dispelling the lack of Mexican-American involvement in city affairs, as is indicated by two other developments. In the spring of 1960, E. C. Muñoz, an insurance salesman, decided to run for the school board, which was and had always been completely Anglo.[52] He decided to run with the goal of finding out what the school board was doing.[53] Muñoz recalled that nobody in the Mexican-American community ever knew what the school board was considering or what issues it was discussing. Since there was rarely any opposition for school-board posts, very few people even knew there was an election, much less voted.

Banking on the fact that very few people would vote, Muñoz thought it would be easy to win if he got his friends to the polls. His candidacy, however, spurred the four Anglo incumbents, all seeking re-election, into making sure that Anglos turned out to vote. But during the campaign no Anglo ever talked to Muñoz about his running for the board, about why he was running, or about what his concerns were. When the April election came, a record 1,034 votes were cast:[54]

1960 School Board Election

Dr. S. S. Peters, President	730
R. E. Boyer	725
B. R. Guyler	722
H. M. Addison	721
E. C. Muñoz	311

Muñoz ran a distant fifth, although his total of over three hundred votes would have been enough to elect him easily in a normal turnout.[55]

According to Muñoz, the Anglos were against allowing a Mexican onto the school board because they didn't want Mexicans to know what the board was doing. Whatever the reasons, however, it seems clear that the Anglos were against having a Mexican on the board, even though by now the school system, including even the high school, was overwhelmingly composed of Mexican American children.[56] By failing to appoint a Mexican of any sort to the school board before 1960, by turning out heavily to defeat Muñoz in 1960, and by continuing the policy after Muñoz ran of not seeking out even a "responsible" Mexican for the school board, the Anglos seemed to indicate their desire to dominate the school board completely.

Shortly after the defeat of Muñoz, however, another event concerning the schools occurred which surprised the Anglo community. Although Crystal City had ended complete elementary-school segregation in the previous decade, the only integrated school in the community was the Anglo elementary. The other elementary schools were totally Mexican American. Only a small number of Mexicans were allowed into the Anglo school, and these were chosen by school administrators generally after testing the Mexican children on their comprehension of English. No similar test was given to Anglo children. In 1960, however, the second son of the Reverend Arnold López, minis-

ter of the Mexican Evangelical Baptist Church, was scheduled to
enter the first grade.[57] The López family had moved to Crystal
City only two years before, having previously lived in Houston,
and they spoke fluent English. The year the Lópezes arrived
their first child had been sent to the Mexican elementary.
Although surprised at this, the Lópezes did nothing, basically
because they were new in the community. In 1960, however,
they were more established and more familiar with the situation. When Mrs. López arrived at the school with her son, she
observed that all the Anglos went to classes while all the
Mexican children had to wait until they were given tests. Although her son scored extremely high on the English comprehension test, he was not allowed to enter the Anglo first grade.

When this happened, the family began to organize the Mexican-American community to protest *de facto* segregation and
the unequal treatment of Mexican children. With the help of
Gerald Saldaña, a mail carrier, what may have been the first
mass action by the Crystal City Mexican-American community
was organized. Although the board and administrators first
indicated intransigence, when it became clear that legal action
seemed imminent and that the protest group had a following of
several hundred, the board agreed to break up the all-Mexican
schools.[58] The grade schools were merged, although individual
classrooms still were heavily Anglo or heavily Mexican American. Having accomplished a large part of their goal, however,
the group disbanded.

The following year the city and school elections reverted to
normal. There was no campaign, and no one opposed the
victorious candidates. Three Anglos were elected to the school
board, and five candidates including Salvador Galván, a Mexican
American, and Ed Ritchie, a candidate whose mother was of
Mexican heritage, were elected to the city council.

A further sign of potential unrest occurred in the winter of
1962. After a severe freeze which destroyed much of the area's
vegetable crops, about 125 Mexican Americans marched to the
County Commissioners Court requesting assistance. They argued that because of the freeze they "had no jobs and no
money to buy food."[59] In this situation the county government approved a surplus-commodities program for an emer-
gency period of thirty days. Altogether 3,623 persons participated in the program, but at the end of the period the Commis-

sioners Court voted three to two not to extend the program, even though many were still out of work. The majority on the board feared that continuing the program might lessen the Mexicans' desire to work.[60]

In the spring of 1962 the Anglo candidates for the school board were again unopposed, but in the county elections in May there was serious Anglo competition.[61] José (Cleto) López ran for county commissioner in precinct two, which included the eastern part of Crystal City. He came in fourth in a field of four, however, and no other Mexican ran for any other office.[62]

A review of the developments in the community through 1962 seemed overall to reveal gradual progress in race relations in the community and a gradual upgrading of the Mexican American—an improvement both absolute and relative to the Anglo population of the town. A look at the politics of the community, studied at the level of campaigns, issues discussed, and decision-making, might have led one to believe that the community was basically stable, yet adaptable to incremental change. The Anglo response to the limited Mexican activity had been to allow some participation in a few areas. The inclusion of two candidates of Mexican heritage on the Anglo slate elected to the city council, the response to the López-Saldaña protest, and the response to the demands during the severe freeze seemed to indicate flexibility by Anglos in recognizing that the Mexican Americans deserved a larger role and improved treatment in the community. Although the school board remained totally Anglo, the number of teachers in the school system with Spanish surnames had increased to seventeen out of a faculty of 106, and the increasing number of Mexican-American graduates confirmed that more and more Mexicans were getting a better education. At the same time, the city's decision to apply for urban renewal seemed to indicate a recognition that steps were needed to be taken to improve city services for the poor in the community and also a willingness to use federal funds for the improvement. Did this limited progress mean that the community would gradually integrate its Mexican-American members into the life of the community, that the Anglos would welcome Mexicans into their political, social, and economic activities? If the Anglos were to offer it to them, would Mexicans want a gradual acculturation that might even lead to assimilation? If the progress did not mean this, did it perhaps still mean that the incremental, gradual improvement would lead to a "pluralist democracy," with all groups sharing in power and all reasonably happy about the outcome?

With the hindsight of a decade, it seems clear that it did not. The progress taking place in the community was not preparing the way for continued stability and incremental change; rather, a subordinate racial group was gradually acquiring the resources to fight for equality, for retribution, and for control of the community. What might have looked to some like a stable, moderately progressive community was in fact a tinder-box. In 1963 the forces of racial and class antagonisms exploded.

2 the revolt

The spark that set off the explosion in Crystal City was in fact an Anglo.[1] Andrew Dickens, a retired oil-field worker, moved to Crystal City in 1961 and shortly thereafter proceeded to set up a doughnut shop. This in itself was hardly a radical step, but it turned out that Dickens' shop was located on property local authorities wanted as a right-of-way. Dickens considered himself to have been "taken" on his property lease, and when he tried to get help in fighting the arrangement, he found that all the officials in the city government and the county government were in agreement. He could get nowhere. This caused him to take a hard look at the local government, and what he found was a small group of families who had been running the county and the town for a long time—a "machine." Outraged, he vowed to the governing officials that he would work to turn the place over to the Mexicans in order to beat the "machine" he saw ruling Crystal City.[2]

As a start Andrew Dickens contacted the union at the Del Monte plant and talked to its business agent, Juan Cornejo. As the local leader of the union, Cornejo had been one of several *jefes* in Crystal City with small followings. Because he controlled a group of voters, his support was occasionally sought after by Anglo politicians. Dickens and Cornejo, together with several others from the union, talked over the idea of organizing against the city government. Although Cornejo had always before been a *jefe* firmly dependent upon the Anglo political structure, he was now seized with the idea of breaking away from these people and forming his own political organization. As a start toward assembling a counter-structure, he and Dickens journeyed to San Antonio to talk with the president and business manager of the Teamsters Local 657 of San Antonio, Ray Shafer. Until that time Shafer had not been interested in putting his union on the line in Crystal City.[3] Because of the local concern for fighting the Anglo rulers, success appeared possible and Shafer therefore was interested. Crystal City might also, he hoped, turn out to be an opportunity to expand the Teamsters Union in South Texas. Shafer thus told the group to begin by launching a poll-tax drive.[4]

The Teamsters provided outside organizational expertise to conduct the drive, including even bookkeeping which allowed some of the Mexicans to pay their $1.75 poll tax in install-ments.[5] During the drive small flyers circulated among the population:

NOTICE TO ALL LATIN AMERICAN CITIZENS
OF CRYSTAL CITY

This is to let you know that a Political party is being formed by the working people of Crystal City to induce each and every eligible Latin American Citizen to purchase his poll tax and vote for an All Latin American Party in 1963, so we can stop discrimination and the procedures of urban renewal in their tearing down of the homes of people who cannot afford to buy a $5,000 or $6,000 home. The all Latin Party will see that justice is done, which will give you better government and representation in Public Schools.

It is your duty to pay your poll tax and vote in the way that will protect you, your family, and your home. Do not allow anyone to pay for your poll tax, as this is against the law and you may be prosecuted. Do not allow anyone to say [*sic*] or bribe you to vote his way. If you do, you are defeating the purpose of your fight for your family and home.

You must have your poll tax to vote in 1963. So pay your Poll Tax now! and urge your neighbor to do the same as this is the last chance you will have.

By the: All Latin Party[6]

The poll-tax drive turned out to be extraordinarily successful. At the end of January, a whopping 1,139 Mexican Americans had paid their poll taxes while only 542 Anglos had. This contrasted starkly with the previous year's figure of 792 Mexican-American and 538 Anglo poll taxes. Thus it was not just that the Teamsters had been unusually successful in their drive; this had occurred at the very time Anglo poll taxes had remained stationary. A quirk of fate allowed the Mexican Americans to increase their registration greatly without any "backlash" in Anglo registrants, and this alone may have been enough to make the difference between victory and defeat for the insurgents. L. L. Williams, the politically skilled city manager, died in the fall of 1962 and was replaced by James Dill. Dill was not familiar with the situation in Crystal City as L. L. Williams had run it. Previously it had been the practice to watch poll-tax payments very closely as they were coming in. The town's Anglos were quite aware that they were in a minority, and a group of the town's businessmen and agricultural leaders had set up a contingency fund to be used to buy Anglo and "safe" Mexican-American poll taxes if the Mexicans began buying too many.[7] James Dill apparently did not keep adequate tabs on poll-tax payments. The result was the disaster of several hundred Anglos not paying their poll taxes at the very time Mexicans had dramatically increased their number of eligible voters.

When the results of the poll-tax drive were made known in early February, Shafer of the Teamsters became even more interested, as he and everyone else working on the drive now sensed victory. In a strategy meeting, Shafer and two of his most helpful lieutenants, Henry Muñoz and Carlos Moore, realized that they had the votes to win the election if they could keep the Mexican Americans from losing confidence in the drive, from being intimidated, or from selling out as had been the custom.[8] All their strategy for the campaign thus revolved around trying to prevent these possibilities from occurring.

The strategists faced two other serious problems related to the above-mentioned dangers. The first of these concerned how to play down the influence of the Teamsters in the election. Aware of their image problems, the Teamster strategists devised a two-fold plan to try to deflect the focus in the election from themselves. First, a local campaign committee was organized, called the "Citizens Committee for Better Government." This local organization, with its innocuous-sounding name, channelled most of the outside help, and was headed by a local union man, Moses Falcón.

In another step to deflect attention from the Teamsters, the union approached the Political Association of Spanish-speaking Organizations (PASO), which was a new and militant political organization that had originated from the Viva Kennedy Clubs during the 1960 presidential campaign. PASO had been having serious troubles following its disastrous attempt to wield influence in the 1962 Democratic primary elections in Texas, and a number of its leaders believed that in order to establish a more solid base, the organization needed to concentrate its activities at the local level.[9] Crystal City fit in perfectly with this strategy. By commissioning the help of PASO the Teamsters were able both to get valuable help and to deflect some of the attention from their own involvement. Albert Fuentes, the state executive secretary of PASO, and Martin García, a district director of PASO who was also employed by the Teamsters, became the main PASO contribution to the campaign. Through providing campaign materials, speakers from San Antonio at rallies, and a small amount of money, as well as the expertise of Fuentes and García, PASO added considerably to the morale and enthusiasm of the whole campaign.

The second serious problem which the strategists faced concerned the selection of candidates. Shafer drove down to Crystal City and called the first of several strategy meetings. But the choosing of candidates to run became more difficult than they had expected. A number of people declined to run, some through fear for their jobs and some through fear for their families. At the same time, it became apparent that the middle-class Mexicans in the community would have nothing to do with the movement. The main reason for this appeared to be because of the Teamster Union involvement which meant that the revolt seemed to revolve only around lower class cannery and migrant workers.[10] The organizers were thus forced to compose a slate from those few candidates who were willing to run. The five candidates for the city council, who were called "Los Cinco," were Juan Cornejo, the business agent for the Teamsters at the Del Monte plant and one who had been involved in the effort from the beginning; Manuel Maldonado, a clerk in a local Economart store; Antonio Cárdenas, a truck driver; Reynaldo Mendoza, operator of a small photography shop; and Mario Hernández, a real-estate salesman. None was well known in the Anglo community; none had graduated from high school. Although these men were not currently migrant workers, none was much above the poverty line. Not one was in any of the Mexican, much less the Anglo, middle-class organizations.

After Los Cinco Mexicanos had been chosen to run for the city council, the Citizens Committee for Better Government also selected two candidates to run for the school board against the two Anglos whose terms were expiring. The candidates chosen, Jesús Maldonado, a warehouse official at the Del Monte cannery, and Lorenzo Olivarez, a barber, had both finished high school and were attending night courses to further their education.[11] Jesús Maldonado had in fact been considered as a possible candidate for the city council, and if he had run he would have been the most educated of the five. He feared, however, that his job, which was in a management position at the canning plant, would be threatened should he run with obvious Teamster backing. In running for the school board, he tried to steer his campaign clear of explicit Teamster support, although it was obvious that the same people supporting Los Cinco would support the two Mexicanos running for the school board.[12] As it was, he nearly lost his job anyway, but after careful explanations to the management concerning why he was running, he was allowed to keep his job.

With the naming of the candidates and the establishment of the local campaign organization, the campaign had broken out into the open. Although worried by the developments taking place in their town, the Anglos still had reasons to be confident. As all Anglos knew, it was one thing for a Mexican to be registered to vote; it was another for him to vote. And if he did vote, the chances were great that he would be amenable to "influence." Not only was the weight of tradition completely on their side and against those Mexicans who would try to gain election without the support of Anglos, but owing to the quality of the Mexican candidates, the middle-class Mexicans were staying rather firmly in line.

Shortly after Los Cinco had announced their intention to run, several of the community's most prominent Anglos approached the local Mexican Evangelical Baptist Minister, Arnold López.[13] Explaining to him that the five candidates running were unqualified and a disgrace to the "better Mexican element" in the town, they convinced the minister that he ought to run for office. Whether these men wished to be able to vote for a responsible Mexican American who was also concerned for the welfare of the community is not clear. None of the Anglos who came to the minister, however, were close to the mayor and his administration. But when the minister began launching attacks upon the five candidates, charging that they were being managed and run from outside and that they were unqualified, it became clear that his support might come more from Anglos, who were charging the same thing, than from Mexicans.[14]

At this point the same Anglos who had talked the Reverend López into running came to him again and urged him to withdraw because he was splitting the anti-Teamster vote. In refusing to withdraw at this point, he added an uncertainty to the Anglo problems of retaining control of the community. And this problem was heightened by the entrance of another independent candidate, Dr. Henry Daly, who also refused to withdraw from the race.

Along with having to come to grips with its inability to control the candidate selection process, the old Anglo elite in Crystal City also quickly had to realize that the traditional apathy toward local government was being shattered. "Los Cinco" candidates were appealing to the poorest, most uneducated Mexicans, those who had never been involved in politics before. In the Anglos' view this could only be happening because outside agitators—Teamster agents and militant Chicanos from San Antonio—were coming into their community to stir up the Mexicans, organize them, and forge them into a powerful challenge to their decades of rule. As this became known, Anglo reaction, which had been remarkably lenient throughout the poll-tax drive (if only because of ineptitude), now stiffened. But the Teamster-PASO strategists had not expected that the Anglos would take all this without striking back. To prepare for this, very early in the campaign the organizers sent Carlos Moore down to Crystal City in a Cadillac, posing as an oilman.[15] Since some oil was being discovered in the area, it was plausible for Moore to say that he was looking for oil in the county. The city officialdom treated him royally, and in gaining their confidence, he began to find out what their strategy for conducting the campaign would be. Although his identity was later discovered when someone spotted him with Cornejo outside of town, he was able to unearth that their strategy would involve intimidation.

True to predictions, a series of incidents followed, testing the very foundation of a democratic order. Earlier there had been trouble in filing for elective office. When the five Mexicanos had gone to file for office, the city clerk had "run out of forms." Los Cinco had surmounted this problem, however, by typing their own forms, which were accepted. But now businesses and finance companies began to put pressure on the Mexicans who owed money and were active in the campaign. In the face of this intimidation, the job for Moore, Muñoz, Fuentes, and García was to put out all these "grass fires" before the local Mexicans panicked and deserted the campaign. As the strategists stayed and fought each harassment with all their resources, the local population began to see that the organizers were not going to abandon them in midstream when the going got rough.

In combating the Anglo tactics, uncertainty over the identity of Carlos Moore proved very helpful. Although the Anglos knew he was on the side of the Mexicans, they still were unsure about what his real profession was. At times Moore pretended to be an attorney, threatening to take the Anglos to court for such things as withholding duplicate automobile titles from their Mexican patrons, or for failing to comply with provisions in the Texas election code. At one point the Anglos feared he was working for the FBI. In their confusion over who he was, the Anglos were afraid that if they did try too much, he might get them into serious trouble.

The most serious case of attempted intimidation occurred at the Del Monte plant during March, with only two weeks to go before election. Several employees were dismissed "for wearing campaign tags."[16] How this incident was handled provided another instance of the crucial role the Teamsters played. Normally in South Texas such firings would have been final, and the men would have been without jobs. Had these workers in Crystal City lost their jobs now, in the middle of the campaign, the morale of the workers would have plummeted and fear would have become central for all those involved in the campaign. Had the Teamsters been unable to protect their own union men, everyone in the town would have realized the implications. The Teamsters, however, were now more than ever willing to put their prestige on the line. The local union people, with the help of higher-up Teamsters officials, interceded with the company and warned the management that the workers would have to be reinstated. The management complied. This victory for economy security in the face of political activity bolstered the campaign activities of Los Cinco and the morale of all their supporters. It was further evidence of the anti-Anglo counterpower being assembled for the campaign.

At the same time that this harassment was proceeding, and perhaps partly because of it, the campaign began to take on a tone that was unusual for a city election: the issue of discrimination was raised. Mexicans began charging that they had been discriminated against on city improvements, such as on sewage connections and the paving and lighting of streets. They noted that no Mexicans had ever been members of the city police force and charged that local justice was such that Latins were punished more severely than Anglos for the same offenses. Rumors spread that the city's swimming pool, which apparently had been segregated until recently, had been disinfected each time after the Latins used it.[17]

These charges put the Anglo community on the defensive, and they began denying that there was racial discrimination now, although many admitted that there had been in the past. But the Anglos did not stop here. They countercharged that outside agitators were coming into the community to stir up the Mexicans, and they argued for local control of the community. The local city attorney, R. A. Taylor, was quoted as saying, "Certainly we're resentful of this union bunch coming in here and stirring up a bunch of rabble."[18] A prominent Anglo lady said:

Why this whole thing is just awful. Those outsiders coming into a little ole bitty town like this. I'm just mortified. People like that coming in and taking over. It just scares you to death. . . . They don't know how to handle money. Haven't handled over a $35 paycheck in their lives. . . . If they take over and spend all this money, who's going to pay for it—the landowners? . . . And young Latin girls, running around to some of our best Mexican people and saying awful things to them, like "Gringo lovers, deserters of your own people"— things like that. That's the kind of thing these outsiders have stirred up—people in this little town hating each other now.[19]

Both the general charges of the Anglos and of the Mexican Americans were essentially correct. The charges against the Anglos of discriminating against Latins on street pavement and sewage, however, might have been more correct had the Mexicans charged that there was discrimination against the poor rather than against Mexican Americans.[20] Crystal City's decisions concerning these matters were based upon the normal American practice in local government of determining whether or not one was rich enough to afford to pay for it. Of course in actual practice this meant that paved streets and sewage connections were located overwhelmingly in the Anglo areas of town, but it upset the Anglos greatly that the Mexicans should have charged discrimination based on race when in fact it was rather discrimination based on poverty.

As to the Anglo charges that outside agitators were coming into the community to mastermind the Latin campaign, this was patently true. Teamster and PASO power, money, and expertise were being used throughout the campaign, and were crucial from the beginning. Without the protective shield of these outside strategists, the campaign would have almost certainly collapsed at any of a number of points. The five council candidates themselves had had no experience in running for office or in running campaigns, and they were watched and coached carefully by the strategists on what to say and what not to say at rallies. This understandably infuriated the Anglo community and was an embarrassment to better-off Mexicans.

Two further issues developed out of the campaign itself, concerning questions of discrimination. During the campaign the local Lions Club announced that it would be supporting an all-Anglo Boy Scout troop.[21] Whereas this normally would have proceeded with scarcely a stir, it was seized upon by organizers and used as proof of Anglo discrimination. A further incident occurred late in the campaign. Martin García, the PASO-

Teamster organizer, was asked to leave a restaurant after having ordered a beer, and he immediately charged racial discrimination. In fact, the incident was somewhat manufactured: the management did not serve beer without food, and when informed of this, García asked for a piece of bread with his beer. At this the management asked him to leave. The management did of course normally serve Mexicans, but it was also most reluctant to serve an aggressive Mexican labor organizer such as García. Realizing the value of such an incident, García in effect created it.

Both these incidents received wide publicity and emphasized the difficulties the Anglo community faced in confronting the Mexican campaign. If the Anglos were going to deny that there was discrimination in a manner that was at all plausible, it meant that they would have to be very careful not to do certain things that came naturally to many of them. And this restraint would have to be exercised at the very time Mexicans were getting "belligerent." This was simply asking too much of the Anglos.

As the council campaign heated up, the enthusiasm for the Latin candidates helped the school-board candidates as well. But the two campaigns were kept somewhat distinct, because of the difference in candidates and difference in the types of jobs the school-board candidates held. Also, the board candidates were running only for the two expiring terms on the seven-man board. Control of the board was thus not in question. Significantly, the question of discrimination was not raised in the school campaign. Jesús Maldonado and Lorenzo Olivares reiterated that they were not trying to gain control of the board, that they were not trying to disrupt the board, that they were not accusing the board of engaging in discrimination, and that they were not running because they held grudges against the Anglos.[22] Instead they argued that they were running because they felt that the Mexican Americans in the community ought to have some representation on the board. Since many in the community did not understand English well, the two candidates declared that they wanted to serve as interpreters for these people unable to speak easily in English.

Regardless of what the two school candidates said, however, the Anglos viewed them with deep suspicion, because they were seen as part of the general Mexican-American activity which threatened to gain control of the community. And even though the two school candidates tried to steer clear of the issue of discrimination in the community, the question of the proper place for the Mexican Americans in the community became the major topic and motivating force behind both the Anglo and the Mexican campaigns. By 1963, however, the Anglos did not rule by discrimination against all Mexican Americans in all areas.[23] A small Mexican-American middle class was developing and was playing a small part in community rule. Indeed there was already one Mexican, Salvador Galván, on the city council, and another councilman, Ed Ritchie, was part Mexican. Thus the issue of racial discrimination was in several respects quite different from the more clear-cut, obvious discrimination existing in the South between Negroes and whites.[24]

In Crystal City, discrimination revolved at least as much around questions of class and of culture as of race. If the Mexicans in the community were willing and—at least as important—were able to shed their culture, then there was a good chance that they would be accepted by many Anglos in the community, at least in a number of activities. But these were important qualifications, for in order to advance, Mexican Americans still had to be willing to relate to Anglos on Anglo terms. The Anglos themselves were willing to admit that social discrimination did exist against Mexicans, but they denied that any basic violation of civil rights occurred.[25] To the great majority of Mexicans, however, the concern was not over whether the discrimination was based upon "subtle" distinctions of class, culture, and social factors rather than upon race. They knew they had been discriminated against, that they were treated as uncivilized "natives," and that was enough. Yet, since it was the Mexicans who were raising the question of discrimination and who were running a slate composed only of Mexican Americans, the Anglos began to charge that it was the Mexicans, not the Anglos, who were the purveyors of racial hatred. This countercharge gained strength, among Anglos at least, as the campaign progressed and raw nerves were exposed.

As the campaign approached its last few days, both Anglos and Mexicans increasingly realized that *los Mexicanos* were becoming more and more involved: Los Cinco rallies were now drawing hundreds, even thousands, of supporters. In response, Anglo women organized a telephone committee to get all 542

Anglos to cast ballots, and the Anglo leadership engaged in more harassing tactics.[26]

They called upon the Texas Rangers to come into Crystal City to maintain order. For over a century the Ranger concept of maintaining order had been quite different from the Mexican-American's idea of what this should entail.[27] Bringing in the Rangers might have panicked the Mexican community into being afraid to turn out for rallies and vote. But again in a brilliant tactical move the Teamster strategists decided to circulate the fallacious rumor that they themselves had requested the Rangers in order to insure that there would be order in the community for the rest of the campaign. Carlos Moore publicly thanked the Rangers for coming to protect the people, and this confused both the Rangers and the Anglos.[28] In truth, the rumor was not as implausible to the community as it might now seem, because talk had been circulating throughout the town that there might be wholesale violence against the Mexican activists. Although Captain A. Y. Allee of the Rangers was extremely upset over the outside agitators in Crystal City, he would not have participated in or allowed the kind of violence that was being rumored as a possibility.

Having failed to get the expected mileage out of calling in the Rangers, the city officials engaged in one final, pre-election harassment. They refused to allow poll-watchers for the election. There had, of course, never been any before, and the city saw no reason for them now. When Carlos Moore, who specialized in Texas election law, showed the city authorities that part of the election code which specified the right of candidates to have poll-watchers, the city relented rather than face legal action.

The campaign from the beginning had been a series of Anglo mistakes, caused first by overconfidence and later by inability to decide upon a coherent strategy to counteract the Mexican activists. Denials of discrimination had been followed by intimidation. Even where the intimidation was effective, it had weakened the credibility of the Anglo leadership with the Mexican population.[29] Basically, the entire campaign had been a series of victories for the Mexicans. Morale in their community was running high and confidence in their right and ability to challenge the city fathers was increasing by the day. The initiative had been so taken by the activists that middle-class

Mexicans were beginning to feel pressured. Several even put up
signs supporting Los Cinco, but the great majority of those
better off continued to side with the Anglos against the "rabble" trying to run for office. In fact, Mexican and Anglo
businessmen were so closely aligned that the week before the
election the Mexican Chamber of Commerce, which was primarily a social club of middle-class Mexican Americans, joined
the Chamber of Commerce in sponsoring the following advertisement:

> We believe that city government should be local, represen-
> tative government.
> We believe in continuing the excellent racial relationships
> we have attained over the years and are against tactics de-
> signed to create racial issues.
> We believe in voting for men who through their education,
> knowledge, business experience and good judgment are best
> qualified to handle the city's affairs.[30]

Although the advertisement did not specifically endorse the
incumbents, it was obvious to all that if one's criteria for voting
were going to be a candidate's education and business experience, there would be no contest at all.

The amazing aspect of the Crystal City election, and that which
made it such a radicalizing election, was that the Mexicans of
the city were not listening to their own acculturated "leaders."
Those Mexicans who were most like the Anglos and whom the
Anglos thus preferred to consider the leaders of the Mexican-
American community were simply not being followed by the
masses. And the system of allowing *jefes* who would do the
bidding of Anglo politicians to rise among the lower-class Mexicans was backfiring. At least one of the *jefes* was setting out on
his own. The historical weakness of the local middle-class Mexicans and the independence of the city's migrant workers were
clearly being felt. Enthusiasm for Los Cinco and respect for
their courage in challenging the Anglo leadership was increasing.
By election eve the final campaign rally for Los Cinco drew
somewhere from 1,500 to 3,000 enthusiastic supporters. Again
outside support was prominent as leading San Antonio liberals
such as State Representatives Jake Johnson and John Alaniz
and PASO organizer Albert Fuentes spoke to the crowd, in-

creasing both their confidence and enthusiasm. Fuentes told them:

> The gringos say they are not afraid of this election. They say they never worry until the day before the election, then they go out and buy the vote. "Give a Mexican a dollar and he will sell himself," they say. But this is no longer true. The mexicanos' eyes are open, and the price is higher now. The man who wants to buy a vote must pay liberty, respect, dignity, education for the children, a higher standard of living for all, and progressive government—that is the new price.
>
> We're going to have people there in the polling booth tomorrow to help you. Do not be afraid. . . . The victory we win tomorrow is here tonight. The Anglos know this now. More important, we know it too.[31]

A nineteen-year-old student from Crystal City, José Angel Gutiérrez, also addressed the crowd. Larry Goodwyn records this as follows:

> Gutiérrez, our interpreter, made his way to the speakers' stand. He told the crowd, "They say there is no discrimination, but we have only to look around us to know the truth. We look at the schools . . . the houses we live in . . . the few opportunities . . . the dirt in the streets . . . and we know." The shock waves again, the strongest of the night, perhaps, for Angel. One of his classmates explained: they are proud of him. He is an honor graduate of Crystal City, and he is with them, not like the middle-class Mexicans supporting the five incumbents.[32]

Martin Garcia, the PASO organizer, also addressed the crowd, telling them, "We're here tonight because deep in our hearts, we're all Mexicans, and tomorrow, we're going to vote for our people."[33] This remark, and a letter from Albert Peña, head of PASO and a county commissioner in San Antonio, which stated that Los Cinco were "the only true 'Mexicanos' in the race" caused tremendous resentment in the Anglo community. Anglos, who were already upset that their opposing candidates were all Latin, charged that Peña's letter and Garcia's statement at the rally were further proof that it was the Latins, not the Anglos, who were discriminating.

Also on election eve, in a final attempt at inducement rather than harassment, the city fathers announced that they had decided to spend $500,000 in bonds on street paving in the Mexican sections of town. Since the issue of street paving had been very much involved in the campaign, they hoped that such a decision would dampen this issue.

Realizing that the election was likely to be very close, the Anglos figured that their best bet for victory still lay in keeping all these newly registered Mexicans from voting. But by the same token, the insurgents also knew that turnout was the key to victory.

Election day was long and tense. In an effort to cut the Mexican vote, Anglo agricultural leaders suddenly doubled wages for that day to the unheard of figure of $2.00 an hour for those working in the fields. Certainly the possibility of making $2.00 an hour presented a painful choice to families who had little money to spare and were always faced with the threat of unemployment. At the same time Del Monte suddenly announced that it was going onto overtime production for election day and that its workers would unfortunately not have time to vote. In both instances, because of careful organization and outside assistance, the Teamster-PASO strategists were ready. At Del Monte the Teamsters pointed out that even on overtime the company had to allow the workers the opportunity to leave their jobs temporarily to vote. Not to do so would have been a violation of the contract and an invitation to legal action or a strike. When mentioning this still did not get the company to change its policy, the Teamster organizers placed a desperate call to Jimmy Hoffa, who throughout the campaign was being kept informed of developments. When notified of what the Del Monte Corporation was doing in Crystal City on election day, Hoffa called their headquarters in San Francisco and notified the management in no uncertain terms that if they did not allow the men time off to vote, there would be action against the company.[34] Because the Teamsters had the muscle and were willing to use it, the management complied.

To handle the wage increases in the fields, the organizers made sure that all migrant crew leaders were to return with their workers by the early afternoon, vote them, and then take them back to the fields. By setting the time early enough in the afternoon, the organizers would have time to send someone else to bring in the workers should the original driver be lured into staying.[35] As it happened, however, all the drivers returned from the fields with plenty of time to spare. Election day was in fact an impressive show of organizational strength by the Teamster-PASO coalition. From poll lists to see who had voted, drivers to bring people to the polls, cards with the candidates' names, and even a marked string to help illiterates know which seven of the twelve candidates to scratch out, the Latins were so well prepared for election day that as many people voted in the city council election as had voted in the entire county in the Nixon-Kennedy presidential race three years before.[36]

The Anglos spent the day uneasily eyeing the long voting lines. The Rangers patrolled throughout the city, but did little more than make themselves very visible. Late that night the results were made known after a long, tense count. They electrified the town and South Texas. Los Cinco had swept to victory in a close count, defeating all five incumbents. The results were as follows:

Manuel Maldonado	864
Juan Cornejo	818
Mario Hernández	799
Antonio Cárdenas	799
Reynaldo Mendoza	795
Ed Ritchie	754
W. P. Brennan	717
Bruce Holsomback	716
J. C. Bookout	694
S. G. Galván	664
Dr. Henry Daly	164
Rev. Arnold López	146

As Goodwyn recorded it, "Within seconds there was pandemonium: the winners were hoisted up on shoulders, so was García, so was Fuentes. Handshaking, horns, a couple of mexicano versions of the rebel yell, and remarkably suddenly they fled to cars and dispersed under the gazes of the Rangers."[37] Soon the results received national and international publicity.

Utilizing the large base of migrant farm laborers through the small Teamsters union at the Del Monte cannery, and playing upon Anglo weaknesses of exclusion and discrimination, the coalition of outside Teamster and PASO organizational expertise had managed to turn the town's political structure upside down. But even the celebrating revealed the precarious position of the victors. The noise of the joy was too much for the Anglos to take. Captain Allee went into action, confronting Cornejo and telling him, "Cornejo, you're going to have to control your people. They must have respect."[38] In order to bring greater "respect" in their followers, Cornejo and others were thus forced to talk to their followers to get them to go home. Quiet settled over the town, with everyone wondering what the election would mean.

The closeness of the vote and the degree of division in the community were re-emphasized three days later when the two Mexican candidates for the school board narrowly lost. The fact that the school district encompassed some rural areas of the county, made up almost exclusively of Anglos and of "controlled" Latin votes, was probably the main reason the two Anglo incumbents were not ousted here as well.

An incident which took place election eve, however, may have weakened the insurgents.[39] As the election eve rally for the two Mexican candidates approached, Lorenzo Olivares was increasingly getting cold feet because his barber-shop business was being affected. He agreed, however, to go to the rally if Jesús Maldonado did most of the talking. Shortly before Maldonado and Olivares were scheduled to go to the rally, they were visited by an unexpected Anglo caller, a dental assistant to the school-board president. By asking the two again why they were running, and why they would try to defeat the venerable dentist, the Anglo engaged the candidates in conversation that became so involved the two were an hour late getting to the rally. By the time they arrived, the crowd had found out that an Anglo had been to see them, and it looked as if the two candidates were afraid to run. Hundreds had already left the rally. The turnout the next day reflected that upwards of two hundred people who had voted in the council elections did not vote in the school elections. Nevertheless, the school vote also set a record, almost doubling the record set three years before when E. C. Muñoz ran. The 1,705 votes were cast as follows:

Dr. S. S. Peters	888
R. E. Boyer	873
Jesús Maldonado	789
Lorenzo Olivares	782

The jubilant Dr. Peters trumpeted, "They haven't got us yet."[40] As events were to prove, he was right.

3 governance, 1963-1965

Unfortunately for those who had worked so hard to bring about the electoral victory, governing the community turned out to be far more difficult than winning the election. The nature of the victory—the inexperience of the candidates, the dependence upon outside help, and the vulnerability of the Mexican community in a town which had always been dominated by Anglos—came back to haunt all those who had worked for the electoral success.

As publicity about the takeover increased, journalists from all over Texas, Mexico, and the nation began flocking to the city for interviews.[1] They quickly sensed the radical implications of what had happened in the town, as this editorial from the *Corpus Christi Caller-Times* reveals:

> Political historians have noted that Latin Americans rarely have been able to agree among themselves on the issue of candidates. Under the patron system voters followed the wishes of their patron. As this system died, a distinctive middle class began to emerge. Ironically, this middle class identified itself with the Anglo population rather than the Latin. Instead of providing a reservoir for political candidates, the middle class tended to stand apart from the politi-

cal struggle, or if they took a part they tended to side with candidates and slates chosen by Anglos.

It now seems apparent that the incident of Crystal City represents a revolt against the "Uncle Toms" of the Latin community. The candidates who won at Crystal City, with the help and financing of the Teamsters Union and PASO . . . represent workers, not the Latin middle class.[2]

With the glare of international publicity focused upon them, the hitherto quiet community was further transformed, and the pressure on both groups increased. More and more the Anglos felt that they had been used as guinea pigs by the Teamsters and PASO. They had been upset by outside involvement and the raising of the issue of discrimination, and this publicity was like pouring salt into their wounds. One by one the defeated Anglos all indicated their stunned amazement at what had happened to their town. Bruce Holsomback, who had been mayor since 1925, said:

> Yes, we were surprised by the way it came out. We didn't have any idea they would use the tactics they did—union tactics. They even intimidated their own people. . . . They spent a lot of money. The Teamsters flew a lot of politicians from San Antonio down here to make speeches. We never had waged a campaign. I drew no salary—I was just trying to do something for the city. I had wanted to quit for several years but couldn't find anyone to take my place. . . . It is pitiful. It wouldn't have been so bad if they had picked intelligent people who knew something about running the city.[3]

W. P. Brennan, city councilman for several decades, commented about opposition charges in a stinging letter to the local paper: ". . . you the MAJORITY of the people, including a few AN-GLOS, could have had all these improvements, but you, the MAJORITY, refused to participate. You would not pay for them." Brennan went on to say that in 1962 the Mexican community in Crystal City paid only "36 percent of the general taxes, while the minority group of 20 percent of the people paid approximately 64 percent of the taxes." He then asked, "Could this be called discrimination?"[4]

While national coverage of the results was generally favorable, the local and statewide press was either shocked or guardedly skeptical. Even the independent liberal weekly, *The Texas Observer*, was uncomfortable with the nature of the campaign the Teamster-PASO coalition had waged. Ronnie Dugger, the editor, remarked that it appeared to him "that sufficient care was not taken to resist the temptation to fight discrimination *with* discrimination." He further commented that "it is true that only mexicanos can speak for mexicanos only if it is also true that the one and entire purpose of politics is serving one's own cause, that is, one's own interest, and that one's own cause is a racial, not a personal, subject."[5]   Qualms that were to sweep the nation's liberal community when "Black Power" became a rallying cry thus swept the liberal community in Texas several years before on account of the Crystal City election. Among Anglo liberals in Texas there was regret that the five winning candidates had all been Mexicans and fear that the defeated Anglos would simply not let the Mexicans get away with it. A short time later in *The Texas Observer*, Hart Stilwell commented that

> There is going to be a brutal tightening down on the Mexican in every town of South Texas because of what PASO and the teamsters union so arrogantly pulled off at Crystal City. Race hatred and discrimination builds back up.
> Whereas if PASO and the teamsters had been content with a mere majority of three and had not completely shut out Anglos, the situation would have been entirely different.[6]

This regret that the slate had not included Anglos, however, reflected a lack of familiarity with the situation in Crystal City. There were no Anglo migrant workers or Anglo stoop labor in Crystal City, and no Anglo in the community was interested in sponsoring, much less running with, a slate of uneducated workers. In 1963 these people were considered by all Anglos, including many with the best of intentions, and by nearly all of the Mexican-American middle class, as persons simply not fit to run for office.

Juan Cornejo, the councilman-elect most willing to speak out, reacted to these charges as best he could.[7] He explained to the press: "I know I'm not educated. I will have to depend on a qualified city manager and city attorney who will cooperate

Statue of Popeye in front of the City Hall of Crystal City, Texas, "The Spinach Capital of the World." Courtesy *The Zavala County Sentinel.*

Unveiling the bust of Benito Juárez, October, 1972. Mayor Frank Benavides is to the right of the statue; the Mexican Consul General is to the left. Courtesy *The Zavala County Sentinel.*

Mayor Juan Cornejo reading of his incident with Texas Ranger Captain A.Y. Allee in April, 1963. Copyright © Express Publishing Co.; printed with permission.

Anglo County officialdom being sworn into office in January, 1971. Irl Taylor, County Judge, second from left. Courtesy *The Zavala County Sentinel.*

with me. But I am educated in the ways of my people. I know my people. And that is better than any college education."[8]

This sort of talk, however, was not going to satisfy the press, or the Anglos, or reduce the qualms of those people who understood what forces and issues had been brought into play in Crystal City. The Anglos were not content to sit around and complain. They struck back quickly. The day after the council election, Manuel Maldonado, the top vote-getter on the ticket and the man ironically most respected by the Anglos, lost his job at the Economart store. Anglo pressure had been strong enough that his employer reluctantly caved in. Another member of Los Cinco, Antonio Cárdenas, found that his wages were halved from $77 to $35 a week. Within a few days a third member of Los Cinco, Mario Hernández, had turned against the other four and began echoing the charges the Anglos were leveling at the council-elect. Financial insecurity was at the core of this difficulty as well. The Anglo leadership confronted him with a series of bad checks he had written, and told him that if he did not say just what they told him to say, he would be prosecuted to the fullest extent of the law. He immediately did what they told him to do, and his "charges" received enormous publicity.[9]

Thus as the Anglos gradually began to realize the implications of their disaster, their opposition to Los Cinco increased to a new level of bitterness. The county attorney, Curtis Jackson, announced that he would conduct an investigation of the vote to look for possible irregularities, and also announced that he was investigating land transferals which had made two of the council candidates eligible to run.[10] The victory of Los Cinco was bringing to the surface deep racial, economic, and political antagonisms that made most people extremely uncomfortable. The five inexperienced and uneducated councilmen-elect were thrown into a situation that would have taxed the minds and the talents of the most seasoned politician. The tremendous resources the Anglo community could marshal were steadily being assembled, and the pressure on Los Cinco increased. The local Anglos may have been defeated in an election that had taken them by surprise, but they had powerful allies whom they now called upon for help. Not only did county and state law-enforcement agencies, for example, continue to patrol the town after the election was over, but their sympathy for the defeated Anglos and their hatred of the Teamster-PASO coalition became obvious. The county sheriff, C. L. Sweeten, noted that "this town is really divided now," and predicted that a similar disaster would never happen again because "the Anglos will really get out and pay their poll taxes now."[11] Texas Rangers also continued to patrol the town, and they too were obviously most upset with the election results. Captain Allee remarked that he was trying only to keep outside agitators from coming into the community, but of course "outside agitators" (in the form of San Antonio expertise) were still essential to the movement.[12]

Although coercion increased, and threats upon the lives of Los Cinco through rumors and anonymous telephone calls continued, Los Cinco were not dissuaded from taking office. But the trauma they were going through had its impact on the selection of mayor for the town. By tradition the candidate named mayor was to be the one with the highest number of votes. This would have been Manuel Maldonado. But with Maldonado fired and his economic weakness exposed, the next highest man, Juan Cornejo, actively sought the post. Aided by his connections with the Teamsters and by Maldonado's own fear for his family, Cornejo managed to persuade a majority of the council to elect him mayor.

In trying to insure that the insurgents would be able to govern, the most important task left for the Teamster-PASO alliance was to select a city manager for Crystal City. Since according to the city charter it was the manager who ran the municipality on a day-to-day basis, the consequences of this selection were sure to be at least as important for the town government as the selection of the five candidates for the council. For this position the alliance found George Ozuna, a Mexican-American engineer from San Antonio who received his degree from the University of Texas. Ozuna was currently working in the public works branch of the San Antonio municipal government, but he had recently been considered for the position of city manager of Terrell Hills, a rich Anglo suburb north of San Antonio. Although in the end he had not been selected from among the three finalists, that he had been considered at all in the suburb indicated that his credentials were excellent. Upon being chosen for Crystal City, Ozuna became the first Mexican-American city manager in Texas.[13]

By selecting Ozuna, a man with no prior connection to either the Teamsters or PASO, the alliance indicated they were aware that they very much needed an efficient, well-organized city manager for Crystal City who could allay the fears of many Anglos throughout the region and who at the same time could prove that Mexican Americans could run the town.

As events were taking place, however, the local Anglos were by no means taking a respite from their counteroffensive. In fact, in the two-week interval between the election and the swearing-in of the candidates, the city government was very nearly reduced to a shambles. When it gradually became clear that the councilmen-elect, in spite of the pressure being put on them, were going to take office, the Anglos decided upon a strategy of trying to protect themselves and also to cripple the city government. Since Del Monte feared that the new government might want to annex them to the city in order to get needed tax revenue, the plant got the lame-duck city council to quickly sign a seven-year contract renouncing the right to annex the plant into the city. As a means of crippling the city government, certain important Anglos tried to get all the city help to resign. They hoped to paralyze the city government until the Latins could be thrown out, in one way or another. Pressure was put on appointive city officials to resign by panicking them into thinking that chaos would break out as soon as the Mexicans took over and that all officials would be fired anyway. The city manager, the city marshall (who had been criticized during the campaign for discriminating against Mexicans), and nearly all appointive officials capitulated. As Ozuna was sworn in as city manager, one by one the superintendents of streets, gas, water, sewage, and garbage handed in their resignations.

In the face of both overwhelming publicity and wholesale Anglo resignations from the city government in the hopes that the new government would topple, George Ozuna thought that his most important task was to keep the city government running. In this he was aided by a few Anglo holdovers who, for one reason or another, did not resign.[14] The most important of these was the city clerk for the last thirty years, June Broadhurst. Miss Broadhurst had been city clerk since before even the time of L. L. Williams. She and the late city manager had been the two most important persons managing the day-to-day affairs of the city. Although the panicked Anglos had written out a letter of resignation for her to sign, she refused to comply on the grounds that she should stay to keep a watch over city expenditures. Ozuna recognized that Miss Broadhurst's knowledge of the city government would be invaluable to the new administration, and Miss Broadhurst soon realized that Ozuna was a competent, dedicated engineer who wanted most to be a responsible, efficient reformer. As the storm swirled around them, the two became fast friends.[15]

Through Miss Broadhurst, Ozuna extended offers to all those who had resigned from the city government in the days after the election. Although this action dispelled the rumor circulated by the Anglos that the new government would fire all Anglos, none who had resigned was willing to return. Ozuna was thus faced with the task of finding replacements. He looked into each department, trying to find lower-level men who thought they could supervise. Using this lower echelon help, Ozuna then worked to get them qualified for the jobs they were to handle. The spirit inside the city government in the early days was thus one of intense cooperation, with Ozuna and the people who remained trying desperately to keep city services going and at the same time trying to prove that they could govern the city as well as the old regime had. When disasters struck, such as a burst in a water main, they all pitched in and tried to help.

It was under these conditions, not very different perhaps from a new nation trying to keep the infrastructure going after the departure of the colonial power,[16] that the government slowly but surely began to establish itself and to institute reforms. The first Mexican-American policemen in the history of the town were appointed, and Rey Pérez became the new city marshal. Jobs that had been considered as reserved for Anglos thus began to open up under the new administration. The city council began to fill appointments to such city boards as the Urban Renewal Commission, the Housing Authority Board, and the Board of Equalization with Mexican Americans, and they gradually began to learn about the running of the city.

Not long after being in office, Ozuna discovered that there were no city maps showing the location of city water, gas, and sewer lines. He also discovered that the city was losing from thirty to sixty percent of its natural gas through leakage. He thus began a painstaking survey of the city and charted the course of the underground mains, giving the city its first accurate maps.[17] Funds made available through urban renewal and the city's bond election two years before were now used for a number of dramatic improvements. Street paving came to the Mexican sections of town, and with this came gutters, curbs, and better drainage facilities. The number of city street lights more than doubled, and new city parks were created. The first traffic lights and speed-limit signs in the city's history were installed, and water, gas, and sewer facilities were extended to a number of Mexican homes in the city.

Within the city government itself, Ozuna instituted wage increases after discovering that many of the city's Mexican help, including water, sewer, and gas workers, were making $27 to $30 for a forty-hour week. Ozuna raised their wage to a dollar an hour. He also bought uniforms for the city police department, bought a police car, and increased the size of the city's police force while appointing qualified Mexicans. Ozuna also initiated a surplus-commodities program for the city's many unemployed and underemployed. This had been something the city government had been reluctant to do earlier because it smacked of welfare.

Ozuna also proved to be a frugal city manager, cutting costs and saving the city money in a number of ways. Taxes were collected more diligently than before, bringing in greater revenue to the city. Because of new members appointed by the city council, the Board of Equalization began working on tax valuations in the city, which Ozuna felt were assessed too low and in a discriminatory manner.[18] By stopping gas leakage, ending car allowances for policemen now that the city had a police car, and improving clerical procedures in the city, he also saved the city money. Certain practices by the old administration of not bringing in revenues when it could have—such as neglecting to collect rents on private hangars at the city's airport—were now ended.

Ozuna thus slowly but surely established himself as a first-rate administrator and manager for the city. When the opposition, simply unable to believe that the Mexicans were not bankrupting the city, charged that the city's credit rating had been ruined, the First of Texas Corporation, which handled Crystal City bonds, issued a stern rebuke. They reported that "the present administration has continued the affairs of the city in a conservative manner. Mr. Ozuna has demonstrated his abilities to supervise the administration. Tax collections to date are the best on record. The financial situation in Crystal City is sound."[19]

It was thus difficult for the Anglos to find fault with Ozuna's improvements. Since many of the changes occurred through the urban renewal program, the Anglos countered that these developments would have taken place regardless of who was in power. Tensions within the city did not diminish and opposition to the new government continued at a high level. It was not so much what the new government did that upset Anglos; it was more the fear of what these Mexicans backed by the Teamsters *might* do that terrified the Anglos. Said one of the leaders of the Anglo opposition, Captain J. A. Loyall:

> Only Latins will determine how tax money will be spent. You can imagine the nightmare this circumstance gives responsible-minded town's people, Latin and Anglo alike. . . . The Teamsters wanted political stooges in government, and the PASO boys were willing to serve. Big unionism has not been able to gain its objectives through collective bargaining and the legal pampering which has been accorded them. In fact, they are losing ground all of the time. Now they are seeking through political yes men in government to gain through legislation what they are unable to gain through salesmanship and service.[20]

Given this degree of opposition to the Mexicans in city hall, improvements were very nearly ignored as political events surrounding the new government prevented any return to stability.

Less than a month after the new council had taken office, Mayor Cornejo charged that Texas Ranger Captain A. Y. Allee (who was still staying in town) had physically attacked and threatened him. Cornejo filed a $15,000 damage suit against him and asked for an injunction permanently restraining him "from assaulting, intimidating, threatening or interfering with" his constitutional rights.[21] The incident occurred after Cornejo had had a heated argument with an Anglo over the Anglo's possible firing of one of the new councilmen. As reported in the *Laredo Times:*

Sheriff C. L. Sweeten, standing nearby, bumped Cornejo with his elbow as Cornejo turned to walk away. Cornejo turned and glared at Sweeten. Captain Allee immediately approached, put his hand on Cornejo's shoulder and told him: "Come here, I want to talk to you." They walked inside an office at city hall; Sweeten followed. The door was slammed hard. The three were inside for twenty minutes.[22]

What exactly happened inside is still disputed, but the county sheriff and Captain Allee did take the mayor into a private room without witnesses.

The suit was dismissed, predictably, for lack of witnesses, but the incident received tremendous publicity. Anglos rallied around the Ranger Captain, who throughout his many years with the Rangers had developed a reputation similar to that J. Edgar Hoover had with the FBI.[23] Crystal City residents journeyed to Austin to talk with Colonel Homer Garrison, head of the Texas Department of Public Safety. They praised Allee and asked for the Rangers to stay in the area. The Zavala county judge and county commissioners passed a resolution praising Allee and Sweeten. Councilman Hernández said that the Rangers were necessary for law enforcement, and he requested Ranger protection for himself. Ultimately the state government was involved in the dispute, as Colonel Garrison and Governor John Connally came to the defense of the Rangers.[24] Senator Ralph Yarborough, however, issued a statement denouncing "men wearing pistols, not a part of a city government, but breathing down the necks of duly elected city commissioners as they exercise the functions of their offices." Such men, Yarborough said, "are a relic of a primitive age in Texas which should have passed away with the frontier."[25]

There was also harassment of the Mexicans on the city's police force. In June city policeman Leonardo Santoya was arrested on charges of contributing to the delinquency of a fourteen-year-old girl. Captain Allee quickly produced a sworn statement made by the girl, which he read to the city manager and police chief. Although Ozuna and Police Chief Pérez had little choice but to suspend Santoya pending investigation, in the course of the investigation the charges appeared clearly to be a frameup, with the girl acting as *agent provocateur*. Santoya was found not guilty and was reinstated with the police force, but Ozuna warned all people working for the city to be extremely wary of further attempts to get them into compromising situations.[26]

While the explosive question of law enforcement and intimidation was being raised, the owner of one of the larger packing sheds in Crystal City announced that he was leaving Crystal City for La Pryor, a nearby town. Terming the Teamsters "a terrible cancer that is spreading," the owner said that the labor market at La Pryor was better.[27]

To compound the problems for the new city government, Anglo politicians were working with county and state law enforcement officers and area businessmen to do all they could to harass the new government. When County Attorney Curtis Jackson was unable to make a case for investigation of the election, or for disqualification of several councilmen on the grounds that they did not own valid property, the Anglos set about trying to force a recall election for the council. Texas law, however, required that for a recall petition to be valid a majority of those who voted in the election must request that a new election be held. The Anglos could not hope to get this many people to sign for a recall. Instead they devised a plan which was nothing short of brilliant in its ability to weight the procedures of governance in their favor. Calling their petition not a recall petition but a "charter revision," so that, under state law, only ten percent of the voters would have to sign the petition, they proposed to increase the number of seats on the council from five to seven. This would amount to a recall petition in that all five councilmen would be forced to run again. The "charter revision" further stipulated that the election had to be held on October 1st, before many of the Mexicans working in the fields up north would have returned, and that henceforth terms for the council would be staggered, lasting four years. Best of all, the "charter revision" stipulated that all future city elections were to be held in July, when it would be next to impossible for Crystal City's many migrants to vote.

The city council, however, refused to call for the elections, arguing that the petition was in effect a recall petition and therefore lacked a sufficient number of signatures.[28] Although the district judge agreed completely that the petition was a "charter revision" rather than a recall petition, legal appeals managed to postpone a decision until the October deadline passed and the question became moot. By appealing the decision, the new government further enraged the Anglos. The local press, which had always been solidly conservative and strongly supportive of Anglo rule, now editorialized that by refusing to order the election the councilmen had gone against God. Stated the editor concerning the revision of the charter, "Surely no right thinking citizen could object to this provision in his government."[29]

Although stymied in this attempt to use institutional procedures to throw out the government, the Anglos also set up a new organization to prepare for the next elections.[30] Realizing that they could no longer rule as they had before the revolt, they began to change their strategy of ruling.[31] Given the historical composition of Crystal City, the Anglos had from the beginning been faced with basically only three ways of ruling: outright intimidation, cooptation of certain Mexicans, and the creation and maintenance of apathy. Their rule always had been a mixture of all three, with a gradual increase in the need and desire for cooptation as the Mexican community began to improve its lot. But the revolt in 1963 upset the Anglo routine and the politics of gradualism and forced the process of cooptation to become far more deliberate, particularly as intimidation could no longer guarantee success. Unless common, ordinary Mexican-American "rabble" who were now voting and participating in the government could be disenfranchised, the Anglos simply had to have Mexican support in order to win. When their attempts at disenfranchisement through the charter revision failed, the Anglos sought more than ever a coalition with the "better Mexican element" which would allow these Mexicans a chance to shoulder many of the visible concerns of the Anglos.

In this strategy the Anglos were aided by the new government's inexperience in ruling, unfamiliarity with keeping together a winning coalition, and by Ozuna's desire to stay out of the swirl of politics. Shortly after the election, representatives from the Mexican Chamber of Commerce approached the Cornejo administration in a conciliatory manner. Cornejo quite understandably resented these businessmen's support of the old Anglo administration, and he rejected their offers to contribute to the new government.[32] Thus the new Mexican government indicated a lack of tact in dealing with the middle-class Mexican community at the very time Anglos were assiduously courting their favor.[33]

The Anglos themselves, who had never been completely monolithic, were faced with several problems in seeking Mexican support. In particular, the question of how to attack the new government became more of a problem as the Anglos increasingly sought and relied upon Mexican support. To have campaigned against the Mexicanos as *Mexicans* would of course have been disastrous. Also, since the new government was instigating many noncontroversial and popular reforms, the Anglos could not hope to build a winning coalition by attacking the policies of the government many of them so clearly hated. Instead, the issue which they settled upon was one of local control versus outside domination. Their enemy was not Mexicans; it was the Teamsters, PASO, and other "outsiders" who were coming into Zavala County and stirring up hatred.

Because of obvious and admitted Teamster-PASO involvement in the whole revolt, and because of the lack of experience of the elected candidates, the question of outside involvement continued to be enormously explosive even after the election. "Advisers" from San Antonio were on hand for almost all meetings of the city council, helping the mayor learn parliamentary procedure, and in general guiding him through the meetings. This infuriated the local Anglos, and because both the Teamsters and PASO were viewed as potential threats to the stability of all South Texas, charges of Teamster-PASO domination drew tremendous amounts of publicity in the regional press.[34]

After Hernández broke with the group, he began charging that Ray Shafer of the Teamsters and Albert Fuentes of PASO were trying to run the town. The wave of publicity given Hernández's charges prompted both the Teamsters and PASO to assert that they were for allowing the local people in Crystal City to run their own government. But these disclaimers could be only partly true. It is possible that both organizations hoped that Crystal City officials would run things smoothly and competently enough, so that they would not need to intervene. But because both the Teamsters and PASO had invested a great deal of prestige in the Crystal City venture, and because both organizations did hope to increase their power in the rest of South Texas, neither organization could claim disinterest in the affairs of the city once the election was over. They both knew that Crystal City could be a vital power base for further expansion.

It was very much in their interest to see Crystal City become a model for other municipal governments in South Texas, a model for reforms which allowed Mexicans, laboring Mexicans at that, a role in government more representative of their actual numbers. This would help the image of both organizations. Further, since both associations knew and understood the tremendous vulnerability of the local Mexican community, they also knew that to leave town and abandon Los Cinco after the election would result in a rout. Thus even if both organizations had genuinely wanted to leave Crystal City alone after the election and to allow the new government to call all the shots, because of the type of candidates chosen and the degree of opposition in the community, to leave Los Cinco completely alone was to risk utter disaster. This they knew, but in the face of tremendous pressure, both began a reluctant pullback.

Even with this gradual retreat, charges of outside domination, or at least of outside influence, were still accurate to some extent. These charges also revealed that there was no easy way out for the outsiders, owing to the vulnerability of the local Mexican community.

Using this constant refrain, then, the Anglos were able to build up a successful coalition with a large part of the Mexican community. For these charges of outside domination did not strain Anglo and middle-class Mexican relations. On the contrary, they reinforced the alliance because the Mexicans who were with the Anglos could be "responsible" and "qualified," which was what most of them had desperately wanted to be anyway. Together, then, the Anglos and the middle-class Mexicans formed a powerful coalition, called the Citizens Association Serving All Americans (CASAA).

Since the local people active in the Teamster-PASO alliance in 1963 had hoped to accomplish a takeover of the county in 1964, CASAA organized on a county-wide basis and announced that its objectives were "to prevent the takeover of Zavala County by outside political pressure groups, to endorse and support local candidates for public office within Zavala County and to rid the county of persons already in public office who are under domination of outside interests."[35] The organization was carefully composed of co-chairmen—one Mexican, one Anglo—and a board of directors with a nearly equal ratio of Anglos and Mexicans.[36]

the 1964 county elections

It was understandable that a fight would soon develop over control of the county. The county government had become quite involved in Crystal City affairs. Not only was the sheriff openly allied with CASAA, but the county judge and commissioners had supported the Rangers and the sheriff against charges of brutality and intimidation. An action in the autumn of 1963 further accented the dispute between the city and the county. In November the federal government approved a grant for the construction of a city-county public building complex. The application had been made the previous year, several months before Los Cinco had been elected. Although the funds had been approved, the county now decided that it no longer wanted to participate in the building complex because it no longer had any confidence in the city administration. The county judge, who along with the commissioners had approved the request for funds the year before, remarked that the county wanted to "stop the tide of socialism and pork barrel legislation."[37] The city was thus forced to prepare another application for funds for the building complex, which was to include a library and public-health unit as well as a new city hall and jail.[38]

Given the hostility of the county government to the city administration, a takeover of the county would have removed one of the main impediments to the new administration. But a takeover was not possible. Because terms for county offices were for four years and were staggered, it was impossible to gain control in 1964. The county judge was not up for re-election, nor were two of the four county commissioners. Only the county attorney, sheriff, tax assessor-collector, and two of the four commissioners had terms expiring in 1964. While these offices could be very valuable to the insurgents, they could not mean control of the county.

All the incumbent county officials were opposed to Los Cinco. The county attorney had of course been bitterly opposed to Los Cinco, and had been instrumental in trying to throw them out of office, first through investigating the voting and their property qualifications, and later through the recall petition. The tax assessor-collector, an aging Anglo, occupied an office which could have been valuable as a means of bringing about more equitable assessment of land values in the county. As it stood, land in the county, overwhelmingly owned by Anglos, was undervalued just as it had been in the city. The sheriff, like the county attorney, had a clear record of opposition to Los Cinco. His statements against them and his support of Captain Allee were well known. Late in the year, however, another incident occurred which increased Mexican-American distrust of the sheriff. Prisiliano Briones, a local Mexicano, while supposedly being taken to the hospital by Sheriff Sweeten, was shot to death in the back of the head. Briones at the time of his death was handcuffed in the back of the sheriff's car. Sheriff Sweeten maintained that Briones wrestled his way into the front seat, got the gun away from the sheriff, and while still handcuffed, managed to commit suicide by shooting himself in the back of the head.[39] Just how many people believed the sheriff's story is unclear, but an interesting aspect is that the story itself, should it have been absolutely correct, might have also been expected to arouse questions about the sheriff's competence. If the sheriff could not keep a handcuffed prisoner from stealing his own gun, could this be a reflection upon his abilities? Apparently not. At least there was no Anglo opponent to Sheriff Sweeten.

In trying to oppose these three county officials, the insurgent Mexicans ran into further trouble. Because of more institutional constraints, they were not able to oppose even all three of the officials up for re-election. By state law the county attorney must be a licensed attorney. Since, not surprisingly, none of the Mexican-Americans in the community had law degrees, none was qualified to run for office.

Aside from the problem of the institutional setup of the county administration, which assured that any attempt to gain control of the county would fail, there were other serious problems lying in the path of a strong challenge to county officialdom. The county, when compared to the city, was not as ripe for political change.[40] In the first place, the Anglo-Mexican demographic ratio for the county was different from the ratio in Crystal City itself. Whereas Anglos were outnumbered six to one in the city, they were outnumbered only three to one in the county. This meant that of those people in the county over twenty-one who had paid their poll taxes, the Anglos were outnumbered by considerably less than two to one.[41] Sec-

ondly, the ranchland and small towns of the county contained
Mexican Americans who were much more dependent on local
Anglos than were those in Crystal City. There were of course no
other unions in the county; furthermore the economic and
social relationships prevailing in the smaller towns and rural
areas tended to be both more intimate and more paternalistic
than in Crystal City.[42] Many farm- and ranch-hands, for example, stayed with their Anglo masters all year rather than migrate.

Thirdly, the takeover of the city, while it had galvanized the
Mexican Americans of the city, had also jolted Anglos out of
their accustomed lethargy and had given them a year to prepare for the battle over the county. The mistake of paying too
little attention to getting Anglos registered and to seeking
Mexican votes would not be repeated. Instead the Anglos,
through CASAA, were armed to the teeth. In their campaign
against "outside domination" they had ironically been able to
garner considerable money from outside the county. Absentee
landlords in the county, and those who owned land in general,
were anxious to prevent the insurgents from getting a foothold
in the county government.[43] With both money and excellent
organization, CASAA was able to sponsor numerous free barbecues, and this brought out as many as two and three thousand
people for their rallies. They were also careful to endorse two
Mexican-American candidates for office. One, Jesus Rodríguez,
an owner of a grocery store, was running for county commissioner. If elected, he would be the first Mexican ever to be a
county commissioner in Zavala County. Yet in endorsing Rod-
rígeuz, CASAA had had to forgo endorsing an Anglo member of
their organization, Busey Coleman, who was running for the
same post. This split emphasized that while the bulk of the
Anglos were ready to make concessions, not all Anglos were
united on the desirability of having Mexicans run for county
office.

All of the above-mentioned factors added up to formidable,
if not insurmountable, obstacles for the insurgents seeking to
expand their control into the county. But an equally serious
factor was the deterioration that had occurred within their own
organization. After the tremendous reaction and adverse publicity which both the Teamsters and PASO had received in
1963, neither organization was prepared to take on another

battle, particularly in a contest where the odds were stacked heavily against them from the beginning. Both organizations had said they were in favor of allowing the local Mexicanos to run the city government. Sending their tacticians back into the community to prepare for the county elections would subject them to even more condemnations. In fact the impact of the Crystal City election had very nearly destroyed PASO as a viable political force in the state. In the aftermath of the victory, the organization was attacked from within by those who felt PASO should never have been involved with the Teamsters, should never have run an all-Mexican slate, and should never have run uneducated workers for office. Shortly after the Crystal City election, most of those who opposed the Crystal City venture left PASO, leaving the organization in no position to attempt another battle of similar magnitude.[44] In Crystal City itself, however, the local organization began to consider itself a local PASO chapter. But it was virtually autonomous from the battered statewide group and received no help from them. Thus at the very time the opposition was mounting a massive campaign against "outside domination," the local political organization for Los Cinco, now called simply PASO, was left increasingly to fend for itself.

Lack of outside assistance and expertise combined with a year in office had also allowed certain enmities to develop among the Mexicanos active in the movement. Many had expected dramatic economic improvements after Los Cinco's victory. When these could not immediately materialize, some became angry and disillusioned. There was also considerable jockeying over who should do the leading and who the following. When Moses Falcón, who had been chairman of the Citizens for Better Government in the campaign of Los Cinco, announced that he was running for county commissioner before the PASO organization had had a chance to vote on whether or not to endorse him, many in the organization were affronted. Mayor Cornejo and Councilmen Mendoza and Cárdenas spoke against this insult to the organization, and the PASO group eventually endorsed Antonio Yanas over Falcón. When Falcón failed to back Yanas, he was expelled from the organization for not endorsing its candidate. This feuding and in-fighting expended a great amount of energy and sapped the morale of the whole campaign effort.

All these factors added up to continued Anglo control of the county. But CASAA had two further advantages. Since the county elections were to be in May rather than in April, fewer migrants would be in the community to vote. And secondly, by being the incumbents CASAA was able to have full control of the voting procedures for the elections.[45] As a means of ensuring their victory, CASAA embarked on an ambitious campaign to garner absentee votes from sick and elderly Mexicans.[46] When Mayor Cornejo requested that a PASO poll-watcher be allowed to watch the absentee voting, the county clerk refused. In the ensuing attempt to become a poll-watcher, Mayor Cornejo was repeatedly turned down because his application did not conform, in one way or another, to the Texas election code.[47] Cornejo also asked that the absentee ballot box be sealed with several signatures until the counting time. This, however, was deemed unnecessary because only the sheriff and the county clerk had the key combination necessary to open the box.[48] This might have calmed PASO's fears of fraud, except that of course both the sheriff and the county clerk were well-known CASAA partisans. Further, Sheriff Sweeten was at the moment locked in a bitter campaign against a PASO candidate, Manuel Garza. Nevertheless, or perhaps because of this fact, Cornejo was continually rebuffed, and CASAA marched seemingly inexorably forward. By the close of absentee voting, over five hundred people, or nearly one-sixth of all those who would vote, had cast absentee ballots.

As the battle over absentee voting indicates, throughout the spring campaign there were charges of impending fraud. The Anglos charged that Mexican nationals were registered to vote and that migrant workers who were leaving before the elections were giving their poll-tax certificates to others to vote for them.[49] PASO charged that absentee balloting was being used to vote feeble and elderly Mexicans who neither requested ballots nor marked them themselves. In June a letter from an anonymous school teacher to the Democratic party chairman, R. A. Taylor, was made public:

> I understand you are checking every angle of crooked voting. I think you should start with your absentee voting. As you probably know it was the most illegal procedure practiced, yes, in the history of this town.

As long as "CASAA" hires women like Mrs. Ofilia Perales and María Cumpian to do their dirty work your election will continue to be a mockery.

It is a known fact all over town that the tactics these women used are a disgrace to our democracy. I had the opportunity as well as many others, of seeing signed affidavits of the persons "The Puppets" (as the above women are called) stole the votes from. "The Puppets" would have these persons sign their names where they should sign it, but that's as far as they participated in preparing their own ballot. These persons like Juan Antonio De Leon and others like him who were easy prey for these women, were told by "The Puppets" that they would take care of completing the ballot. . . .[50]

The letter was signed, "A Crystal City Teacher— If I sign I might as well resign. . . ." R. A. Taylor dutifully announced that he would carefully investigate these charges, but of course he was a prominent CASAA man himself. Although the letter states that CASAA was using the absentee ballots illegally, nothing was done to stop the practice. Thus charges of fraud flew thick and heavy. These charges were to continue beyond 1964.[51]

As the overwhelming preponderance of the factors sighted here indicate, the 1964 campaign for control of the county was in general a reversal of the 1963 city campaign. Lacking significant outside support, lacking the unity and enthusiasm which had ignited them the year before, unable to take their opponents by surprise, and forced to campaign in terrain that was less favorable to them for both demographic and institutional reasons, the local PASO group was beaten.[52] In a record turnout of 3,416 votes cast in the county, PASO won only two minor offices and forced CASAA into a runoff in two others. In their two victories, Julian Salas was elected justice of the peace in precinct three (western Crystal City, which is heavily Mexican), and Alfredo Terán was elected precinct chairman for the Democratic party in this same precinct. Although the Mexicano candidates had garnered over forty percent of the vote, both the sheriff and tax assessor-collector were re-elected, and PASO failed to take over control of the local Democratic party organization.

A runoff was required in the hotly contested race for county commissioner of precinct three. Antonio Yanas (PASO) had led the pack, followed by Jesus Rodríguez (CASAA) and the Anglo CASAA had refused to endorse, Busey Coleman. Moses Falcón had pulled out of the race shortly before the voting began. Because of a tie vote in the race for constable of precinct three, Rannie Hale and Santos Alcozer were also forced to run in the June runoff. But as everyone knew, just as there were fewer migrants in the community in May than in April, so there would be even fewer in June.

The June runoff thus found both CASAA candidates winning. Because of the selective drop revealed in the support for PASO and CASAA candidates between the May primary and the June runoff, the results are produced in the table below.

Office	May Primary	June Runoff	Drop In Turnout
Constable of Precinct Three			
Santos Alcozer (PASO)	489	315	35%
Rannie Hale (CASAA)	489	461	6%
Commissioner of Precinct Three			
Antonio Yanas (PASO)	448	306	32%*
Moses Falcón (ex-PASO)	4		
Jesus Rodríguez (CASAA)	363	474	8%**
Busey Coleman (CASAA member, but unendorsed)	155		

*combined vote of Yanas and Falcón.
**combined vote of Rodríguez and Coleman.

As the table indicates, in the race for constable support for the PASO candidate dropped thirty-five percent while support for the CASAA candidate dropped only six percent. In the race for commissioner of precinct three the differential rate of decline in turnout was similar. A comparison of the May primary and June runoff election thus very likely indicates the degree to which the migrant workers were overwhelmingly behind the PASO candidates. The figures also indicate the devastating effect the CASAA-backed charter revision (which specified city elections for July) would have had upon Mexican participation had the revision become law.

The county returns also showed definite indications that the whole county had been polarized not only for local offices, but for state-wide offices as well. In the statewide Democratic primary U.S. Senator Ralph Yarborough was running against a radio station owner and strong conservative, Gordon McLendon. Governor John B. Connally, who only shortly before had been injured in the assassination of President Kennedy, was running for re-election against a Houston liberal, Don Yarborough (no relation to the Senator). For Lieutenant Governor Preston Smith was running for re-election against Albert Fuentes, the PASO organizer instrumental in the campaign for Los Cinco in 1963. In their state-wide races the three liberal candidates (Yarborough, Yarborough, and Fuentes) fared very differently, garnering vote totals ranging from fifty-eight percent to twenty-one percent of the vote. In Zavala County, however, the three liberal candidates were generally perceived as a coalition and they received remarkably similar vote totals. All three of the liberals lost, although by fairly close margins. At the same time their totals were remarkably similar to the totals received by the Mexican-American challengers to the county sheriff and tax assessor-collector.[53] This would seem to indicate that, for the overwhelming majority of voters in the county, to be a supporter of one of the liberals (whether statewide or local) was to be a supporter of all.[54]

In particular, Senator Yarborough's Anglo support, which had never been large, simply vanished. He received only one percent more of the votes than Albert Fuentes received, although statewide he received three times as many votes as Fuentes. Of all the Senator's actions, his criticism of the Rangers seems to have done most to make him anathema to the local Anglos.[55] The degree to which the countywide polarization extended to statewide offices, then, seems to be a further indication of the degree to which the county was going through an extremely bitter struggle, with ideological and racial themes almost universally recognized by the voters.

the aftermath of the county elections

Viewed in totality, Los Cinco and their organization, PASO, emerged weakened from the 1964 county electoral battle.

Office	Statewide Totals	Statewide Percentage	County Totals	County %	County % Difference From State
U.S. Senator					
Ralph Yarborough	905,000	58%	1,355	46%	-12%
Gordon McLendon	673,000	42%	1,600	54%	+12%
Governor					
Don Yarborough	471,000	30%	1,199	40%	+10%
John Connally	1,125,000	70%	1,769	60%	-10%
Lieutenant Governor					
Albert Fuentes	304,000	21%	1,325	45%	+24%
Preston Smith	1,160,000	79%	1,633	55%	-24%
County Sheriff					
Manuel Garza			1,377	42%	
C. L. Sweeten			1,865	58%	
County Tax Assessor					
Raul Flores			1,485	48%	
M. C. Morris			1,630	52%	

Note: Because of the intense Mexican opposition to Sheriff Sweeten, one might have expected the sheriff to do more poorly than any of the other Anglo candidates. In fact, however, he did better than M. C. Morris, both because the Anglos in turn seem to have been more concerned to see him rather than Morris re-elected, and because Raul Flores, the candidate against Morris, ran an independent campaign, stressing that while he would work for change he would not be tied to either the Teamsters or PASO. Flores therefore does not seem to have aroused the opposition as much as the challenger to Sweeten did.

64

Given the hostility between the city and county government, it was not surprising that PASO had tried to take county offices. But because of the tremendous handicaps they faced, it was also not surprising that they lost. Their losses were not by great margins, and given their inexperience, the new terrain they had to cover, and the other factors mentioned earlier which were working against them, it would not be difficult to argue that their showing was credible.[56] The county had always been dominated by Anglos. Now suddenly Mexicans were running for office, capturing over forty percent of the vote, and forcing the Anglos into coalition building and campaigning. Because PASO had such high hopes, however, their loss was viewed as a serious defeat, and it seemed to compound their problems. Their morale had been damaged and incipient factionalism had broken out into the open.

In particular, the spring elections seem to have taken their toll on Mayor Cornejo. He had never been fully able to reconcile himself to the city-manager form of government—to the idea that the city manager, not the mayor, ran the city government. It had been Cornejo who had campaigned, who had put his name, and very nearly his life, on the line. He had been the one with the courage and dedication to make the try back in late 1962. To have done all that and then have to take a back seat to an engineer from San Antonio went against his grain. He was the mayor, yet he received no salary and was not even supposed to concern himself with day-to-day affairs of the city. The city-manager form of government, set up to provide businesslike administration for the town, seemed designed also to prevent new political leadership from developing authority.

He further was not really able to understand the complexity of the problems the city faced. Cornejo tended to view Ozuna as a technician who was to fix or repair whatever it was Cornejo thought needed improvement. When Ozuna wasn't able to do everything right away, Cornejo would get mad. This problem was compounded by the high expectations Cornejo's followers had after the victory.

The increased publicity about events in Crystal City also aggravated Cornejo's irritation with his lack of authority in the city government's affairs. From being a dutiful worker at the Del Monte cannery, a union man who as a *jefe* had controlled a small following of votes which Anglo politicians had sought,

Cornejo after 1963 had been thrust into international publicity as the leader of a political revolution sweeping South Texas. Soon he was making speeches around the area and was flown to Los Angeles for a talk. There he had ended his speech with the phrase: "Today Crystal City, tomorrow the world!"[57] In the end this transformation turned out to be disastrous for him, for George Ozuna lay in the path of his aspirations for bigger and better things. In the struggle that followed, the revolution in Crystal City was destroyed from within.

Less than one month after the June runoff the issue of who was to run the city was very nearly brought to a head when Ozuna fired one of the city's new policemen. Leonardo Santoya either had refused or had been unable to pay off debts he had incurred, and because of this Ozuna fired him. "I felt that a policeman who can't meet his financial responsibilities has no business serving the public," Ozuna was quoted as saying.[58] This firing infuriated Cornejo, and he tried to fire Ozuna in retaliation. Although Cornejo had the votes on the council to pass a motion to fire Ozuna, the intervention of Mrs. Ray Shafer, wife of the Teamsters official, dissuaded Cornejo from calling the meeting to fire Ozuna.[59]

An uneasy truce between Ozuna and Cornejo followed for a little over a month, with Cornejo increasingly resentful of his subordinate status in the city government. The issue which finally brought the clash to a head, and which clearly signified the two different styles of governance exemplified by Ozuna and Cornejo, involved the pay raise for city employees.[60] Ever since his victory in 1963 Cornejo had as his goal the building of a *patrón* system in Crystal City with himself as *jefe*.[61] Cornejo viewed each political development from the point of view of building a machine. Never having had much money, Cornejo dreamed of using his office to become wealthy and powerful the way others had. Thus after the city pay raise, Cornejo had expected the employees to contribute part of their raise back to him, for the creation and maintenance of a political organization. When twenty-three of the employees refused to contribute to his fund, Cornejo told Ozuna that they should be fired.[62]

Ozuna's basic concern, however, was to provide efficient, businesslike management while initiating reforms. He felt that most important of all was the need for the new regime to be proof that Mexican Americans could govern Crystal City well, disproving Anglo fears and allegations. For Cornejo to institute a boss-type machine similar to that in other areas of South Texas would not only defeat his purpose; it would almost assuredly receive widespread publicity because of the interest Crystal City had already generated. Besides, since Ozuna thought that the twenty-three people Cornejo wanted fired were doing their jobs adequately, he felt that to fire them would be unjust and improper.

When Ozuna refused to fire the employees, Cornejo got the council to fire Ozuna. At the same time the council also fired the police chief, Rey Pérez, who had been a supporter of Ozuna. Hired in his place was the policeman Ozuna had fired, Leonardo Santoya.

When Cornejo announced to the world that Ozuna had been fired, Mrs. Ray Shafer, after an acrimonious meeting with Cornejo, announced that the mayor had been fired by the Teamsters as business agent for the union at Del Monte. Into Cornejo's job for the union the Teamsters picked Moses Falcón, already an enemy of Cornejo's. The Teamsters thus reluctantly felt they had to thrust themselves into the dispute between Ozuna and Cornejo to try to preserve the respectability of the government. In so doing, they exacerbated the divisions in the local Mexican community and many Anglos felt this was confirmation that the Teamsters had really been running the whole show since the election.

Cornejo, in trying to fire Ozuna, was fired himself. Because of this he understandably took on the Teamsters as well as Ozuna. Responding to a question about his newfound enemies, the furious Cornejo responded: "I'm not sorry I told them to go to hell. Nobody is going to tell me what to do with my government."[63]

It turned out, however, that there were plenty of people who were going to tell Cornejo what to do with his government. The city attorney, a liberal-labor lawyer from San Antonio brought in with George Ozuna, sided with Ozuna, and the firing of Ozuna was immediately contested. The district judge, Ross E. Doughty, nullified Cornejo's actions on the grounds that no reasons were given for the firing and that therefore it was not done within the framework of the city charter. At the same time Doughty removed from office councilman Reynaldo Mendoza, one of the two councilmen supporting Cornejo, because

Mendoza owed the city $125.98 in utility bills. The city char-
ter, it seems, also required that no councilmen could owe any
money to the city. Thus not only did the charter require that
councilmen own property, the charter also assumed that councilmen would be rich enough to require no salary while serving
and it made sure that any councilman not rich enough to pay
his bills would be prevented from continuing on the council.
The struggle between Cornejo and Ozuna, thus as a side product, revealed the extent to which the whole institutional procedure for governance in the town was premised upon middle-
class and business-oriented Anglo ideas. The charter came quickly to be labelled by Cornejo's supporters as a "rich man's
charter."

By ending Mendoza's tenure on the council, Judge Doughty
had also deprived Cornejo of a majority on the council. This
seemingly assured that Cornejo would not be able to fire Ozuna,
especially since E. C. Muñoz, appointed to fill the vacancy,
sided with Manuel Maldonado and Antonio Cárdenas against
Cornejo.

After the judicial reprimand, Cornejo became more moody
and resentful. Fired from his job with the Teamsters, he became
unemployed. His new car was repossessed, and soon he was the
only mayor in Texas drawing unemployment compensation.[64]

With Mendoza being knocked off the council, the financial
squeeze which had hit Los Cinco immediately after their victory
and had continued throughout their term of office began to
take its toll, aggravated by the charter's provisions. By the fall
of 1964 Councilman Hernández had outlived his usefulness for
the Anglos. His charges against the Teamsters and PASO, and
his disclaimers of discrimination in Crystal City had proved
invaluable to Anglos in 1963, but Hernández soon became a
liability. He was arrested by Police Chief Pérez for carrying a
concealed weapon, and was expelled from the CASAA organization. Anglos were no longer willing to bail him out of his
financial difficulties or to protect him from hot-check charges.
He therefore was soon thrown off the council because he
likewise owed the city money. Although Hernández was replaced by a Cornejo man, Antonio Yanas, this still left the
council set three to two against Cornejo.

Shortly before Christmas of 1964, Antonio Cárdenas, who

was unable to find any employment after injuring his back and having to spend time in the hospital, was ousted from the council because he also was unable to pay his utility bills.

With Cárdenas joining Hernández and Mendoza in being expelled from the council, only two of the original five remained. The council was split two against two over the firing of Ozuna: Manuel Maldonado and E. C. Muñoz against Cornejo and Antonio Yanas. Because of this deadlock, however, the council was unable to agree upon a replacement for Cárdenas, and an attempt by Cornejo to have Mrs. Virginia Musquiz appointed to the vacancy ended in a tie vote. Ozuna's tenure continued, precariously supported only by a court order and a tie vote of the council.

the attempted reforms

Throughout this period, however, George Ozuna continued to work diligently for the new programs and reforms he was trying to institute. Although he was successful in a number of areas, he, like Cornejo, was hampered by the structures. His most serious constraints concerned the city's taxing powers. In particular, he thought that the whole tax structure was unfair and that a systematic re-evaluation and reassessment of all property in the city should be undertaken. Ozuna found, however, that such a program would have to be undertaken by an experienced appraiser who could make his reassessments stand up in court. To get an appraiser of this sort would cost the city around $55,000.[65] Because the county would of course not be willing to participate in the reassessment of the whole property-tax system, Ozuna knew that the city alone would have to pay for it. He felt the city simply could not afford it. A vicious circle of poverty from revenues was thus perpetuated. This poverty was reinforced through the city's being unable to annex the large Del Monte plant on the edge of town. The lame-duck Anglo city council had thrown up an effective roadblock to the annexation shortly before Ozuna took office. Recognizing this roadblock, Ozuna had wanted to go to San Francisco and "lay the cards on the table" to the management of Del Monte, explaining to them about the inequity of their not contributing a penny to city taxes. The council, however, was afraid to treat Del Monte in this way, fearing that reprisals by the company might be severe and that therefore the issue was simply too dangerous to touch.

In trying to institute reforms which required money, Ozuna had to rely increasingly on federal programs. He also had to work before the advent of the Eighty-Ninth Congress and before the time the poverty problem was in vogue. Nevertheless, through federal programs, particularly urban renewal, funds flowed into the community and many needed improvements were made. Ozuna, however, felt hampered by having to deal with the program's director, Sam Anderson. Anderson had been a realtor before he became the director of the program when it was adopted in 1958, and he had close personal ties to important Anglos in the community and to various federal officials with whom he dealt. Although Anderson was a competent administrator, Ozuna resented his connections and his domination of the whole project. Ozuna could not afford, however, to try to have him removed because there seemed to be no one else of a more sympathetic nature in the community who was qualified to take over the job.

Not all federal programs worked out to be the qualified success urban renewal was. Seeking to becoming affiliated with the Manpower Development Training Program, which might have helped a number of the city's unskilled and semiskilled workers who were migrants, Ozuna invited an official for the program to meet with area businessmen to explain how it would function. Because the program required that jobs be guaranteed to the individuals going through the training, not a single one of the twenty businessmen present was interested in working with the program.[66]

Juan Cornejo was thus not the only person frustrated in many of his undertakings. George Ozuna, in his own quieter way, continued to run into a number of obstacles. But overall he was still able to venture into a number of areas needing reform. Shortly before the council elections in 1965 Ozuna issued a summary of his accomplishments and hopes for the future. Citing the new public-building complex the city was now constructing, the extensive work by urban renewal in expanding paving, eliminating several hundred outhouses, adding street lights and improving water and gas lines, Ozuna nonetheless noted that much work remained to be done.[67] His top priorities included finding new sources for the city's water supply (which would also be vital in the attempt to attract jobs to the area), improving police and fire protection, expanding the city library, developing a master planning program for the city's expansion, and participating in the federal government's Anti-Poverty War. Ozuna further stated that he hoped the city could build a community swimming pool and build more school sidewalks. As this indicates, under Ozuna Crystal City began an era of considerable upgrading. Ozuna clearly hoped to be able to continue working to improve the quality of life in the city.

the 1965 political struggle

While Ozuna was trying to continue and expand his reforms, a clerical error managed to provide Cornejo with his last chance to get Ozuna. It was discovered that Manuel Maldonado, because of a billing error, owed $2.94 to the city. Cornejo therefore immediately moved that Maldonado be expelled from the council. Although the vote was deadlocked at two each, with Maldonado voting (as well as taking a couple of swings at Cornejo), Cornejo charged that Maldonado could not vote, and that therefore the motion carried, two votes to one. He and Yanas then removed Maldonado, filled his "vacant" seat and also filled the vacant seat caused earlier by the expulsion of Cárdenas. Hilario Lozano and José de la Fuente, the two men appointed to the council, were strong supporters of the mayor. With a majority now of four to one, Cornejo proceeded to fire George Ozuna and to hire another city manager. Ozuna and the city attorney, Arthur Gochman, however, again got District Judge Ross E. Doughty to enjoin Cornejo from throwing Maldonado off the council and from proceeding to conduct business with only two votes (his own and Yanas').[68] Thus again Cornejo was thwarted in his attempt to fire Ozuna.

Had Cornejo been able to gain control of the government, he would in several important ways have tried to produce greater changes than Ozuna did in the city government. Although Cornejo was not an ideological thinker, in wishing to institute a machine in Crystal City with himself as *jefe*, he would have ended up firing far more people than Ozuna did. And in being much less concerned about "experience" and "qualifications" than Ozuna, he would have insured that there was greater

Mexican and greater lower-class participation in the city government. It is unclear whether the city administration could have
continued to operate under these changes, particularly in view
of the local opposition, the constant intervention of the judi-
ciary, and the implied threat from such outside forces as the
city's bond company. Cornejo might have ended up with chaos,
and with fewer reforms than Ozuna was able to institute. But
through such disputes as that occurring over the surplus-
commodities program, the differences between the competent
engineer and the third-grade dropout were underscored. And at
the same time the implicitly greater demand for change by
Cornejo, and its resultant confusion, was also highlighted.
Shortly before the 1965 election, the city's surplus-
commodities program, which had been instituted under Ozuna,
was temporarily halted. Ozuna charged that Cornejo was responsible for sabotaging the project and was quoted as saying
that Cornejo "failed to see that we have residential and income
regulations on who gets the food. Cornejo thinks everyone
should get it."[69]

This struggle between Cornejo and Ozuna and the two different concepts of government they represented went on until the
council elections of April, 1965. The feuding greatly weakened
the strength and prestige of the new government and to many it
reduced the image of Cornejo, who after the victorious election
had been viewed as a hero and savior, to that of a would-be
tyrant willing to wreck everything he couldn't control. Even
though he retained a group of loyal followers, his overall support in the community waned throughout the struggle, and he
was at times made to look ridiculous.

George Ozuna, however, was no real political alternative to
Cornejo, and he did not intend to be. He was not interested in
being a politician. He was not interested in building a machine.
He was not even interested in building an organization, and as
such he had no real understanding of the need the migrants had
for a political organization. He had hoped, through the power
of his own actions, to justify himself and the revolt. This was
not the sort of leader the migrants could be expected to follow;
nor did it indicate he understood the degree of wrath the
Anglos felt for the revolt and all that was connected with it.
Although many Anglos might grudgingly respect him and agree

that the reforms were needed, Ozuna was still an outsider who had come in with the Teamsters and PASO. To many citizens, both Anglo and Mexican, Ozuna seemed to have an insufferable air of superiority. In spite of this, he was respected for his competence and knowledge in a way that Cornejo could never be respected. Both men recognized their differences. Cornejo resented Ozuna, an outside city slicker who had not suffered through the spinach fields and the migrant trails, and Ozuna could not help but think of Cornejo as a bumbling politician. By the end they were hardly on speaking terms.

Thus the unity under which the whole 1963 electoral campaign had flourished so amazingly now crumbled. The waves of publicity and raised expectations had changed the lives of all the men involved. And the business-oriented procedural arrangements of the city government had brought with them irreconcilable differences which made the coalition impossible to hold together. Throughout the two years, Anglo threats and inducements and the strategic retreat of the Teamsters and PASO had also taken their toll upon the revolt. The significant reforms that had been undertaken in such areas as paving, lighting, sewage and water connections, police policy, and job opportunities were somehow lost in all the personal squabbles, rivalries, charges and countercharges.[70] Instead, the bitter factionalism wracking the city government became the political issue, and the Anglos and CASAA found themselves more eager than ever for the confrontation which the April, 1965, elections would bring.

Primed for the fight and increasingly confident, the CASAA organization chose three Mexican Americans and two Anglos to run on its slate for the city council. In this way they wanted to disprove charges that there had been discrimination in the community. Their five candidates were Carlos Avila, an electrician; Bill Leonard, a funeral director well known and respected by the Mexican community; Ed Stocking, a Chevrolet dealer; Ed Salinas, a ranch foreman; and Humberto Castillo, a gas-station owner. Of all five candidates, none had been closely associated with the old Holsomback regime, and in fact none had been very active in politics before the 1963 election. All were middle-class; all were respectable. And the three Mexicans, as was the practice with CASAA, were chosen because of their willingness to work with Anglos and because they came from large, extended families which they would hopefully convince to vote for the ticket.

Cornejo, on the other hand, had been so busy fighting people in his own organization that much less effort went into the campaign. Neither he, nor anyone connected with the Teamsters or PASO, conducted a poll-tax drive. Both the Teamsters and the statewide PASO issued statements saying they would not be involved in the 1965 campaign. Moses Falcón, the new Teamster business manager at the Del Monte plant, also issued a statement saying he would not be supporting Cornejo.

Although Cornejo had been able to maintain control over the local PASO organization, this had been possible only through seriously weakening the organization. The 1964 countywide campaign had taken its toll on the organization, as Moses Falcón, Natividad Granados, and others active in the earlier effort were expelled. As the spring elections in 1965 approached, still others active in the revolt, such as Enriqueta Palacios, a stalwart who was head of the PASO organization, resigned in disgust. Cornejo's tactics of rule or ruin increasingly irritated his would-be followers.[71] Yet because of the enemies he had made among the Anglos, because of his unquestioned courage, and because of many of the goals he had sought, such as ending discriminatory employment practices and hiring more Mexicans, Cornejo was still enormously popular among segments of the Mexican community.

Being in control of the local organization, Cornejo picked for his slate people who were sure to back him. Running with him were Antonio Yanas (the cannery worker already on the council), Hilario Lozano and José de la Fuente, and Mrs. Virginia Musquiz. All three of the new candidates—Lozano, De la Fuente, and Musquiz—Cornejo had tried unsuccessfully to appoint to the council earlier.

E. C. Muñoz, who had sided with Ozuna against Cornejo, chose not to run for office. Manuel Maldonado, who had been Ozuna's closest supporter and had been the only other councilman besides Cornejo to last the full two years, chose to run as an independent. In running with two other independents, Maldonado gave those Mexicans in the community a chance to support Ozuna. But he had little chance of victory. The presence of the independents primarily helped to assure that Cornejo would be beaten. If Cornejo were to win, it was obvious that Ozuna would be fired. Should CASAA win, the future of Ozuna was not so clear, although it was probable that he would still be fired. There were, however, within the CASAA organization, mainly among the Mexican-American and younger members, people who had a great deal of admiration for the quiet competence of the San Antonio engineer.

The CASAA campaign was supremely well organized from start to finish. With considerable funds and with many workers, they had poll-tax lists and data carefully analyzed in preparation for the spring election. A number of Anglo housewives devoted a great many hours to manning the organization. As in 1964, CASAA also wanted to make heavy use of absentee voting. CASAA, however, realized that the person in charge of absentee voting for the city was devoted to George Ozuna. Consequently, several very important people in the CASAA organization went to this person, confiding that if CASAA won, George Ozuna would be retained as city manager.[72] On the basis of this information, this person was willing to help CASAA and to engage in a number of less than legal actions concerning the absentee voting. As with 1964 it appears that an important part of the strategy was to take, without requests, absentee ballots to elderly and dependent Mexican Americans, get them to sign their names, and then mark the ballots for them. Certain Mexican-American women were paid by the CASAA organization to do this. This practice, it turned out, was even more successful than their effort in 1964. Altogether 561 people, or approximately one quarter of all voters, voted by absentee ballot.

Although Cornejo's tactics had alienated many of his original followers and he was now forced to confront a much better prepared counterorganization, he now had working for him a Mexican-American community which was becoming used to participating, and who knew that victory was possible. Taking all factors together, however, he was not strong enough to withstand the challenge of CASAA and the independents. The mayor and his battered and divided forces were defeated by a united, confident coalition of Anglos and middle-class Mexican Americans.

Significantly, of those people who voted on election day, a majority supported the Cornejo slate, not CASAA. Cornejo was

1965 CITY COUNCIL ELECTIONS

Candidates	Absentee Ballots	Election Day Vote	Total
CASAA Slate			
Carlos Avila	505	743	1248
Bill Leonard	508	723	1231
Ed Stocking	496	691	1187
Humberto Castillo	477	650	1127
Ed Salinas	502	624	1126
PASO Slate			
Juan Cornejo	30	945	975
José de la Fuente	24	933	957
Hilario Lozano	29	895	924
Antonio Yanas	24	890	914
Virginia Musquiz	25	829	854
Independent Slate			
Manuel Maldonado	41	239	280
Ramón Garza	19	123	142
Joseph Varner	13	49	62

defeated only by the large number of absentee votes. A comparison of the absentee balloting for the 1964 and 1965 elections is revealing. Although CASAA carried the absentee balloting in 1964, after engaging in what clearly seems to have been fraud, its margin of victory in 1964 was nowhere comparable to its more than ten to one victory over PASO in 1965. CASAA increased its strength while support for PASO candidates, in absolute figures, dropped considerably. It is difficult to offer any legal explanation for why the votes for PASO candidates dropped so sharply while CASAA candidates increased their strength. All this does not mean, however, that the irregularities occurring in the absentee voting were necessarily enough to make the difference between victory and defeat for Cornejo. There is strong evidence to believe that the absentee voting would have gone heavily for the CASAA candidates without fraud. Since Cornejo had refused to allow more than one polling place on election day, many Anglos voted by absentee ballot simply because they did not want to have to wait in a long line to vote.[73] But the irregularities do indicate that the Cornejo slate, if it did in fact lose, lost by a more narrow margin than the election returns suggest.

Secondly, it is significant that the PASO slate in losing still garnered more votes than in its winning campaign in 1963. The enormous turnout in 1965, which was almost double the total *countywide* turnout in the 1960 Kennedy-Nixon presidential race, signified that although Cornejo had lost, a sizeable opposition to the CASAA organization existed. It seemed clear that Mexican Americans in the community, through both CASAA and PASO, had solidified their role as participants and that the *ancien régime* could not be restored.

conclusion

Pausing in 1965 to assess the two years of revolt in the community, certain factors crucial to the success and later to the failure of the revolt become apparent. In the beginning the revolt was completely dependent upon outside support and assistance, although local dissatisfaction and the small Teamsters union were already present. Because of the lack of opportunities and consequent inexperience of the local Mexican population, the Teamsters and PASO shouldered the questions of organization and of strategy for the revolt. They at the same time provided protection for the local population and limited the degree to which the Anglos could engage in successful threats and coercion. Throughout the campaign, however, the outside organizers seem to have devoted little attention to the kind of rule the new government should strive to implement or to what its goals should be once it was in power. It was, of course, understood that a new government would institute reforms in the areas where they were charging discrimination, but the manner in which these reforms would be carried out was not seriously planned.

When faced with choosing candidates to run, the organizers were forced to choose from the very narrow field of those willing to run. They could not get experienced candidates with high-school or college education. Both the Teamsters and PASO hoped and assumed that they would be getting candidates they would be able to work with and continue to advise. But with their very success, factors came into play which they were not able to handle. The intensity of Anglo outrage and the general condemnation of both outside groups from people all over the area surprised both PASO and the Teamsters. As we have noted, it very nearly destroyed PASO as an organization.

Both groups responded logically to this publicity and pressure by finding a capable, nonpolitical engineer to be city manager for the community. If either organization had wanted to use Crystal City as a base for the development of a machine or powerful organization in the area, they gave up that wish with the selection of George Ozuna. He was honest and businesslike, and from the beginning ran the city in an incorruptible manner. But the Teamsters and PASO couldn't select George Ozuna as city manager and then make a complete retreat in the face of all the unfavorable publicity. They were caught in the bind of having to help educate and prepare the local people they had chosen to be leaders.

While they were trying to give advice, the local candidate they most trusted, Juan Cornejo, began to realize that he was now a famous person, sought-after for interviews, asked to speak on college campuses, and instantly a hero to the local Mexicanos. In his instant transition into a celebrity, Cornejo found at the same time that he was to receive no salary, get no payoffs at all, and in fact was not even supposed to run the city. The office of mayor was set up to be a figurehead. The conflict between Cornejo's expectations and his actual condition led to his assault upon the setup of government in the community. At the same time it meant an end to his willingness to accept advice and take a back seat to the city manager. His goal was the establishment of a machine with himself as ruler and everyone else his loyal and obligated servant. This desire of course was not unusual for South Texas, or for political life in general. But because of the limitations upon his personality and the office he held, he was not able to accomplish his goal, for the new government was in far too precarious a position from the beginning to attempt to change the institutional procedures of government found in the city charter. What he was able to do, however, was to bring the new government crashing down, defeating himself and everyone else who had worked so hard for success. His fixation on personal power and material betterment, when combined with his lack of experience in the politi-

cal process, meant that he was a very poor leader who antagonized a number of people he could not afford to affront. He
increasingly found himself in situations he could not handle.
This, together with the institutional arrangements which were
designed more for Anglo businessmen than for Mexican-
American workers, led to the defeat of the new city government.

Although within the Mexican community there have since
been attempts to blame various individuals for the failure of the
revolt, the Crystal City story of 1963 to 1965 was a story of
failure mainly because of the very inexperience and lack of
opportunity which had produced these leaders. In the end the
force of change and of revolution is contingent upon the local
people who must do the leading and the following.[74] And here
the vicious circle of inequality and inexperience cuts in, for the
ability of the local people is conditioned by the type of rule
they have known. For a future movement to succeed, more
effort would need to be spent building up local, indigenous
organizations and leadership.

The uniqueness of the Crystal City organizational base of
Teamsters supported by migrants was enough to win an election, but it was not enough to govern. If it was the uniqueness
of Crystal City that allowed for the revolution in 1963, it was
its very similarity with the rest of South Texas—similarities
regarding poverty, inexperience, and vulnerability—that brought
about its downfall.

4 the reaction

The Citizens Association Serving All Americans, a coalition of Anglos and middle-class Mexicans, had swept to victory in the April, 1965, city elections.[1] United in their desire to restore qualified, businesslike leadership to the community, the powerful, well-financed, and well-organized coalition had ousted the embarrassing and unbusinesslike mayor and his coterie. In an action which the Anglos felt further vindicated them from all the previous charges of racism and discrimination, Carlos Avila, as the strongest vote-getter on the CASAA slate, was elected mayor of the city. Thus a Mexicano succeeded Cornejo as mayor.

The questions CASAA now faced were many, however, and they all centered around the fundamental question of what their victory had meant. Had it meant that the people were fed up with the programs and policies of the last two years, with the reforms that George Ozuna had initiated? How much did the people of Crystal City want to erase the last two years and the Mexican participation that had come with the revolt?

The organization of CASAA from the very first had been an indication that Anglos recognized the old way of governing could not be completely restored. Perhaps the best indication of the change in Anglo thinking came from the following conversation:

"Wouldn't it have been wonderful to have had a CASAA slate two years ago, when Cornejo won?" someone mused. Bill Leonard, a councilman-elect, looked a bit startled, then replied thoughtfully, "It wasn't possible two years ago. We knew there was a machine that had been in power for years, but nobody was interested in running for city office, so they just kept on."[2]

CASAA was thus different from the pre-Cornejo city administration. Besides including a hefty number of Mexicans, their candidates were men who had not been active in city politics before 1963 and who therefore felt no need to defend all the actions taken in the decades of Anglo rule. The victory for CASAA meant that after two years of being locked out of city government, the Anglos now at last had a chance to prove their good intentions.[3]

Although CASAA represented basically only Anglos and middle-class Mexicans, there were diverse opinions within the organization. In fact, the Anglos had never been as monolithic as the running of the city government had seemed to indicate. Although at the local and the county level a small group of old Anglo families had run things with only occasional opposition, there had always been some heterogeneity among the Anglos. An examination of certain economic and social characteristics of the tiny Anglo minority reveals that although none of the Anglos were poor in comparison to the migrants, there were considerable differences in wealth and education in the community. Among those more wealthy, the town's businessmen seem to have at times disagreed with the farmers and ranchers of the area, especially over the desirability of attracting industry.[4] Socially there were also differences. The ethnic background of the Anglos varied more than in the state as a whole, with German and some Eastern European immigrants present along with the Anglo-Saxons. In part because of this there was also religious diversity, although the two primary Anglo denominations were, as in the rest of Texas, Methodist and Baptist. Although political diversity was rarely revealed at the local level, the town had always included a large number of Republicans, almost all of whom were Anglos. Even though most Anglos voted Democratic in state and local elections, at the level of presidential elections the Republicans did well. Eisenhower carried the city decisively, and in 1960 the city split almost evenly between Kennedy and Nixon.[5] But it was only with the overthrow of the old Anglo city leadership that most Anglos began to take an active part in local politics. In spite of their heterogeneity, they could nearly all agree in their dislike for the Teamsters, PASO, and the Cornejo government, and thus almost all sympathized with CASAA. There was, however, difference of opinion over what the response to the rise of the town's Mexican Americans should be.

The predominant Anglo attitude toward the town's Mexicans was perhaps most clearly stated by Captain Jack Loyall, one of the men who had successfully engineered the CASAA victory. At the time CASAA was first organized he had said:

> The Anglos of Crystal City have all the pride of blood that the Latin has. He is dedicated to the American ideal of justice, and is most willing for his Latin brother to gain and to hold public office, provided he is properly qualified and has the correct patriotic impulses. If the government of Crystal City and Zavala County are won by qualified Latins, then so be it. As one old timer put it: I have no objection to responsible Latins being in public office. In fact, I think it would be a good thing, and I know they would treat the Anglos as well as we treated the Latins when we had control of the government, and that should be good enough for anyone.[6]

The general Anglo attitude, then, was that the radical Mexicans had done the Anglos a grave injustice by accusing them of treating Mexicans unfairly. These Anglos stated repeatedly that they had no objection to the proper sort of Mexicans participating in government, and they resented criticism implying that their treatment of Mexicans had been less than fair and just.[7]

Although the CASAA officialdom were considered moderates by local standards, in having complete Anglo support, CASAA also had considerable conservative pressure placed on it. In fact, one of the Anglo candidates revealed that during the campaign CASAA officials had had to spend considerable energy convincing some Anglos to support "qualified, respectable" and anti-Cornejo Mexican candidates. In the end nearly all Anglos did, but there were some who simply could not bring themselves to vote for any Mexicans, regardless of what the candidates' views might be.

Besides shouldering within the organization all Anglo attitudes in the community, CASAA also had middle-class Mexican support. In general the Mexicans who were in CASAA were there because, as one of them related, they were "more like the Anglos." They were the more acculturated, wealthier, middle-class Mexicans of the community, those who were no longer migrants. Although these Mexicans were thus rather monolithic when compared to the majority of the Mexicans in the community, they nevertheless represented some diversity in their attitudes. Many Mexicans were in CASAA because they wanted to be like Anglos and they wanted to be accepted by the Anglos. There were also Mexicans, however, who were not so willing to ignore the mass base of migrants and their own heritage even though they had "made it."[8] These Mexicans were in CASAA for a number of reasons. Some were embarrassed by Cornejo and Los Cinco, and wanted to present to the community a better image of the Mexican community. Others had deep compassion for their poor, migrant *compadres*, but felt that true progress could only occur through racial cooperation rather than through racial antagonism and polarization. When approached by Anglos to join the CASAA organization, these Mexicans welcomed the chance to present their own point of view. Of course, other Mexicans were CASAA supporters only because of direct financial gain.[9] But for whatever reasons, all Mexicans in CASAA wanted to see race relations improved.

The Anglos worked with this desire for acceptance, often reminding their Mexican friends how important it was for Mexicans to set a good example and to pull themselves up by their own bootstraps. Because of the tremendous differences in background between the Anglo and Mexican American in Crystal City, and the wide gulf that still separated the two groups economically, culturally, and educationally, it was difficult for any Anglo to avoid viewing Mexicans in a paternalistic way. Some Anglos commented that they had tried to help Mexicans but too often found it impossible to break down the wall of superstition and ignorance they encountered. Others said that the Mexicans were happier without being "civilized." Most Anglos, at any rate, placed a heavy emphasis upon individual

Mexican success, regarding any other kind of upgrading as illegitimate. Through insisting upon individual betterment, they were also able to determine which Mexicans would be allowed the rewards of their Anglo society. Thus, from the beginning of the CASAA organization the Anglos had chosen the Mexicans they wanted in CASAA. Although the Anglos wanted the votes of any Mexicans they could get, for leadership positions they were much more discriminating. They wanted only those who, as Captain Loyall had so concisely stated, were "properly qualified" and showed the "correct patriotic impulses."

Recognizing these differences within the CASAA organization, CASAA was faced with the task of governing as well as with holding together their own coalition. The organization's underlying *raison d'être* had been to combat racial hatred and outside agitators. Now that they were victorious, they had to decide some questions which many might have preferred to avoid, for in the process they had to define their own principles more clearly.

The first, and certainly one of the most important issues which CASAA faced after its victory, was that of what to do about George Ozuna. CASAA had argued vociferously that they weren't against Mexicans *per se*. They were merely against unqualified, irresponsible Mexicans. George Ozuna, however, was an example of a well-educated, responsible Mexican. Everyone in CASAA knew that Ozuna alone had prevented mass Anglo firings and the creation of a machine. He alone had thwarted Cornejo's desires and had kept the city government on a sound, stable, businesslike course. In his undemagogic, quiet way he had overseen reforms in the city which most people recognized as good. Within CASAA there was considerable Mexican sentiment for keeping Ozuna. No less than two of the three Mexican councilmen-elect were in favor of retaining Ozuna as city manager. Further, Ozuna himself had made it clear that he hoped to continue his job. He had also said to the press, "I just want to get rid of one man—Cornejo."[10] Ozuna thus seemed to be a perfect example of an anti-Cornejo, well-qualified and responsible Mexican American. But to many Anglos in the community, Ozuna was still associated with the Teamster-PASO alliance.[11] He had in fact been chosen by them to be the city manager. Some, although certainly not all Anglos, thought of him as an arrogant, uppity Mexican, or in the words of one of the Anglo councilmen-elect, an "egotistical, smart aleck man."[12] Accordingly, a majority of Anglos were in favor of firing Ozuna and of starting off the new city government with a clean slate.

The locus of power within the CASAA organization was revealed when the Anglos had their way. Ozuna, seeing that the council-elect did not want him to continue, resigned "with due reservation and consideration."[13] Significantly, however, Mayor Carlos Avila, one of the two councilmen in favor of keeping Ozuna, voted not to accept Ozuna's resignation, which, however, was accepted by a four to one vote.

This decision turned out to have wide repercussions because the council after accepting Ozuna's resignation found itself in the difficult position of trying to find a satisfactory replacement. Their first choice did not want to be city manager. They therefore ended up sifting through around forty applications and interviewing about five. Their final choice was a retired Air Force Colonel, R. H. Marshall. Marshall, an Anglo, had retired from the Air Force only two years previously, and had had no experience as a city manager. Almost immediately the council realized it had made a mistake. Having spent twenty-eight of his last thirty years in the Air Force, Marshall found it quite normal to treat the people of Crystal City like Air Force personnel beneath him. Within a very short time, Marshall had managed to antagonize practically everyone through his imperious manner and poor public relations.[14] He lasted only a year.

Chastened by this experience, the council began searching for another manager. This time they settled upon Jack Whitley, a retired Army Colonel who was active in the American Legion. In spite of these qualifications, which were remarkably similar to Marshall's, the council thought he would be an improvement because he had had experience as a city manager in Arkansas. Whitley, however, turned out to be a repetition of Marshall—antagonizing the city staff, the council, and nearly everyone. He also lasted only a year. The job seems to have taken its toll on Whitley as well as on the city personnel, because he gave as his reason for resigning: "I have twice been a victim of ulcers and feel that if I continue here this situation will again result. I cannot allow this to happen."[15] One of the Anglo councilmen, thinking back over the days of Marshall and Whitley, lamented, "Don't ever hire military people."[16]

This inability to find a competent, qualified city manager, the lynchpin of the whole city government, prevented CASAA from introducing the kind of powerful stability they had intended. It prevented them from establishing their legitimacy as quickly as possible and was at the same time embarrassing because they had earlier asked Ozuna to resign. This failure to keep Ozuna, however, stemmed not from an accidental quirk of the CASAA organization. On the contrary, the firing of Ozuna, signalled the dominant policy line in the CASAA organization. Not only did they go after Ozuna; they also wanted to fire everyone who had been connected with the Cornejo-Ozuna administration. Just how this policy line was arrived at—who the most important persons pushing for this hard line were and who the most influential opponents were—have been questions difficult to determine. There must have been a struggle of sorts, however, since no less than two of the three Mexican councilmen were against the decision to fire Ozuna. It seems most likely that a group of Anglos inside the CASAA directorate were responsible for the assumption of a hard line against those Mexicans (and a few Anglos) who had not been in consistent opposition to the Cornejo-Ozuna government or who had been independent of the CASAA organization. It also seems likely that this policy decision was opposed by the moderate Mexican-American group in CASAA which included the mayor himself.[17]

This desire for a purge by those most powerful in CASAA created an irony. Whereas earlier CASAA had been shocked and appalled at Cornejo's desire to fire people and appoint his friends, now CASAA was intent upon doing very nearly the same thing. A number of qualified Mexican employees who had been brought into the city administration under Ozuna or who had been appointed by the council to various governing boards were also forced to resign. Even an Anglo member of the city administration who was outspoken in opposition to Cornejo, but who had developed a friendship with Ozuna, was denied a pay raise because of her suspected "disloyalties" and her unwillingness to discredit the previous two years. Looking back upon this period, she commented, "Hate was so thick in this town!"[18] One of the Anglo councilmen later commented that those in control of the CASAA organization were "mad because we hadn't fired even more!"[19] In their desire to eradicate the influence of the last two years, the Anglos running CASAA were forming a powerful organization which to many did not appear different from a machine.

The organization certainly knew how to exert pressure. One CASAA councilman in later disillusionment commented that it was not so much that CASAA engaged in mismanagement that upset him as that in the firings and hirings "there were no issues involved." It was more a vendetta, and the replacements were always to people who were "friendly." He commented later in disgust: "They wanted too many favors."[20] After such a trauma as the Cornejo years, then, the pressure in the Anglo community for the reassertion of control and for punishing those who had been less than firm in their opposition to the revolt was strong.

Although it might at first appear that this policy of vengeance was shortsighted and doomed to failure, it was not at all inevitable that the firings would lead to a successful backlash among the Mexican Americans. To the extreme CASAA partisans it appeared wisest to eliminate as thoroughly as possible those who had been influential in the Cornejo-Ozuna administration and to build up a powerful organization to prevent such a recurrence. People who might become alternate sources of influence and those who could not be trusted were thus best removed from and kept from positions of power. Because large-scale participation in the community was still new, was most unusual for the area, and presumably couldn't last forever, CASAA figured it was following a safe, successful strategy. Further, since the Teamsters and PASO had both been damaged by their ventures in Crystal City, it was a good bet that these two sources of outside agitation could no longer serve to stir up the Mexicans or to protect them.

It would be unfair to say that revenge was the only, or even the most important, desire motivating CASAA. As noted earlier, among both the Anglos and the Mexicans within the organization, there were different goals among the partisans. Many Anglos felt an overwhelming desire to prove their good intentions to Mexicans by allowing the right sort of Mexican a much greater say in the affairs of the city. CASAA, for example, generally tended to replace those Mexicans they had fired with other Mexicans, albeit more "reliable, trustworthy" ones. These moderate Anglos were also willing to work for and support federal programs to upgrade the Mexican community and to promote acculturation, but they also expected and demanded that they play the dominant role in the administration of these federal programs. In other words, help to the Mexican community through benevolent paternalism seems to have motivated at least as many Anglos in CASAA as revenge or the conscious desire to exploit naive, well-intentioned Mexican moderates.

There were inevitably some Anglos, however, to whom the strain and shock of the Cornejo years had served to reinforce their own anti-Mexican sentiments and had confirmed their belief that no Mexican was responsible enough to be trusted. This latter group of Anglos, often also opposed to all forms of "welfare" for Mexicans, was a minority, no doubt in part because most Anglos realized that to follow such a policy would mean political suicide in a community where Anglos were such a minority. For these Anglo extremists, however, the Anglo restoration was incomplete. Anglo dominance had not been reasserted decisively and commandingly. Cornejo had been replaced by another Mexican. These Anglos were to cause the moderates in CASAA a great deal of embarrassment and anguish, and were to threaten the coalition which CASAA had built.

Not long after Carlos Avila had become mayor, one of these bitter Anglos came in to see the mayor, propping his feet up on his desk. When Mayor Avila asked him to take his feet off the desk, the man became infuriated and a scene occurred. The Anglo finally condescended to take his feet off the mayor's desk, with city and county personnel watching anxiously. But having a Mexican tell him what or what not to do was something this Anglo could not stand. In order to avenge his honor, he and a group of his friends came looking for Mayor Avila that night. Either because they could not find him, or because the mayor had a bad back, they agreed to go after Carlos's brother, Luis Avila, as a surrogate. They beat up the mayor's brother brutally and were preparing to drag him through town when a Black filling-station attendant saw what was happening and held a gun on them until they ceased.[21] Luis Avila was badly injured and required hospitalization in San Antonio.

This sort of Anglo response to "qualified, responsible" Mexican leadership created a public-relations disaster for the Anglos. It was severely embarrassing to them. We find that the Anglo leadership in CASAA responded to this incident in a revealing way. Rather than purging themselves of these sorts of Anglos by prosecuting the men involved, they instead desired to hush the incident up. The Anglo attackers were never brought to trial, because pressure was put on Mayor Avila not to file charges and because the county attorney refused to take the case.[22] It was pointed out to the mayor that if he pressed charges it would endanger all CASAA had worked for and create an even bigger scandal. Mayor Avila thus capitulated and nothing was done. But from then on, things were never quite the same for the mayor. His belief in Anglo sincerity and good intentions had been badly shaken by the attack on his brother and the Anglo response to it. Although he did not turn against CASAA, at the end of his two-year term he resigned and withdrew from politics.

Hardly had this public-relations disaster for the Anglos occurred than another respected Mexican American, also of moderate persuasion, was beaten. In August, 1965, the father of Jesús Maldonado was charged with disturbing the peace.[23] According to the son, it had been "an altercation with friends." Jesús Maldonado was concerned about his father, both because his father did not understand very much English and because he was blind in one eye. He therefore went to the judge, Harold ("Stormy") Davis, trying to explain what had happened and urging him to be lenient. While Maldonado was talking to the judge, Sheriff C. L. Sweeten came into the room, poked his gun into Maldonado's ribs, and told him to get out of the courthouse. When the startled Maldonado refused to move, the Sheriff poked him several more times. At this Maldonado went after the sheriff. The ensuing struggle ended only when the judge, in perhaps less than classical judicial behavior, landed a blow on Maldonado's head. The sheriff and the judge then proceeded to lock the injured Maldonado in jail, although he wanted to be taken to the hospital. Only later, with great reluctance, was he taken to the hospital, where he had to spend several days.

Maldonado filed charges against Sheriff Sweeten and Davis, and the FBI came and took statements from him. When the jury was able to render only a partial verdict, however, District Judge Doughty ruled that Maldonado was not entitled to any damages and had to pay court costs.[24] This incident, however, served to radicalize Maldonado and his friends, as they felt the law had been discredited by a double standard.[25]

As these incidents indicate, CASAA found itself beset with certain internal contradictions which made the job of governing and of holding together its coalition more difficult than it had expected. The frustrations within the organization and in the community-at-large led to explosive situations which CASAA could not always control. Each confrontation tended to chip away at the moderates' credibility, negating many of their attempts at establishing more harmonious race relations.

CASAA also had to contend with a growing movement toward selective economic boycotting by Mexicans in the community. The Lone Star Beer distributor in town found his business suffering, both because of his often-voiced attitudes toward certain Mexicans and because his wife was one of those teachers in the schools whom many considered a racist. Perhaps the best known boycott, however, was against the grocery store owned by CASAA official Jesús Rodríguez. This boycott crippled his business so badly that in 1968 he announced he would not run for re-election to his county-commissioners post.

Other boycotts occurred throughout this period and were enough to make businessmen edgy. They also indicated to Mexican-American businessmen that there could be costs involved in joining the Anglos. As all of this indicates, politics did not cool down appreciably in the community after the first CASAA victory in 1965.

In spite of these internal and external pressures on CASAA, however, the city government managed to accomplish a number of things. Federal programs continued to expand, and the urban renewal project proceeded rather smoothly under the continued direction of Sam Anderson. A neighborhood center with swimming pool was completed, and parks were improved. In the school system Project Head Start was begun, and a migrant program which concentrated the school year into six months was inaugurated through Title One of the Elementary and Secondary Education Act. Because of the advent of the Eighty-Ninth Congress, then, CASAA was able to inaugurate some programs which were not available under the Cornejo-Ozuna administration. Another federal program which developed while CASAA was in power, the poverty program, was allowed into the county and was supported by many in CASAA. The program gradually began to have an impact on Crystal City, but its influence was unsettling. Those parts which penetrated soon began to upset the conservatives. The Neighborhood Youth Corps began employing unemployed youths at $1.25 an hour. This soon brought scathing criticism from some Anglos. One letter to the editor expressed the point clearly, stating that the work the youths were doing "does not merit $1.25 an hour, when hardly any business in town could pay employees that much." The irate letter then went on to call the whole poverty war a "political sugar daddy deal."[26]

As conservatives had feared, the poverty war soon began involving poor people in protest activity. Among those elected to represent the poor was Mrs. Irma Benavides, the sister of Mayor Carlos Avila and of Luis Avila. When the school board denied school facilities for the Adult Migrant Education Program, Mrs. Benavides staged a protest march through town. Some school personnel, according to Mrs. Benavides, were outraged that money was to be given to the adults to attend school and did not want school facilities used for such "giveaway" programs. They also seemed to hold the attitude that it was too late to do anything about illiterate adults in the community anyway.[27] The protest march failed. At the confrontation many of the women were asked by school officials to identify themselves, and this frightened them. Not only were their demands not met, but pressure was put on many who had been involved in the march, and some maids lost their jobs.[28]

Although the march failed, it did keep the community from settling back into the political apathy it had known before 1963. This protest, and the beating of her brother Luis, turned Mrs. Benavides into an active opponent of the CASAA organization, even though her brother was mayor. Shortly after the beating, Mrs. Benavides began trying to reconstruct the battered, bickering forces that had been defeated by CASAA in 1965. She relates:

> I had all the Mexican American leaders, men, meet at my brother Luis's house. Moses [Falcón] and Juan [Cornejo] were there. I started making up strategy—how we were going to win the April [1967] election. So Moses started fighting with Juan, and at that time Juan was going to run again and

so was his brother, Robert. So I was just sitting there and hearing their arguments out. And then I got up and said, "Listen people! You better stop that damn fighting because we'll never get anything or anywhere. That's exactly how they are dividing us, because you people won't get together and iron out your differences. We have to win this election, because they beat my brother up. . . . They have beaten Mr. Maldonado up. Next time they are going to kill someone! They were just getting ready to kill my brother! Next time they will really kill or blow somebody's brains out!" So they stopped their feuding and we drew up our complete plans for strategy. . . . We got everybody registered, of course. We got it by precincts, and then we got it by neighborhoods. And then we gave each person a neighborhood to work on. We made sure they went and told them to vote, and if they didn't have transportation we would take them to the polls.[29]

As Mrs. Benavides says, the two-year reign of CASAA had brought about a fragile union of the anti-CASAA forces which were ready to try to retake the city.[30] The relations between Moses Falcón and Juan Cornejo had been particularly strained because Falcón had taken over Cornejo's job with the Teamsters after Cornejo was fired, and the enmity between these two men who had worked together for victory in 1963 was never really overcome, but it was circumvented. Each man ran on his own slate, but together the two slates equalled only five candidates. Cornejo ran with his younger brother, Roberto, and with Hilario Lozano, one of the men who had run with Cornejo on his losing slate in 1965. Moses Falcón ran with Natividad Granados, one who had been active in the successful poll tax drive in 1962 and who had been ousted with Falcón from the local PASO chapter by the Cornejo forces in 1964. Falcón and Cornejo, then, did not run against each other even though they did not run together. Instead they concentrated their fire on the mistakes CASAA had made.

One further mistake was made by CASAA which served to galvanize further the Mexican-American community. This offense was committed by the second CASAA city manager, Jack Whitley, shortly after he took office, and involved Robert Díaz, the city policeman who was made police chief when Rey Pérez resigned to continue his education. Robert Díaz was using some property salvaged by the city from urban renewal projects; in particular, he was using some leftover tin to build a chicken house. This practice had been customary for city officials and was considered as "fringe benefits." When the new CASAA city manager got word of this, however, he wanted Díaz arrested for theft of city property. Sheriff Sweeten was apparently reluctant to make the arrest, so Whitley called in the Texas Rangers for the job. Although a complaint was filed against Díaz, the case was never brought up for trial. Díaz, however, lost his job with the city and left town. This action outraged many Mexican Americans in the community, who felt that Díaz had been the victim of a frame-up and singled out by the city manager for doing something which had been common practice for Anglo city employees.[31]

The mistakes of overzealousness on the part of CASAA officials and Anglos in general—mistakes that included firing George Ozuna and other qualified Mexicans in the city government, ending the career of Police Chief Díaz, and attacking Luis Avila and Jesús Maldonado—all helped to unite the opposing Mexican Americans. Although CASAA still had nearly total Anglo support and heavy support among middle-class Mexicans, their two years in office had disillusioned some people who had no affection for the "radical" Mexicans. A number of Mexicans in CASAA, including the mayor, apparently felt they were being used by the Anglos in CASAA. Because of various practices during the two years of CASAA rule, these moderate Mexicans began to feel that not all the Anglos were sincere in their relations with the Mexicans in CASAA. This taking advantage of the moderate Mexicans who wanted to be accepted by Anglos was confirmed later by one of the most important Anglo leaders in CASAA. According to him, many (although by no means all) of the Anglos were still, in his words, "racists." Time and again he was told by other Anglos, "We've got to *use* the Mexicans."[32] Thus many Anglos in CASAA were willing to work with Mexicans only because it was necessary for political survival, and a number of moderate Mexicans began to sense this.

This practice may have become more obvious because, after the defeat of Cornejo and "outside domination," many Anglos began to lose interest in politics. The incentive to work with Mexicans and to prove Anglo goodwill declined, and more "normal" race relations began to reappear.

the city council elections of 1967

In 1967, then, CASAA rule more than counter-initiatives by the defeated Mexicans seemed to lead to a weakening of the Anglo position and a consequent strengthening of the Mexican forces opposed to CASAA. The five-man city council reflected the weakening of CASAA and the pressures that had been on all of them. Mayor Avila refused to run for re-election. Ed Stocking, an Anglo businessman, announced that he too was resigning because he wanted to devote more time to his business.[33] Bill Leonard, the mortician, also wanted to retire from the council, but was prevailed upon by CASAA leaders to run again.[34] In the end only Ed Salinas and Humberto Castillo and a reluctant Bill Leonard ran for re-election.[35] To replace Avila and Stocking, CASAA nominated Paulino Mata, a high-school math teacher, and Charlie Crawford, a manager at the Del Monte cannery.

The campaign was again intense. CASAA held more free barbecues and went to work on the absentee ballots. PASO, as they were still generally called, held numerous rallies at La Placita, an open-air meeting place in their section of town. The *Sentinel* editor again warned about the danger of irresponsible Mexicans being in control. In trying to arouse the Anglos and anti-PASO supporters, he asked of the PASO candidates: "Can they offer a stable, dignified city government? Can they offer ability and successful business experience?"[36] Later he editoralized: "Some have forgotten the days of 'Los Cinco,' when there was no understanding of the business community, no real interest in the welfare of the city, and little concern for anything except power."[37]

The election turned out to be extremely close. The CASAA coalition had indeed been severely strained. With over 2,000 people voting, only seventy-two votes separated the strongest vote-getter from the weakest.[38] Although two CASAA Mexicans led the voting, three anti-CASAA Mexicans came in next and were also elected to the city council.

Of interest, Juan Cornejo's lesser-known younger brother, Roberto, did better than Juan himself. This indicated that Juan Cornejo was continuing to antagonize people who might have been his supporters. Bill Leonard was defeated in his bid for re-election, and since the other CASAA Anglo was also defeated, the city council became as in 1963 all Mexican.

1967 CITY COUNCIL ELECTION RESULTS

Name	Faction	Absentee Votes	Election Day Vote	Total
Paulino Mata	(CASAA)	305	812	1,117
Ed Salinas*	(CASAA)	313	800	1,113
Hilario Lozano	(PASO—Cornejo)	55	1,039	1,094
Roberto Cornejo	(PASO—Cornejo)	58	1,036	1,094
Moses Falcón	(PASO—Falcon)	57	1,028	1,085
Juan Cornejo	(PASO—Cornejo)	59	1,025	1,084
Charlie Crawford	(CASAA)	301	778	1,079
Bill Leonard*	(CASAA)	306	765	1,071
Natividad Granados	(PASO—Falcon)	53	1,015	1,068
Humberto Castillo*	(CASAA)	302	743	1,045

*Indicates incumbent

The election was so close, however, that election suits were filed. Since Juan Cornejo had only one vote less than the successful Moses Falcón, Cornejo filed suit to challenge the results, claiming fraud by CASAA in the absentee ballots. Among the numerous claims of fraud alleged in the absentee balloting, the suit contended that specific individuals had "received assistance from María Cumpian or Julia Mendoza or Helen Mayer or Ofilia Perales in obtaining their applications and in completing them." These women, the suit stated, "marked the ballots expressing their choices instead of those of the voters."[39]

When Cornejo filed this suit, the defeated CASAA candidates felt they had to file suit also.[40] Consequently, the three losing CASAA candidates contested the election results, claiming that ineligible people—noncitizens, unknown people with unknown addresses, etc.—had voted. Shortly before the district judge gave his ruling, Cornejo rather mysteriously withdrew his suit. The district judge eventually decided that of all the claims of illegality brought, he would act upon only one.[41] He ordered that the ballot boxes be opened and that all those who had failed to sign their name to the back of their voting stub have their ballots removed.[42] Of the 2,280 voters, the judge found twenty-seven

voters had left their stubs blank, had signed with an "X," or had
signed only their initials. Not surprisingly, a disproportionate
number of these individuals, many of whom were presumably
illiterate, had voted for the PASO slate. By subtracting these
twenty-seven voters from the totals, Moses Falcón lost his seat
on the council and Charlie Crawford replaced him.

Although Juan Cornejo could presumably be consoled in
knowing that if he could not be on the council, Moses Falcón
could not be on either, it seems that the shift giving CASAA a
majority did not have a tremendous impact on city politics.
Moses Falcón had already sided with the two CASAA candidates against Roberto Cornejo and Lozano in the selection of
mayor. Paulino Mata, the highest vote-getter and a newcomer to
the CASAA slate, became mayor. Although Falcón presumably
would have been an independent swing vote on the council, he
had already shown that he was willing to work with CASAA on
at least some important matters.[43]

the schools: successful cooptation

Intense campaigning was thus continuing over places on the
city council, and CASAA had not been able to solidify its
position within the city. Yet at least as important during this
period was the lack of campaigns for school-board positions.
Not since 1963 had any attempt been made to gain control of
the board. After Maldonado and Olivarez narrowly lost in the
race for the board in 1963 and Los Cinco won control of the
council, the Anglos began to recognize that changes also needed
to be made in the school board to protect themselves from
Mexican candidates. The Anglo board decided it would be a
liability to continue as an all-Anglo board. Since the school
board was considered less salient in the community than the
council, it was not, however, considered necessary to have a
majority of the board members be Mexicans. Instead one would
be enough, and one that they could choose. Because Maldonado
had impressed the board with his moderate campaign, he was
contacted through a Mexican intermediary about being appointed to the board at the time that an Anglo resigned. He
reluctantly told the intermediary that to accept appointment
rather than election would look like he had sold out. It would

also, he said, make him feel indebted to the Anglo majority that appointed him.[44] He consequently declined the offer to be named the first Mexican-American member of the school board. The Anglos continued their search, wanting to be careful in selecting their Mexican. They finally settled upon Frank Guajardo, an active member of the Mexican Chamber of Commerce who had been a postal employee. Accordingly when Mills Addison resigned in the fall of 1963, Guajardo was appointed to the board in his place.

This step seems to have been a brilliant stroke of cooptation, because while PASO was conducting its concerted campaign for county offices in 1964, they left unchallenged the school-board slate of Guajardo and two Anglos. Again in 1965 no challenge was offered to the board candidates, even though both candidates running were Anglos. This indicated that for less salient positions than the city council, Anglo cooptation was more likely to succeed.

Guajardo's term on the board, however, ended abruptly. Within a year of his appointment, he was charged with misuse of funds at a credit union where he had been working. He resigned from the board and eventually was sentenced to six months in the federal penitentiary. Although his term of office was cut short, his stay on the board was successful from the Anglos' point of view, for he had served to deflect Mexicans from campaigning for the school board. Guajardo was subsequently replaced by Urbano Esquivel, a Mexican-American businessman who ran a cleaners and also worked for the editor of the *Zavala County Sentinel.* Esquivel's stay on the board was much longer, and he quickly proved himself to be as conservative as any Anglo on the board.

After the CASAA victory in the city elections of 1965, the Anglos decided that maybe they should have another Mexican on the seven-man board. Consequently, the same procedures were followed. Instead of choosing a Mexican American to run for office with the Anglos when a term expired, the Anglos selected a Mexican and appointed him to the board during the middle of the year. This method of selection allowed the Anglos to make sure their choice was suitable before he was elected, and it also emphasized the Mexican's obligation to the Anglos on the board. This procedure helped make the Mexicans pliant and also had the consequence of weeding out any candidates who intended to be too independent or who wanted to be leaders. As the example of Jesús Maldonado indicated, independent Mexicans refused to submit to the kind of selection process the Anglos required.

Selected as the second Mexican member of the board was Francisco Benavides, a grocer, who was also the brother-in-law of Irma Benavides. Before Benavides had ever run for election to the board, however, he moved to Laredo and resigned his seat. The appointment of a second Mexican, however, again kept any contest from developing over school-board places. In 1966, as in 1965, less than three hundred people voted for the all-Anglo candidates running for the board. When Benavides resigned from the board, Eddie Treviño, a worker at the Del Monte cannery, was selected to take his place. Treviño was the first worker ever selected by the Anglos to a position as important as the school board or city council, and his selection perhaps indicated a gradual liberalization of the process of selection. At the time he was chosen, Treviño was as surprised as anyone, and later thought he was chosen because Ed Mayer, a Del Monte supervisor and member of the board, thought he would be a good man to appoint.[45] His appointment again kept school-board elections quiet. In 1968, as in 1967, there was no opposition for the board places, and even fewer people bothered to vote.

At the level of preventing challenges to the board, then, the process of cooptation worked astoundingly well. At the very time hot battles were raging over county and city offices, the school board was left untouched. No opposition candidates filed, and only a few people voted. The school board thus remained relatively uncontroversial and less salient throughout the period of struggle from 1963 on.[46]

This Anglo process of cooptation was designed not only to prevent a general Mexican-American challenge to the board, but also to develop stable, responsible and trustworthy Mexican leadership which could serve to counter the more radical Mexicans. Anglos hoped the selection of these Mexicans could be used as proof of their good intentions. It was hoped and expected that these Mexicans would serve as examples to the whole Mexican community and be proof that the establishment was indeed open to Mexicans.

the second casaa term

The second term for CASAA showed definite signs of becoming more stable and less controversial. The term was considerably easier than their first, although their victory in 1967 had been much more precarious than in 1965. Depoliticization seems to have occurred primarily because there were no more grievous Anglo mistakes such as those that shook the community in 1965 and 1966. The Anglos seem to have adjusted to their role in the city government as the powers not in the spotlight but behind the scenes. Their use of "responsible, trustworthy" Mexicans was now grudgingly accepted by even the most bitter Anglo racists. With the lack of beatings and frame-ups to unite the dissident Mexicans, a gradual fractionalization of the opposition continued. The people active in CASAA solidified their position while at the same time the CASAA organization gradually withered. It was no longer deemed necessary to have such an elaborate organization, since there was no longer a threat from the old PASO organization. This lessening of community polarization allowed Anglo controversies to surface. The rumor that CASAA money had been used to support a Democratic candidate for Congress, Chick Kazen, angered the numerous Republicans in the organization and seems to have sounded the death knell to the nearly defunct organization.

As CASAA declined, however, no strong leader emerged in place of the organization. This lack of a strong, number-one man in community politics had been noticeable since the beginning of CASAA. Almost by definition an Anglo could not serve as overt leader of the organization. The Anglos were too small a minority and the whole purpose of the organization was to prove that Anglos did not object to Mexican-American participation. But the Mexicans in CASAA were either too closely tied to the Anglos to receive general Mexican support or if they were somewhat independent, lost their Anglo support and withdrew from politics rather than take on both the Anglos and the militants.[47] No powerful leadership thus developed among the moderate, middle-class Mexicans, who were caught between the Anglos and the radicals.

As in the first term of CASAA rule, between 1967 and 1969 progress continued in the redevelopment and renewal of the city, although not without some setbacks. The inauguration of the Model Cities program in 1967 brought great hopes to Crystal City, with the urban renewal director thinking the city had an excellent chance to be chosen. The program, which allowed for a more comprehensive and coordinated attack on poverty than urban renewal alone provided, was to be even more heavily funded by the federal government. The staff at the urban renewal office, with the help of various city personnel, compiled an application explaining in detail the problems of poverty in the community. The application attested not only to the competence of the people working on the report, but indicated a striking awareness of many of the problems Crystal City faced. The report revealed that authorities, including the urban renewal director and his staff, recognized that while there had been progress, much work remained to be done.

The application boldly used census reports to document the city's poverty. It noted that the 1960 census had found over sixty percent of Crystal City's families making less than $3,000 a year, which was twice the average for the state of Texas as a whole (see Appendix 1).[48] They used the same census to document that nearly half of the labor force in Zavala County worked less than half the year (see Appendix 1). Eighty-five percent of the work force needed permanent employment; eighty percent were classified as migratory workers; and seventy-three percent could not do work other than stoop labor. The Model Cities application also revealed that sixty-five percent of that part of the work force with jobs did not receive even the minimum wage of $1.25 an hour.[49]

Concerning schools, the application again used 1960 census figures, which showed that for the county as a whole the median number of school years completed for the population over twenty-five was 4.5 years. In terms of housing, the Census Bureau had classified between eighty-five and eighty-seven percent of all homes as substandard or dilapidated.

Besides reciting census statistics, however, the Model Cities application also contained reports from various city officials on their major problems. The Superintendent of Schools, M. D. Ray, wrote:

The parents of . . . migratory children are able to pay very little in the way of tax money for the support of our schools and they will be here only for a period of five or six months; however we must maintain classrooms, books, teachers, and other supplies, and equipment for the maximum number of children. As you can readily see the financial burden of a community such as ours is great, and we are in immediate need of classrooms and equipment. In the last ten years the school district has voted $600,000 in bonds for the construction of 40 classrooms, one Homemaking building, and one cafeteria. We now need, in order to comply with the intent of the Federal Aid to Education Act, a minimum of 39 more classrooms. Many of the classrooms we are now using might be classed as substandard. During World War II the federal government constructed an internment camp here in Crystal City to house German and Japanese families who were enemy aliens. When the war was over and the camp closed the government gave the school buildings to the school district. These buildings were built as temporary structures; however, with constant maintenance we are able to hold them together and still use them as classrooms.[50]

A report on the need for low-cost credit for migrants stated that prices in the fall were often raised twenty to thirty percent when the migrants returned. The report stated that migrants were desperately in need of loans, and noted that it was impossible for migrants to get low-interest government loans because the Federal Housing Authority had declared "a migrant worker with steady *jobs* ineligible because he does not have a steady job." The report continued: "Unfortunately the Federal Housing Authority is not interested in loans to the poor Mexican-Americans dominating the South Texas region, as evidenced by the lack of mortgage insurance in any urban renewal project in South Texas."[51] The only avenue left for the migrants had to be high-interest-rate, short-term mortgages through private lenders. This form of credit, the report concluded, "is essential, costly, a means of control (a form of debt slavery), and degrading."[52]

The reports on health in the community were perhaps the most shocking. It was found that

Of the 108 Head Start children, over 7% had bad ears or eyes; 3% suffered from malnutrition; over 47% had pin worms; and 34% suffered dental defects. In the migrant school, 21% suffered from heart murmurs, 61% had dental problems, and

36% suffered malnutrition. The city also experiences a high tuberculosis rate, with over 677 positive skin reactions with an incidence of 14% per 1,000 population, and the infant diarrhea is always high with 6.4% infant deaths per total births.[53]

Dr. Mary Brittain, the medical director of the Family Planning Clinic, reported that nearly all their patients

> . . . answer yes, that they are in good health, yet 100% of our patients have diseased or damaged child-bearing parts. On the average the lady has lost three children by death—mean age at death is six weeks. The cause of death is usually unknown; diarrhea and pneumonia are the only listed causes of death and represent 14% of the deaths.[54]

This sort of report, drawn up by the leaders of Crystal City under the direction of Sam Anderson, thus documented some of the major problems the community faced in education, health, housing, finance, and employment. It was nearly inconceivable that the city leadership would have compiled such a report in the early 1960's, when conditions were most likely even worse.[55] The Model Cities program, in being designed to deal with these varied problems in a comprehensive manner, in itself served as a spur to the city.

Crystal City was originally chosen for the Model Cities program and was assured by various Washington bureaucrats that they could count on the program. At the last moment, however, President Johnson decided to switch the program from Crystal City to Eagle Pass to fit in with his Border Beautification program. Eagle Pass, located on the border with Mexico some forty miles from Crystal City, had made only a one-page application for the program. Crystal City officials therefore had to sit through the humiliation of having Eagle Pass personnel journey to Crystal City to see how an application form should be compiled so that Eagle Pass could then be awarded the program.[56]

Federal funds, or lack of them, thus played an increasingly important role in the development of the community. This failure to get Model Cities, however, was not because of Anglo incompetence or reluctance. It occurred in spite of the diligence the city had shown in applying for these federal funds.

Another setback occurred when the school administration

missed the deadline for applying for a continuation of Project Head Start in 1967.[57] Project Head Start was thus discontinued for the year, although the city set up a similar, but less comprehensive program for the summer. This slip-up angered many Mexican-American parents, who felt that the ending of the program had happened either through mismanagement or because the Anglo administration secretly wanted the program discontinued.[58]

The influx of new federal programs did not always occur smoothly, and without rancoring either the Mexicans, the Anglos, or both. Even the urban renewal program came in for more criticism. Councilman Roberto Cornejo said that people were being forced out of their homes and into more expensive homes which they couldn't afford. "You are going to have a beautiful city with no one living in it," he commented.[59] Anderson answered this charge by saying that he would be happy to meet with anyone about the program and their individual difficulties, but only on a one-to-one basis. Through consenting to see people only on this basis, Anderson was able to use his considerable personal skill and could dampen, as he had in the past, any serious movement against the program.

It continued to be around the poverty program, however, that the greatest unrest formed. Anglos, as we have seen, were upset with the wages the program was paying to Mexicans, and Mexicans were upset with the school administration for refusing to cooperate on the Adult Migrant Education program. Soon, however, dissatisfaction broadened. The administrative personnel of the poverty program became the subject of protests by the local Mexicans. Dissatisfied Mexicans demanded and got the resignation of several members of the personnel in the local office, from the head of the Community Action Project (Captain Jack Loyall) down to a secretary. The local Mexicans resented the salaries these administrators were drawing and considered some of their proposals—such as a class for Mexican women on how to cook beans and cornbread—insulting.[60]

At the same time Anglos were putting pressure on the poverty officials, wanting to assert more control over the programs. The county officialdom voted to reorganize the poverty program and managed to get removed several officials whom they also disliked. This prompted Bernard Weinberg, one of the few VISTA workers in the county, to write an angry letter to the county officials in charge of dismantling the program and end-ing the VISTA program for the area. Weinberg noted that ninety percent of the cost of the program was federal, and charged that what success the program had known had been in spite of, rather than because of, the county. Rather than help-ing, certain county officials had spent their energies attacking the program through "false charges" and "allegations," he as-serted.[61]

Although a hearing was held by the county-commissioners court over the proposal to reorganize the poverty program, and a number of Mexicans showed up for the hearing, County Judge Irl Taylor assured the protesters that regardless of what they said or did, the court had "already made up its mind" before the public hearing.[62] At this public hearing the Rev. Arnold López, who had been active in the program, noted that the county had not contributed a cent to the poverty program. Instead it had only been the city, urban renewal, and churches who had helped. Judge Taylor, however, responded that the county had not been "asked" to participate. Rev. López ex-pressed his anxiety by saying, "Our concern is that the poor will be used as a political tool."[63] But Taylor had already told the group before the hearing that the county was going to reorga-nize the administration of the program, and this was now done.[64]

As this struggle indicated, in the years after the 1967 city elections, federal programs came to play a more important role in local affairs. Mexicans began to be dissatisfied with programs that were supposed to be for them, and Anglos reacted by wanting to oversee the administration of these programs more carefully, or, if the programs were deemed too upsetting (such as VISTA), to end them altogether.

This controversy over federal programs did not, however, spill over into organized political action against city officials. Within the city administration itself, the three CASAA council-men seemed to do little that antagonized broad segments of the community. This was true perhaps mainly because the city government was doing very little and thus maintained a much lower salience than actions surrounding the new federal pro-grams. The city, however, was still not able to find a successful city manager who might have been able to stabilize politics and run the city government the way the late L. L. Williams had.

After Jack Whitley resigned because of the threat of ulcers, the council hired Charles Rogers. Rogers did not get along with the city staff, and he also resigned after serving only one year. Unlike Whitley, he gave no reasons for his resignation.

Hired to replace Rogers was E. W. Marlowe, a man who had been city manager in a number of communities in the area and whom CASAA had originally wanted back in 1965. Marlowe was widely respected by the Anglos in the community, and had a reputation as a frugal, efficient administrator.[65] With his appointment, the city government seemed at last to be on the road to recovery from a string of unsatisfactory managers caused by the forced resignation of Ozuna.

A city sales tax authorized by state law during this time was overwhelmingly approved by the voters. Although some Mexican members of the council had indicated disapproval of the sales tax, an extraordinarily light turnout saw the tax pass by nearly ten to one.[66] Jack Whitley and Charles Rogers had both urged its passage, arguing that with a sales tax the city might even be able to revise its property taxes downward. That a tax as regressive as this could have been passed with hardly a ripple from the Mexican community was yet another indication that the community was finally beginning to settle back into "normalcy," with the Mexicans unorganized and fractionalized. The poverty protests had not been sustained or made generalizable into a broad political attack on local Anglo officials. In fact the Mexican protests had ended up backfiring as the county saw the dangers of the program.

Given this situation, the CASAA coalition, although now rarely referred to as CASAA, continued to run the community and to strengthen its relative position as the Mexican militants weakened. The opposition to the Anglo-Mexican coalition became even more fragmented into feuding fiefdoms and its leadership was increasingly discredited through self-destructive battles.

The 1968 county elections provided a good example of this fragmentation and feuding. Sheriff C. L. Sweeten was again up for re-election, and like perhaps no other Anglo in the county, he could have been expected to unify the Mexican community against him. Ramón Garza, a Mexican who had run a write-in campaign against Sweeten in the 1964 general election and had run as an independent supporting Ozuna on the slate with

Manuel Maldonado in 1965, decided to run against Sweeten in the May Democratic primary.

Juan Cornejo, however, announced that he too would run against Sweeten—only not in the Democratic primary, where there might be a runoff if the two Mexican candidates out-polled Sweeten. He would run as a third-party candidate in the November election. Why Cornejo chose to do this has been the subject of intense speculation. Having tried and failed to win election to county office via the Democratic primary, he may have thought that a third-party race would be a better route, especially if the Republicans were to run someone against Sweeten. Many Mexicans in the community, however, later felt that Cornejo's motives were more sinister—that he was prevailed upon by Anglos to run as a means of splitting the Mexican vote.[67] In order to be a third-party candidate, Cornejo needed signatures from people who would not vote in the Democratic primary in May. Accordingly, each signature meant one less person eligible to vote in the Democratic primary. When the primary election came, Ramón Garza was defeated by Sweeten, 1,399 to 1,016. Although fewer people voted in the primary than in previous years, presumably in part because of the several hundred ineligible Cornejo-ites, Garza had done credibly, receiving forty-two percent of the countywide vote. But Sweeten was still renominated.[68]

When the time came for the November campaign, Cornejo apparently had done little or nothing about getting his name listed on the ballot as a third-party candidate. He in fact did not run at all, and the several hundred people who had signed petitions in his behalf were left with no one to vote for. Cornejo maintained legal restrictions prevented him from running, but this did not allay people's suspicions. Sweeten sailed into another four-year term as sheriff.

As the April, 1969, elections approached, Cornejo again decided he was going to run for the council. He ran on a slate with Hilario Lozano, an incumbent councilman, and Ramón de la Fuente and Alfred Terán. Juan Cornejo's brother, Roberto, did not seek re-election to the council, and according to the *Sentinel* had attended only half the meetings of the city council in the previous two years. The people, however, were apparently tired of Cornejo. Increasingly the Mexican-American community realized they could never win with Cornejo as their leader.

While the Cornejo slate thus represented discredited leadership in the Mexican community, no other group of militants filed for office. Although it is not absolutely clear why no others chose to run, one of the leaders of those Mexicans who were against both CASAA and Cornejo commented that at this point no one was willing to run because they realized they would have had to take on so many different forces: the Anglos, the CASAA-Mexicans, and Cornejo. To do this, argued this Mexican, would have meant being embroiled in a great deal of in-fighting. And because this struggle was likely to be dirty and one's reputation was likely to be attacked and sullied, no one was willing to risk making the effort.[69] Because none of these Mexicans were willing to run, the CASAA group, now referred to as the "Mata Team," expanded its position in the community. There had been no major mistakes of the magnitude of those taking place in their first term of office. In fact, the Anglo and middle-class Mexican coalition seemed to be more willing to extend itself and to run candidates on its slate who were not absolutely bound to the team. As an indication of this, one of the "Mata Team" candidates was Francisco Benavides, the grocer who had earlier served a short time on the school board before leaving for Laredo. Benavides had since returned, and was approached by an influential Anglo concerning his running for the council.[70] Benavides was told by the Anglo that "a group of people" wanted him to run for the council, but that it was "no organization" and that they would not try to tell him what to do. Benavides was considered by the Anglo strategists as an independent who would lend strength to their ticket without being any threat to them. He was certainly no radical, but he was also not associated with the CASAA organization even though he had earlier been on the school board.

The fact that Benavides was on the slate may have been a reason the Cornejo faction ran only four candidates. At any rate, Benavides emerged as the top vote-getter of all the council candidates, and Cornejo and his slate suffered the most humiliating defeat of their careers.[71] They were beaten nearly two to one, and many Mexicans apparently expressed their disgust for the slate by not voting at all. The turnout for the council races was the smallest since the PASO era began. Further signaling their failure, a city charter change providing for staggered terms was at last approved by the voters.

conclusion

The anti-CASAA, working-class Mexicans, now without effective leadership, were thoroughly beaten by a coalition which
showed every sign of being more sophisticated and confident.
Because discredited leadership had alienated many potential
supporters and had in part sold out or been induced to support
the Anglos, the working-class and migrant Mexicans were once
again basically leaderless and demoralized. A return to apathy
finally seemed to be recurring, as the voter turnouts for city
council, school board, and countywide offices all declined. In a
community of such poverty and inexperience, it had of course
been most unusual for the lower-class Mexicans to have political
leadership or political unity at all. That this leadership now
declined was an indication that the community was reverting to
more normal political behavior, where businessmen and skilled
professionals ruled. As the events of the last decade had clearly
indicated, the political system was not designed for the poor.
They did not have the knowledge or the resources to understand and master the system of governance. From their sudden
emergence onto the political scene, the poor had not been able
to develop leadership that could master the political process.
Consequently, given time, political sophistication, and firm control of the social and economic institutions of the area, the
Anglos, working primarily in concert with middle-class Mexicans, had been able to regain control of the political structures
of the community.

It should be noted that the defeat of the radicals had by no
means left them with no successes to point to. The Anglos had
learned in the decade of struggle. No longer would they run
all-Anglo slates for the school board and city council (although
for county offices it was still considered safe to do this). The
Anglos had learned the importance of working with and developing "responsible, trustworthy" Mexican leadership who could
handle many of the affairs of the local government. Further, a
majority of Anglos were beginning to overcome their distaste
for federal "handouts" for the poor and were learning to use
federal programs to help alleviate some of the problems they
realized existed in their community. Urban renewal in the
community was proceeding at a rapid pace. In fact Crystal

City's urban renewal program was fast becoming one of the most comprehensive in the country. By the end of the decade, nearly $14,000,000, or an average of about $600 per capita, had been spent in the community on urban renewal and low-cost housing.[72] The city's serious attempt to become part of the Model Cities program had further indicated Anglo concern and desire to help upgrade the community. Federal funds for migrant schooling were being sought and used, and federal aid to the school district became more important with each passing year.[73]

The Anglos seemed to have adjusted to the initial rapid expansion of the electorate in the community. Not only were Anglo assaults on Mexicans over, but the Anglos seemed to recognize that a strong, well-trained and experienced Mexican-American middle-class represented their best strength against the "rabble" which had been aroused to unusual activity by the Teamster-PASO coalition.[74]

Looking at the community in the spring of 1969 immediately after the council elections, one would have found the indicators pointing towards a return to stability, a return to politics more normal for Crystal City and the area. Through gradual, incremental adaptations, combined with inducements and "tempered" by repression, authorities were recognizing and dealing with many of the issues the Mexicans had first raised.

One might have concluded that the system, with the help of federal developments, had responded and was making changes. Slowly but surely it was working towards integrating an ever greater part of the Crystal City Mexican population into the life of the community. All groups were now having an influence on the governmental process and its policies, although of course not all could be winners. Government was by coalition, compromise, and negotiation. Crystal City had become more democratic and its governmental process more pluralistic as a result of the revolt. Although the leadership of the revolt had failed, we could be reassured that many of the ideas lying behind the revolt were succeeding.

But ironically, at the very moment when events seemed to indicate that Crystal City was settling down into a newly-found stability, the whole community was swept up in another catharsis, far greater and more radical than the first. With hindsight it

is still hard to believe that many social scientists would have
been any more prepared for this revolt than were the Anglos.
Indicators in the community were pointing towards accommodation, adjustment, and depoliticization. How could the community be blown apart again?

5   the second revolt

In a period of seeming quiescence, when the Anglos and moderate Mexicans appeared to have consolidated and solidified their position in the community, a revolt began which eventually sent the community into a trauma greater than the revolt of 1963. To understand how this could have happened, it is necessary to examine the community in a deeper, more critical light, for the revolt did not begin in or around a political structure, nor did it come from the same sources as the 1963 revolt. Because of this, the Anglos were essentially unprepared.

This second revolt signified a great deal about the community—the degree to which changes had and had not occurred, the extent to which the changes had been successful, and the differing attitudes Mexicans and Anglos held towards these innovations. As we have noted, in almost all areas of public life Crystal City had been moving toward greater integration, greater accommodation, and what looked like greater harmony between the races. The city council had a Mexican-American majority since 1963. The Anglos had adjusted to this, and in fact had restrained themselves from seeking more offices. The school board had moved from being all Anglo to including two Mexicans on the seven-man board. The school faculty had changed from being only ten percent Spanish-surnamed at the beginning of the decade to being more than one-fourth Spanish by the fall of 1969. New federal programs utilized by the schools and the city government indicated a growing concern among the city leadership over poverty and other problems confronting Mexican-Americans.

All these measures revealed that Crystal City had clearly made progress between 1963 and 1969. The city now took racial integration more seriously than any of the surrounding communities which had not been shaken by revolts. Uvalde, Carrizo Springs, and Cotulla—all communities near Crystal City and all located in or near the Winter Garden Area—had not proceeded nearly as far in racial accommodation. If one were to examine communities in the Winter Garden Area for objective measures of discrimination, it would be difficult to show that discrimination was as noticeable or serious, or that the Anglo leadership was as intransigent in Crystal City as in these other communities.[1] For all these reasons, the Anglos felt confident that another revolt would never occur.

The Anglos had seemingly defused the explosive 1963 situation of nearly complete Anglo rule in an overwhelmingly Mexican-American community. Now Crystal City seemed to be moving toward the pattern developed along the border in such towns as Laredo and Eagle Pass, where Mexican Americans had always played an important part in the government and where Anglos had never expected to run things completely on their own. Other structural and institutional factors which produced the explosion in 1963 also seemed by 1969 to have been either defused or to have at least become no worse. The community was still overwhelmingly Mexican American, by roughly the same amount, and Crystal City still was headquarters for a large number of migrants. In fact a 1969 migrant labor report for the state of Texas revealed that Zavala County had a higher proportion of migrants than any other county in the state.[2] But migrants probably made up slightly less of the community's population in 1969 than in 1963. During this period migrants had been forced more and more to hunt for other means of employment as their opportunities for work continued to decline.[3] A number of migrants left the community for relocation elsewhere. Some families had moved to San Antonio; some had relocated as far away as Milwaukee. In addition to this family migration, many of the most talented young Mexicans, those who might have been the biggest potential threats to the continued moderate-conservative rule, were leaving the community in search of better opportunities elsewhere.

Del Monte was still an anomaly in the area, continuing to employ hundreds of Mexican Americans and to pay wages better than others in the area. The union, however, had become increasingly lethargic since its activism in 1963. Because of the trouble the Teamsters had found themselves in from 1963 to 1965, it was inconceivable that the national and state Teamster leadership would again serve as a fulcrum for the revolt.

An examination of all the institutional and structural factors which had created the unique powder keg in Crystal City and had led to the revolt in 1963 thus allowed the Anglo-Mexican coalition to feel confident and secure. If revolts were always based on objective measures of racial discrimination and exploitation, with communities most guilty of ill treatment always being the ones experiencing revolt, then Crystal City Anglos could remain confident. Revolts, however, are not based on these factors alone, as has been observed by scholars from de Tocqueville on.[4] That is, along with the institutional changes in the years since the 1963 revolt, attitudes in the Mexican-American community were also changing greatly. The constant Anglo disclaimers of discrimination and their increased talk of the need for racial harmony had not fallen on deaf ears. By 1969, Mexicans no longer judged success or failure, discrimination or equality, by the same standards they had used in 1963.[5] As the second revolt was to make clear, their attitudes and their resources had changed far more rapidly than the incremental and token reforms Anglos had allowed. And hidden behind the emphasis on change between 1963 and 1969 were still enormous differences in the quality of life in the Mexican and Anglo communities of the town. These differences were to become paramount as the revolt caught fire. At the same time they were to serve as a warning to those observers who in focusing on the few areas of reforms had ignored the far larger areas where there had been little or no substantive change.

developments outside crystal city

Between 1963 and 1969 Mexican Americans throughout the Southwest had done a great deal of thinking over their place in

American society and the purposes and need for a Mexican-American, or Chicano, movement.[6] This was in part spurred on by the rising militancy of the Black movement.[7] Tokenism, or gradualist reforms instituted by well-meaning Anglos, became less and less satisfactory to the intellectuals who claimed to speak for the Mexican American. At the same time integration became less of a goal than the recovery and protection of their own identity. A rebirth in history led to an increased awareness of the Chicano's prior claims to the Southwest, to North American imperialism, and to such offshoots as American violations of the treaty of Guadalupe Hidalgo. This activity led to increased militancy, and ironically, their own "Anglicization" gave them greater confidence in confrontations with "the gringo."[8] In this process of seeking to become the "masters of their own destiny," new organizations of Mexican Americans were founded with new leadership and new goals.[9] The most visible of these new organizations in South Texas was the Mexican-American Youth Organization (MAYO), which was founded in 1967. As MAYO described itself:

> The founders of MAYO felt a need for an active and aggressive organization that would offer the Mexican American youth a vehicle with which to effect meaningful social change. It was felt that the traditional Mexican American organizations were not recruiting young Mexican Americans in order to develop leadership and expertise among the youth. These elder organizations had failed to engage in direct action projects and community organization.[10]

Composed of young militants, often quite well-educated, MAYO adopted as goals a program to fulfill "the destiny of La Raza."[11] These goals consisted of forming third parties separate from either the Democrats or the Republicans, gaining control of the educational systems in Chicano communities, and ending Anglo economic domination by the development of their own businesses and cooperatives.[12] Although these goals were still largely talked about rather than acted upon, and thus few people could know how much they represented the masses of Mexican Americans, there did seem by the late 1960's to be restlessness and dissatisfaction spreading through many of the barrios [Mexican-American ghettos] of the Southwest. This unrest was best indicated by a series of school walkouts which swept through several communities, including such metropolitan centers as Los Angeles and Denver.[13] As a tactic, school boycotts appeared to be a wise choice for militant Chicanos because they mobilized their most active members—young people in their teens and early twenties. School boycotts also appeared to be tactically sound because they could revolve around the family, which had always been a central focus in Chicano culture.[14] Thus the children and their parents could hopefully unite in working to bring greater opportunity to the school children.

Whereas all these reasons were probably important in the singling out of schools for protest against the general condition of Mexican Americans in American society, perhaps the most important reason for choosing the schools was that their policies and procedures seemed to be especially resented by many Mexicans. As the primary Anglicizing institutions for the Mexican American, the schools had long determined who would be successful and who would fail, who would be accepted and who would be rejected and humiliated.[15] And because the Chicano movement was increasingly questioning their own place in society and the desirability of being completely integrated into Anglo culture, resentment against the school's definition of success seemed to build in many parts of the Southwest.

The spread of protest in the Southwest, then, indicated that Chicano experience and intellectual thought had developed substantially in the six years between 1963 and 1969. This was to have its impact on Crystal City. Dissatisfied Mexican Americans knew that Crystal City had been the greatest success story in the Chicano political movement, and also its biggest failure. These Mexicans, not unlike the Anglos, seemed determined to try to learn from the failure as well as from the success. Thus developments affecting Mexican Americans in the Southwest which Crystal City had furthered through its own revolt in turn fed back into the community, intensifying Chicano consciousness. Even without these external developments, however, the community would never have been the same after 1963—not only because of the changes that had been made by the Anglos and moderate Mexicans, but because in Crystal City the Mexican community knew that revolt was possible. It had happened. Everyone had seen it happen. Even though it had ended in bitter disappointment and humiliation, the revolt could never be forgotten. It had become a part of the political history and culture of the community, as all great political crises do. In the ashes of the revolt remained a self-consciousness in the community among all groups. Mexicans in Crystal City were more aware of their condition, of what they had tried to do, and of what had been done to them. Even though their voter turnout was gradually dropping from its 1965 pinnacle, Mexican Americans continued to vote in much higher numbers than in surrounding communities. In spite of the pessimism and cynicism which had followed their defeat, many Mexicans kept to the belief that with better leadership and more auspicious circumstances, another revolt by the migrant and working-class majority of the community might be possible.[16]

It was the Anglos' job, of course, to see that these auspicious circumstances never recurred and that leadership never developed. But because of the different setting for the revolt and because of the changes in attitudes among Mexicans toward what constituted discrimination and what constituted equality, the Anglos were caught off guard. Clearer goals, a different organizational base with a different strategy for mobilizing the Chicano community, and a vastly different kind of leadership not only bewildered the Anglo and middle-class Mexican coalition; it also seemed to make the second revolt more revolutionary and more exportable to the rest of South Texas.

the precipitating event

The second revolt in Crystal City differed from the first in that it was organized around specific examples of discrimination in the school system. Instead of being based as in 1963 upon the anomaly of the Teamsters union, the second revolution had its organizational base in school children and their families. The second revolt differed further in that leadership was not based upon outside organizational experts trying to lead inexperienced local representatives. The new revolution was begun by high-school students, who were the main educational resource in the Mexican community, and was later led by José Angel Gutiérrez, a native of Crystal City who had graduated from high school in the early 1960's. Gutiérrez had gone on to receive a master's degree in political science at St. Mary's University in San Antonio, and had developed political expertise as president of MAYO.[17] With Gutiérrez the revolution had a young man who was far more ideological, far more confident, and far more capable than his predecessor, Juan Cornejo.

To trace the origins of the second revolt, the school system must be examined more closely. As we have noted in previous chapters, much progress had occurred in the schools since the foundation of the community in 1907. From no schools for Mexicans, the school system had moved to the point where an increasing majority of high-school graduates were Mexicans. Mexicans had also made progress on the school board and on the school faculty, as we have noted. The dropout rate for Chicano children also declined. Although for the 1951 entering class of first-graders only nine percent graduated from high school, of the entering class in 1958 seventeen percent graduated.[18] The 1960 census figures had also shown improvement. In 1950 the median number of school years completed by the Spanish-surnamed population over 25 was 1.8 years. By 1960 this figure had moved up to 2.3 years.[19] So there was improvement, but to many Mexicans the rate of progress seemed slow indeed. A dropout rate of over eighty percent was by national standards phenomenal, and the median increase for the population over twenty-five was such that if conditions continued at the same rate of improvement, by the turn of the century most adult Mexicans still would not have graduated from the fifth grade.[20] The figure was made all the more outrageous to Mexicans because their 2.3 year median compared to the Anglo median of 11.2 years.[21] Concerning faculty change, the gradual increase in Spanish-surnamed teachers still left the faculty enormously unreflective of the composition of the student body. By the fall of 1968 eighty-seven percent of the student body were Mexican Americans.[22] And even as the faculty changed, all principals remained Anglo. Thus although there had been changes in the schools, tremendous differences between the two racial groups still remained in faculty and administrative positions, in dropout rates, and in Anglo domination of school-board policies. These statistics all seemed to reveal that a powerful barrier still existed which Mexican Americans could not cross.

Among the faculty there were also certain Anglo teachers and administrators who were almost universally recognized as "Mexican haters."[23] These teachers had precipitated many incidents in their classrooms, occasionally lashing out at all Mexicans, telling them they "should feel privileged to sit next to whites," and in general doing their best to make the Mexicans feel insecure and inferior.[24] One teacher had reportedly told a Mexican who had just been elected to school office, "You Mexicans had better not elect too many, because if you do, Anglos will stop paying their school taxes!"[25] There had even occurred walkouts in individual classrooms over things teachers had said to Mexicans in their classes.[26] Groups of students had visited the school superintendent over these practices, but nothing had occurred except threats of expulsion should the students do anything.[27] Both the Mexican and the Anglo community were aware who these particular Anglo teachers were, but the school board always renewed the contracts of these people, and they continued teaching year after year.

Further, even though the school system had shown clear signs of accommodating Mexican Americans in some areas of school activity, special areas within the schools continued to be Anglo preserves. The United States Civil Rights Commission, which held hearings in Crystal City in March, 1970, found numerous examples of discrimination and segregation. Their report found that segregation was accomplished by five different ways: through different sections or classes of the same subject, through preschool testing, through counseling, through subjects taught, and through tracking.[28] Through examination of textbooks, curriculum, and teacher education and attitudes, the commission found numerous examples of "Anglo ethnocentrism" in the schools. Especially in school-sponsored, extracurricular activities the commission found examples of discrimination. Their report stated in part:

> Generally, it was discovered that the percentage of Mexican American students receiving academic awards was unusually low when compared with the student population. This is the case especially where the school alone has the sole power of selection. . . .
> The selection process of students for popularity/social honors tends to reveal a conflict in the attitude of the teachers and those of the student regarding the just recipients of the popularity and social honors. In those cases where the selection is done strictly by the students the recipients are usually Mexican American, but when the teachers or others

participate in the selection, the recipients are usually Anglo. For example, the "most popular" student during five of the six years studies was Mexican American, while the "most representative" in five of the six years was Anglo. The "most popular" is selected by the students while the "most representative" is selected by the teachers. . . .

Mexican American student participation in drama, speech and debate, and similar activities is unusually low. One base factor appears to be an over emphasis on properly accented pronunciation and the mastery of the English language. . . . This training is, of course most valuable in preparation for public leadership. Anglo participation in each of these activities on the other hand is very high. . . .[29]

Reflecting further on the school system in Crystal City, Calvin Trillin has noted:

Gradually, the percentage of Mexican-Americans in the high school grew, until it nearly reflected the Mexican-American majority in the town. But the student organizations and activities remained basically Anglo—partly because the Anglos had the self-confidence that comes from having always run things, partly because a lot of Mexican-American students didn't take much interest, partly because the overwhelmingly Anglo faculty and administration arranged it that way. The football team, which was ordinarily dominated by Anglos, elected its own Football Sweetheart, but the baseball team, which always had a Mexican-American majority, was told to elect two Baseball Sweethearts—one Mexican-American and one Anglo. . . . And the teachers selecting cheerleaders always seemed to settle on one Mexican-American and three Anglos. In Crystal City, having Anglo cheerleaders was one symbol to the Anglos that their high school was still effectively Anglo even after becoming predominantly Mexican-American. It happened to be the same kind of symbol to the Mexican-American students. . . .[30]

Change in the school system was thus uneven, indicating the limit of Anglo moderation. Anglos were willing to allow Mexicans some token participation, but the Anglos still got nearly all the coveted awards, particularly when these awards involved beauty or glamor. As the Mexicans gradually upgraded themselves in the community, these restrictions became more and more offensive. At the same time the Mexicans began to gain the resources to do something about it.

The spark which set off the second revolt was the election of
cheerleaders at the high school in the spring of 1969. Mexicans
in town claimed that for most of the history of the community
cheerleaders had been elected by the student body. As more
and more Chicanos began to enter high school, however, the
system apparently changed so that a select committee of the
faculty would choose those who they thought were the best
cheerleaders.[31] As Calvin Trillin noted, an unofficial system
was devised so that three Anglos and one Mexican girl were
always chosen. In the spring of 1969 the normal, routine
practice again occurred. This time, however, two of the Anglo
cheerleaders had graduated leaving vacancies, and a Mexican
girl, Diana Palacios, was considered by the student body to be
at least as good as any of the Anglos trying out.[32] The Mexicans, however, already had their "quota" in Diana Pérez, so the
faculty judges again chose two Anglos to fill the vacancies.[33]
The system of discrimination in the selection was thus exposed
to the student body in an unusually clear manner. Since the
protest was over the retention of the status quo, however, this
also indicated that along with the basic developments in Mexican-American thought in the 1960's, Chicanos were becoming
increasingly rigorous in their definition of what constituted
discrimination and were more willing and able to act on their
views.

After the new cheerleaders were announced, a group of
Chicano students protested to the high-school principal. He
considered the matter to be a bunch of "phooey."[34] The
students then went over his head to the school superintendent,
John Billings, at the same time broadening their demands to
other issues involving discrimination. Billings discussed the matter with the students and agreed to adopt an explicit quota
system for cheerleader selection: Three Anglos and three Chicanos. The other demands, concerning the election of twirlers,
high-school favorites, and the establishment of bilingual and
bicultural education, were met either with more quota systems
or with a commitment to "check" what other communities in
the area were doing (see Appendix 3).[35]

The reaction of the Chicano students to their meeting with
Billings was mixed, but most of them were pleased with what
had occurred. Open segregation with separate but equal treat-

ment seemed about the best they could hope for. Although throughout this period of agitation there had been talk of a walkout, none occurred, and Billings considered that he had been successful in avoiding a walkout. Dampening the students' desire for a walkout as well, however, was the realization that since school was almost over they would have little leverage and might all be flunked.

The Anglo reaction to Billings' concessions was generally one of concern and disapproval, and a group of Anglo students and parents went to see him. The old method of cheerleader selection seemed fair to them, and they felt that in adding two Mexican cheerleaders, the superintendent was not being fair to the four cheerleaders already selected. The Anglos also feared that by pandering to the hot-headed students Billings might be opening a pandora's box. Giving in seemed to acknowledge that the system had indeed been discriminatory. Although every Anglo realized that the demands had to be handled carefully, majority sentiment was against giving in to the "arrogant" students.

In June the school board nullified Billings' concessions to the students and also passed a resolution dealing sternly with student unrest.[36] The resolution stated that if any disturbance in the schools occurred, the students involved would lose all credit for their courses and be suspended for the semester.[37] June was considered a safe time for the board to act because school was closed and many students and their families were on the migrant trail. Given these conditions, nothing was done at the time to protest the board's reversal of the superintendent's policy. But with hindsight this action seems to have strengthened the hands of radical students, for the radicals were no longer tied to a position of separate but equal quotas. At the same time, in rejecting the moderate compromise made between the students and the superintendent, the board appeared completely insensitive to Chicano students. In overriding the promises of the school superintendent, the board had also exposed the weakness of the superintendent and had revealed a split in the Anglo community over how to handle the students. During the rest of the summer, word spread among the students that the board had cancelled the agreements, and plans for a school boycott were again discussed.[38]

In this same month of June, José Angel Gutiérrez and his wife returned to Crystal City from San Antonio, at the close of his tenure as president of MAYO.[39] He returned hoping to put into practice the principles of the militant youth organization. Immediately he set about re-establishing connections and re-cruiting a staff to coordinate the effort, not only in Crystal City but in the neighboring counties of the Winter Garden Area. His timing was important. As the spring elections had shown, the original Chicano leadership was by now almost completely discredited. Although local Mexicans recognized their weak leadership, the bitter infighting and factionalism had so weak-ened the sources of radical leadership that none could enter the fray without risking their reputations. Yet the school trouble had indicated that the community was dissatisfied with the status quo and that the students were beginning to fill the void. The situation was thus ripe for new leadership, because many Chicanos in the community seemed to recognize that new people and new issues were necessary if they were to beat the Anglo-backed coalition government.

Gutiérrez had outstanding credentials for uniting the warring factions and for becoming a leader in Crystal City, although his credentials were sometimes contradictory. The son of a doctor from Mexico who had died when the child was still a young boy, Gutiérrez had been well known and popular in the community before he went away to college. As president of the high-school student body and as a debater, he had conducted himself in a manner many Anglos found commendable and reassuring, and the Anglos tended to look upon him as a good leader of the community.[40] As Trillin has commented, "Gutiérrez had been the kind of student Anglos liked to point to as an example of how a bright and ambitious Mexican-American could get ahead."[41] In his high-school days he had many Anglo friends, and he was not involved in the disputes between Mexican students and the school administration over racist statements by Anglo teachers.[42] After leaving the community to attend col-lege, however, he became more radical, and he was one of the few well-educated Mexicans to support Los Cinco in 1963.[43] In 1964 he published an anonymous pamphlet heaping scorn on CASAA and those Mexicans who were in it, and as a result was kidnapped, coerced, and threatened with death.[44] The pam-phlet, reeking with sarcasm, said in part:

The real puppets are [not Cornejo and Los Cinco, but] the Uncle Toms in CASAA. The so-called "smart" Mexicano, these people who feel elevated in status because Mr. White-man treats them to coffee . . . because Mr. Anglo tells him he is smarter than the other Mexicanos. . . .

"There is no discrimination . . ." said the man from Uval-de. Why two cemeteries? Why is the Catholic Church the only integrated church . . . sounds like Alabama. . . .

Our schools where the basic fundamentals of democracy are taught, where brotherhood is preached, where responsibil-ity is stressed, where Meskins vote to elect Meskins and teachers vote to elect little gringoes . . . what about the cheer-leaders? the most handsome and beautiful? The National Honor Society? Why doesn't the school have dances? . . . not private at the Country Club, but mixed in the gym? You can take your shoes off!!! But Muskins do stink, don't they. . . .

For 30 some odd years you had it, now we do! Why do you whine? It's democracy in action, brother! We are all brothers, aren't we? What's the matter, are you a Christian and believe the Bible? Face facts! Either you're a hypocrite or an atheist. . . .[45]

As the bitter sarcasm shows, Gutiérrez had changed from being a nice, moderate Mexican into a bitter radical. That Gutiérrez could have been so "ungrateful" a Mexican surprised the An-glos, but they later developed all sorts of reasons to explain this radicalization.[46] And since he had left the community for San Antonio, he did not appear as a clear threat to the hometown folks. But in the summer of 1969, as we have noted, Gutiérrez returned. His activity in MAYO had given him experience and a chance to develop a strategy for change. As to this strategy, Gutiérrez himself has commented:

. . . MAYO was not intended to be a mass membership orga-nization; nor, a constipated civic group of reformists. . . .

We were not misguided and mal-informed VISTA volun-teers; nor, were we white-knighted Latin Americans that sought to manage the affairs of the gringo for the gringo. We were young Chicanos who saw and felt things like Chicanos should. We loved and accepted our Mexicanismo and saw brighter things for La Raza. . . .

The primary goal was to force the educational system to extend to the Mexican student. . . .

The second goal was to bring democracy to those counties

[where a majority of the people were Mexican-Americans] —
in other words—rule by the majority. . . .

. . . our third goal was a direct confrontation with the
gringo. We sought to expose, confront, and eliminate the
gringo. We felt that it was necessary to polarize the community over issues into Chicano versus gringos.

Basically, the difference between the Chicano and gringo,
aside from the bad guy-good guy criteria is one of attitude.
The attitude gringos have of racial superiority; of paternalism; of divine right; of xenophobia; of bigotry; and of animal-
ism is well-known to La Raza.

After the gringo was exposed publicly, the next step was
to confront their security—status, business, and morality in
order to recognize the enemy in all their involvements of
policies, roles and power manipulations. Once the Chicano
community recognized the enemy, then he had the power to
eliminate gringo attitudes by not voting for the gringo and
not buying from the gringo. Hence, the Chicano community
would limit the primitives. Consequently, the Chicano would
take power available to the gringo and then attack the colo-
nist states so evident in South Texas.

The fourth goal of our Aztlán[47] model would be a program of rural economic development since colonialism still
exists in South Texas. Under this economic development the
first step would be to replace the existing white managerial
functions with Chicano expertise. The transfer of existing
businesses from gringo hands to Chicano hands would be the
second step. In the last step, La Raza would set upon the
agri-business, the oil and gas industry, and the modern day
land and cattle barons—the real subversives in America today. . . .[48]

As this long passage indicates, Gutiérrez was light years
beyond Cornejo. He was an articulate, self-confident, well-
educated Chicano with a very definite program ready to be
implemented. Fundamental to his strategy, and to the MAYO
strategy, was a Saul Alinsky-type interest in direct confrontation.[49]

Not surprisingly, the development of this strategy of direct
confrontation and the assertion of racial pride had not come
about without tremendous opposition from Anglos and from
many Mexicans. Gutiérrez's most notable foe was in fact Congressman Henry González of San Antonio, the most prominent
Mexican-American politician in Texas. González had been the

first Mexican-American state senator in over one hundred years, and had later become the first Mexican-American congressman as well.[50] He had established himself as an independent, liberal politician, with the courage to filibuster against state segregation laws while in the state senate. González was both liberal and enormously popular in San Antonio, but he was very much his own man. Many liberals charged that he seemed to dislike any other Mexican leadership in San Antonio which might bring increased representation and power to Mexican Americans or that might threaten his position as the leading politician of the city.[51] His attitude toward the younger Chicano leadership was that it was "reverse racism" which "jeopardizes the progress that's been made."[52] Referring to MAYO pamphlets espousing their philosophy, González was quoted in the spring of 1969 as saying, "These sheets reflect the language of Castro and incorporate language that is alien to our area of the country."[53]

Because the Ford Foundation had been instrumental in supporting MAYO and community-betterment activities run by militants in the San Antonio barrio, González launched into an attack on the Ford Foundation as well.[54] After considerable pressure was brought to bear, the Ford Foundation announced that it was withdrawing support from Gutiérrez and MAYO.[55]

Gutiérrez's well-publicized press conferences, where he had been liberal with "obscenity" and "gringo-baiting," seemed to confirm to many Mexicans and nearly all Anglos the charges that González was bringing against him (see Appendix 2). By the time Gutiérrez left San Antonio in 1969, he was twenty-four years old, well known, and generally considered a dangerous extremist. His flamboyant language, while perhaps necessary to get publicity, had meant that nearly all influential people in San Antonio wanted nothing to do with him.[56] It would have been difficult, if not impossible, for Gutiérrez to have engaged in successful political action in San Antonio. In San Antonio, Mexican Americans were not even a majority of the population. There was also much more diversity than in his hometown of Crystal City. San Antonio's Jewish community and organized labor had, for example, meant that Anglos were not without liberal spokesmen. To use the word "gringo," no matter how carefully defined, could not help but alienate a majority of the city's population. The Mexican-American community in San Antonio was likewise much more diverse than the community in Crystal City. In San Antonio there were many fewer migrants, considerably more middle-class Mexicans, such as González, and many more bases for political leadership. Thus San Antonio was considerably different from Crystal City in ways important to radical organization. These demographic and structural differences were important in Gutiérrez's decision to leave San Antonio and return to Crystal City, but there were other reasons for his return. In Crystal City Gutiérrez was personally known by nearly everyone in the community. Charges of atheism, communism, and extremism—while they needed to be answered—would not be an insurmountable barrier. He was, for one thing, more careful. No more "kill the gringo" speeches emanated from him, and with his shortly cropped hair and horn-rimmed glasses, he looked like a big, healthy scholar. Instead of flaunting his radicalism and his MAYO background, he set about trying to help the Mexican-American community, and in the process he exhibited his considerable intellectual, debating, and organizational talents for all to see.

Becoming the leader in the Chicano community was for Gutiérrez neither obvious nor immediate. The community had been badly bruised by the struggles of the first revolt, and many Mexicans were skeptical of any potential political leader. His ideas and skills were examined and tested in numerous discussions and meeting places around the community.[57] His wife and his staff (including Bill Richey, an Anglo who was a former VISTA volunteer and a fellow graduate student; and Viviana Santiago, a Robert F. Kennedy Foundation Fellow who was concerned with attracting jobs to the community) found their ideas and talents similarly tested by the local population. He was still able to procure foundation support, although the sources were often undisclosed. With this financial support, he, his wife, and the staff were able to be independent of the economic power structure and at the same time begin to make valuable community improvements. They were active in setting up a day-care center for children and in participating in the Head Start program. In the fall he was elected one of the representatives of the poor in the poverty program elections.[58]

The high-school students active in the spring protest also came quickly to appreciate his ideas on organization and tactics. Gutiérrez realized the errors the students had made in their spring negotiations with the school administration: In waiting until very close to the end of the school term to threaten a boycott, their timing was bad; and they should never have accepted separate but equal quota systems, particularly when Anglos constituted only fifteen percent of the student body. He therefore set about counseling the students and adding to their political sophistication. Most important of all, his confidence and competence were quickly realized by all who were around him. There was within the radical Mexican community no significant opposition to him as he dispelled their skepticism by starting a Spanish-language newspaper and undertaking activities that others in the community had thought were impossible. He thus began to mobilize an already dissatisfied community by showing them that he could get things done.[59]

the confrontation

The school system turned out to be precisely the issue around which to mobilize the community in "direct confrontation with the gringo." Not only had the school board during the summer reversed the superintendent's compromise policy of open but equal segregation; that fall a new example of school discrimination presented itself. The Crystal City High School Ex-Students Association decided to have their own queen and court at the annual homecoming football game. In previous years they had always considered the football queen to be their queen as well, but to increase interest in the organization, the Ex-Students decided to have their own election. Again hoping to further interest among Ex-Students, and perhaps also hoping to influence who the queen would be, the organization established a rule that for a girl to be eligible to run in their election, one of her parents had to have graduated from the Crystal City high school. Chicano students, already restive over the unresolved issues of the spring, seized upon this issue as a clear-cut example of Anglo discrimination, and the ruling was quickly labelled a "grandfather clause." As the discussion of the history of Mexican-American education should have made clear, very few of the Chicano girls were daughters of parents who had graduated from high school. In fact, of the twenty-six eligible candidates, only five were Mexican Americans.[60] When Severita Lara, one of the high-school activists in the spring, insisted on distributing a flyer on the injustices of the election procedure, the school authorities suspended her from school. Only the intervention of the Mexican-American Legal Defense Fund in San Antonio, another Ford-funded organization, got her reinstated in school.[61] When in the midst of rising clamor Superintendent Billings gave the Ex-Students Association permission to have their coronation at the homecoming game, school-board complicity in the discrimination seemed clear.

As the issue of discrimination was again rearing its head, Gutiérrez counseled the students in what action they should take to confront the school leadership and the community, and his advice was recognized by both sides as being extremely important.[62] In a move designed to bolster the protest movement through the family structure, students were encouraged and instructed to talk to their parents about the indignities they were suffering in school. Many of the parents remembered discrimination they had encountered in the schools, and although they were more cautious than their children, and more afraid of economic intimidation, they gradually became willing to back the students if a showdown occurred.[63]

In early November over one hundred Mexican-American students and parents presented to the school board a list of grievances, headed by the demand that the Ex-Students not present their queen at a school-sponsored event because of the association's restrictive clause (see Appendix 3). At the packed board meeting, made all the more crowded because the school board refused to move the meeting to a larger area, Gutiérrez threatened that if the crowning of the queen did take place, students would disrupt it. He told the board, "There will be no coronation."[64] Under the pressure of disruption by an increasingly organized Chicano community, the school board became unsure of what action to take. Although earlier in the year they had indicated intransigence, now in the face of obvious power a majority of the board voted reluctantly to deny the Ex-Students Association the right to the field. The outraged Ex-Students were forced to hold their coronation at a local packing shed. Not surprisingly, the queen and her court were all Anglo girls.

Having voted to comply with the students' most explosive request, the board then announced that it would postpone consideration of the other demands until their December board meeting. It hoped, no doubt, that by then the protest movement would have cooled off.

The granting of the students' first demand, however, did not take the steam out of the protest. Because the board had so clearly reversed itself only under Chicano pressure, it was made to look weak. Having won one of their demands, student attention now focused on those which had been objects of contention since the preceding spring. Anticipating that the board would turn them down on their long list of demands, students began preparing for a boycott. Enthusiasm and determination among the students grew during this period, helped by numerous rallies. Their initial success gave them confidence, and the reaction of the Anglo community also began to play into their hands. By developing a siege mentality of uniting in the face of such a hostile threat, the Anglo community seemed to support all the radical students' claims of discrimination. The Anglos also appeared to confirm Gutiérrez's claim that "the gringos" would end discrimination only if Chicanos exerted pressure through direct action.[65]

Although many of the Anglos thought the Ex-Students Association had made a colossal tactical blunder, even more thought that the board had "sold out" and knuckled under to the pressure, and scathing attacks were made upon those Anglos thought guilty of being soft. None were in fact madder than Ex-Students Association members themselves. One member, in an acrimonious letter to the editor epitomizing this attitude, charged that the school board had

> denied my sons and daughter their future rights in our school by allowing this small fraction of the student body to dictate, with the threat of violence, the administration of our school affairs. I cannot conceive how a group of intelligent people can be so easily "led down the road" by a pair, in my opinion, of disturbed young men like Angel Gutiérrez and Jesse Gámez [a San Antonio attorney who was raised in Crystal City and who attended the November board meeting]—two of our "local boys" whose early education, for the most part, was paid for by taxes from the farmers and ranchers of this community.... Crystal City has been good to these young men, and they return now to spread racial hate and threaten violence that will eventually divide our

Latin people and destroy the tremendous progress they have made here in the past twenty years. I do not believe the responsible Latin people will allow them to continue.

I am now more than ever convinced that our only salvation for getting more for our Latin people, or any people for that matter, is through education. Please explain to me how a school board plans to offer a balanced educational program when that program is constantly disrupted with threats of violence, walkouts, and the degrading of our teachers with vicious accusations of discrimination? How can they allow this to continue? . . .

I am but one of several who do not intend to let this matter rest if people concerned continue to create problems for our schools, and the School Board continues to appease this small fraction. In one of my conversations with [Superintendent] Billings, he asked me to be careful, and, as he put it, "don't rock the boat." We do not plan to "rock the boat," but it does look as if we may need to change the crew![66]

Besides the school board, other Anglos thought to be soft were sought after and harassed. The minister with the most influential congregation in the town, the Reverend Kenneth Newcomer of the First United Methodist Church, had worked tirelessly in his year and a half in the community to develop a spirit of reconciliation in his totally Anglo congregation. Now, however, he was to see his congregation slowly but surely pull back from any form of compromise in the face of such an obvious radical threat.[67] What the Anglos in their panic did not realize, however, was that Gutiérrez and his movement thrived on, indeed were premised upon, confrontation. By reacting with grim determination and intransigence, the Anglos were helping to polarize the community in exactly the manner the radical Chicanos wanted: "gringo" versus Chicano.

When the school board met in December, before them was the question of what to do with the remaining thirteen demands. These included the selection of cheerleaders, school favorites, and band twirlers, which the students wanted to be chosen by the student body and the band, respectively; demanding that Mr. Harbin, the junior-high principal, retire "because he is unfair and discriminates"; wanting to prevent teachers from calling students "names like animals, stupid idiots, ignorants" and from discriminating against students; requesting that September 16th (Mexican Independence Day) be recognized as a school holiday; desiring a Mexican-American counselor along with the current Anglo one; instituting a bilingual education program and a course on the history of "Los Mexicanos"; and wanting the right to organize peacefully, to develop a student organization to help the poor in the community, to publish and sell a newspaper with diverse viewpoints, to allow girls to wear pants in cold weather, and to install showers in the dressing rooms (see Appendix 3).

At the unusually short board meeting, the school board announced that it felt the charges of discrimination as set forth in the remaining demands were false, and that the board would therefore grant none of the demands. In a classic attempt to remove themselves from the spotlight, the board announced that it also felt many of the concerns were "administrative" rather than board problems.[68] With this announcement, a bitter exchange followed between the board president, Ed Mayer, and one of the students, with the board president reportedly shouting, "Boy, you're out of order!"[69] This action shocked and offended many of the parents. The students, however, were prepared for the board's actions: They immediately presented a new list of grievances, even longer than the first. At the top of the new list of eighteen demands, the students warned that "the School Board Administration cannot deny responsibility for the consequences of negating the petition."[70]

The next morning the school strike began. By class time over two hundred students had gathered in front of the school, parading with signs, and by afternoon their numbers had swelled to over five hundred. A number of parents had gathered nearby to protect their children and to help keep them orderly. The preparation in the Chicano community for the boycott had in fact been excellent. Although many students and even more parents were worried about engaging in direct confrontation, particularly since the school had a clear policy of taking off two points on grades for each day missed and of giving all boycotting students zeros for any exams missed, the proven leadership of Gutiérrez, the presence of sympathetic lawyers, and the rudeness which many Mexicans felt the board had exhibited toward their students, all combined to lead to an amazingly well-executed walkout. Parents were standing solidly behind their children, and in this manner the confrontation was strongly buttressed by a united family structure. For both parents and children, the aim was to prevent the children from suffering the indignities the parents had endured. One mother explained to newsmen:

> I went to high school here. We were in the minority then, so we didn't complain. We felt they had the right to run things. We have had the feeling of inferiority. We're made to feel that way.
>
> When my kids came and complained, I said maybe we should take it, even though we know it's wrong. I didn't want to push them until they were ready for it.
>
> What we're doing now, we're expressing to our children something we know has been important for a long time. Something good is bound to come. At least they have spoken. You can't keep people down.[71]

The organizers were careful to plan for the boycott to increase with each passing day. From the high school the boycott extended to the junior high and then even to the elementary schools. At first some representatives for the striking students were left in classrooms to report on activities within the schools, but then these too were pulled out. This tactic increased the morale of the Chicanos and demoralized the Anglos. As the boycott became larger and more effective, journalists and television commentators began to pour into the community and observe the strike. Each morning the students would gather in front of the high-school building, and in response to charges that they were "Un-American" or "communists," would raise the American flag, and recite the pledge of allegiance. They would then march around the school buildings, journeying from one to the other around the community, but with the main effort centered around the high school.

On the second day of the boycott school officials reported that one-third of the entire school enrollment was absent from classes. After marching around the school, the students obtained a police permit and marched downtown with placards waving and observers from the Mexican-American Legal Defense Fund following nearby. On this same day student walkout leaders met with Superintendent Billings in the evening to try to work out an agreement for return to classes. The meeting, however, brought no results and the leaders vowed to continue their boycott.[72]

With the boycott gaining momentum and the Superintendent unable to get the students to return to classes, the school board realized it would have to act. The boycott was too effective to be ignored. The board therefore contacted the Administrative Services Division of the Texas Education Agency, requesting help in investigating the causes of the walkout and in bringing about a settlement. Gilbert Conoley and Juan Ibarra arrived on the third day of the walkout and for the next two days interviewed the participants. They were unable to bring about a settlement, and on Friday, December 12, they returned to Austin after suggesting to the board that the school "be closed early for the Christmas holidays because of fear of someone being harmed. . . ." They further noted that "the tension there seems to be building by the hour."[73] School officials, however, refused to close down the schools.

Although officials had expressed a willingness to develop a course in Mexican-American culture, they were still adamant on the other demands and were insisting that the students be penalized according to school regulations. By the third day of the walkout, however, there were 416 absences from the high school out of a total enrollment of 673. Nearly two-thirds of all high-school students were thus either joining the boycott or staying home from school.[74]

On Sunday a giant rally was held in the city park, with over 1,000 attending to hear Gutiérrez and others speak. Albert Peña, the San Antonio commissioner who had been active in PASO since its formation in 1961, and the Rev. Henry Casso of the organization of Spanish priests were both on hand. These rallies and marches kept morale in the Chicano community at a high level and brought even more publicity to the walkout. At the same time parents who were supporting the boycott were organized into *Ciudadanos Unidos* (United Citizens) to lend further support to their children, to provide food at the rallies, and to increase their own confidence and morale. The boycott thus served as a further means of organizing and mobilizing the Chicano community. Although Gutiérrez was constantly on hand to advise the students of their legal rights, he remained in the background, wishing the students themselves and their parents to shoulder as much of the responsibility and publicity as possible.

Pressure and counterpressure continued to build within the community. Those Mexican-American students who did continue to go to classes were often jeered when they walked past the picket lines, but almost no physical violence occurred. The students, their parents, and the students inside the schools all wanted to keep the community from exploding. One Anglo girl reported her tires slashed, but in general Chicano pressure against Anglo students seems to have been minimal. They had never expected the Anglo students to support them, and none joined their picket lines. What counterpressure the Anglos did exert came from parents rather than children. Several Mexican families did not let their children participate in the boycott because of fear for their jobs. But law-enforcement agencies of the city and the county, while present, did not intervene, and the Texas Rangers were not called in. With the help of parents, the boycott was kept absolutely nonviolent.

Within the Anglo community itself the siege mentality became all the stronger. The Rev. Kenneth Newcomer, who tried to serve as a mediator, reported that "the social stigma involved in doing this was considerable. Any kind of association with the students was interpreted as alignment with them."[75] As an example, he cited rumors that had occurred concerning his activity:

> One of my church members saw me talking with the student demonstrators the first day of the walkout in the morning. She reported to others in the community that I had taken the part of the students, when in fact I was asking student leaders what was going on. The next day, when the students marched through the business section of Crystal City, I was a sidewalk observer, and was looking for my fellow Methodist pastor, Rev. Samuel Blanco, who had alerted me to the downtown march. That evening it was being reported along the grapevine that I had marched with the students.[76]

The second week of the strike began with tension rising even more in the community. On Tuesday three of the student leaders—Diana Serna, Severita Lara, and Mario Treviño—announced that they were flying to Washington to talk with senators and government officials about conditions in the

schools. This action, which Gutiérrez seems to have been instrumental in arranging, not only served to draw even more
attention to the boycott; it also disquieted the Anglos, who
feared what federal supervision might mean.[77] Senator Yarborough received the students cordially, and put them in touch
with both Senators Ted Kennedy and George McGovern. The
students also talked with officials in the civil-rights divisions of
the Departments of Justice and of Health, Education, and
Welfare.

Amid all this publicity and continued activity, the school
board again requested the Texas Education Agency to come
down to help mediate the dispute. When the team of Conoley
and Ibarra again arrived, there seemed to be an opening for
negotiations as the school board announced that it was willing
to meet and discuss the walkout with a group of the students'
parents. The board refused, however, to talk to the striking
students or to grant them immunity from their penalties for
unexcused absences. It was understandable that the board
wished at all costs to refuse to recognize the students themselves. To have sat down at a negotiating table with a bunch of
teenagers, much less Mexican rabble, was too much for the
school board to stomach. It would have meant complete humiliation. The board's refusal to talk to the students, however,
angered the students even more. They felt that the demands
were theirs and that they should be the ones to discuss the
matter with the board. The students also realized that their
parents would be more vulnerable to the board because of lack
of education and fear for their jobs. Students thus asked the
parents not to attend, and the parents stood fast with their
children by refusing to attend a meeting with the board without
students present. Conditions remained at an impasse; the TEA
negotiating team had no meeting to attend.

Further attempts to get negotiations started occurred when a
committee of churchmen was formed in the hopes of mediating
the dispute. Laity and clergy from Catholic, Methodist, and
Baptist churches participated in separate sessions with the students and with the board to try to find areas for compromise.
In the end, however, the Churchmen's Committee was unsuccessful because of polarization within the group and the resentment of the school board and administrators toward the
purpose of the group. With tensions mounting and the com-

munity divided, attempts by local people to negotiate a settlement were doomed.[78]

The community continued to polarize as the strike went on
and the Chicanos became more organized. At the same time
shifts in power between and within the Anglo and Chicano
communities became clear. Having chosen what to the Chicanos
were clear-cut examples of discrimination in the schools, the
radicals were successfully neutralizing many of the middle-class
Mexicans who were in the city government. The sympathy of
Mexican moderates with many, if not all, of the students'
demands left them unable or unwilling to help the intransigent
Anglos and yet frightened of the growing power of the radicals.
Individuals in the city government, after a few attempts to
moderate the dispute to get the children back into school,
lapsed into a painful silence. The mayor of the city, Paul Mata,
who also happened to be vice-principal of the high school, tried
to maintain neutrality as events swirled around him.[79]

To those Mexicans who had worked so hard to win acceptance by the Anglos and to pull themselves up by their own
bootstraps, the mobilization of the Chicano community and the
launching of the school boycott meant pain and anguish. The
students were threatening all that the "moderate, responsible"
Mexicans had worked so hard to attain. One prominent Mexican
was seen close to tears as he ranted and raved about the "thugs"
who were destroying the harmonious race relations in the
town.[80]   One of the two Mexican-American school-board
members was quoted as saying, "Man, am I disturbed. I have
had to take tranquilizers. It has taken us a good many years to
bring our students to the level they are at, and then to have all
this undermined in a matter of a few days. . . ."[81]

As the school boycott continued throughout the second
week, both sides realized that the stakes in the confrontation
were rising with each passing day. By the last day before the
Christmas holidays, from half to two-thirds of the entire school
enrollment were absent from classes, but still no negotiations
were taking place. Since the school board had already announced at their December board meeting that they would not
negotiate on the students' demands, they realized that to begin
negotiations at all would represent a clear defeat.[82] Hoping that
something would happen to weaken the strike, they waited. But
to compound their problems, more events followed which bol-

stered the publicity and morale of the strikers. At the onset of the holidays, Texans for the Educational Advancement of Mexican-Americans (TEAM) announced that they were sending educators into the community to teach the striking students during the holidays. Although TEAM announced that its purpose was not to interfere with the internal affairs of the Crystal City school district but to help the young people catch up in their studies, the Anglos knew that their presence could only put more pressure on the beleaguered school board.[83]

At the onset of the holidays more than TEAM educators arrived in town. The Community Relations Service of the U.S. Department of Justice sent two mediators to the community, reportedly at the invitation of both the board and the students. Although it is not clear exactly how the Justice Department became involved, the visit by the three student leaders to Washington earlier in the week was probably of great importance.[84] With the strike over two weeks old, growing stronger by the day, and with the Justice Department in town, the school board at last agreed to meet with the students, if a representative group of parents were also present.

With the school board, the students, the parents, and three observers from the Churchmen's Committee present, the Justice Department negotiations began. The role of the Justice Department in the negotiations seems to have been important, although it must also be remembered that a great deal of struggle had already taken place in the community before their negotiations began. It does seem, however, that on several points the negotiators were very much in sympathy with the student demands, and that on at least one occasion while meeting privately with the school board, they condemned the board for their seeming intransigence.[85] Through several days of tense and often bitter conflict and bargaining which lasted hours upon end, the Justice Department team of Bob Greenwald and Tom Mata eventually hammered out an agreement acceptable to the students and the board. Continuing support and involvement by the students and their families in the boycott and in the settlement talks led the school board to capitulate on practically all the demands. But also involved were the increasing publicity about the walkout, and state and federal presence (if not pressure). By the time the board had capitulated, not only was the Justice Department involved, but the Regional

Office of Health, Education, and Welfare was expressing concern over the tremendous number of children who were missing school, and the Texas Education Agency was wondering how much financial support the school district would lose because of the drop in school attendance. Fear was also present among the board members, as talk began circulating that Chicano supporters from around the area were going to converge on Crystal City to add strength to *la causa* if the strike was not settled by the end of the holidays.[86]

With the resolution of the conflict, what may have been the most successful Chicano walkout in the history of Mexican Americans in the Southwest came to an end (see Appendix 3). No disciplinary procedures were taken against the striking students. They did not receive unexcused absences with resulting grade penalties, and teachers were to provide make-up examinations for the strikers. The board agreed to work for the establishment of bilingual and bicultural programs in the school system, and agreed to try to find new means of testing preschool youngsters and of ending ethnic isolation in the schools. The board further consented to cheerleaders and nearly all school favorites being elected by the student body, agreed to hire a Mexican-American counselor for the high school if funds were available, and promised to give "appropriate consideration" at the time of contract renewal to school personnel accused of discriminating against the Mexican students. Dress codes and the censoring of the student paper were to be reviewed. The board even consented to the establishment of an assembly period on September 16th in recognition of the Mexican national holiday. By making some of the demands seem contingent upon other factors such as federal funds, the agreement allowed the board to engage in some face-saving. But as the months passed it became all the more clear that except for a few points, such as the election of twirlers and Most Representative Student, the students had scored a stunning victory.

With the realization that the students had won, a tremendous outpouring of elation and pride swept through the Chicano community. To them *La Justicia* and the righting of ancient wrongs had at last occurred, through their own power and resources.

The Anglo community was shocked and stunned. A deep sense of bitterness and frustration, compounded by fear of what their defeat would mean for the future, made them uneasy. Particularly hard for the Anglo parents and students to take was the realization that the boycotting students were to receive no punishment. Rabble-rousing, irresponsible Mexican teenagers were to be rewarded rather than condemned. An angry group of Anglo parents and children met with the board chairman to criticize the board for giving in so soon, but they all realized that it was too late to change the disaster.[87] It was also difficult for the Anglo students and teachers to face the returning Mexican students, many of whom they felt were arrogant, obnoxious, and undisciplined. Teachers in particular were upset over not being informed by the school administration of the results of the negotiations. Only that part dealing with amnesty was given to the teachers, with no clarification. Aware that the settlement had come only through their own humiliation, the school administration did not want to discuss the matter further. Even when Bob Greenwald of the Justice Department offered to return and explain to the teachers the results of the negotiations, the Superintendent firmly turned him down.[88] The results were thus a bitter, humiliating experience for the Anglo school teachers, students, administration, and the entire Anglo community. All the tactics that had worked for them before—and everything they thought they had learned from the 1963 revolt—now suddenly no longer sustained them. Frightened by the loss of power and unsure of what retribution would mean, they found their right to rule and their invincibility had been shattered simultaneously. Their legitimacy and their authority had crumbled.

Concomitant developments kept the Anglos from entertaining any serious thoughts of sabotaging the negotiations.[89] For the Chicanos were not resting upon their victory. As with the victory over the Ex-Students Association in the preceding months, their successful boycott did not lessen their momentum. Gutiérrez himself had commented that "after the gringo was exposed publicly, the next step was to confront their security—status, business, and morality in order to recognize the enemy in all their involvements of policies, roles and power manipulations."[90] With this in mind, the Chicano community began a selective economic boycott towards the end of the strike. The targets were Urbano Esquivel, the Mexican-American schoolboard member unwilling to support the strike, and an

Anglo businessman who had tried to pressure the students by firing two of his employees involved in the strike. Shortly after picketing of these establishments started the Anglos retaliated by arresting four of the students engaged in the picketing. They were charged with "intimidating customers going into the two businesses and with creating a general disturbance," but the youths were released and never brought to trial.[91] Although the arrests created much excitement at the time, they seem to have been more an indication of nervousness of the Anglo leadership over this reversal of roles in economic intimidation rather than a successful intimidation of the students.[92] For even though picketing of these establishments did not last, boycotting of certain businesses did continue.

This reversal of economic intimidation further threatened the security of the Anglo business community and also threatened Mexican-American businessmen who were not willing to help in the strike. As Gutiérrez commented later, "The fact that several businesses were the object of effective boycotts made the white business community cool the rhetoric of racism and reflect a bit for fear that their businesses might be hit next."[93]

In the midst of the struggle against Anglo economic dominance, one might have expected the Teamsters union to have been in the forefront again in support of the community's Mexican Americans. But in contrast to 1963, the Teamsters union at the Del Monte plant was completely inactive. Feeling grew within the plant and in the Chicano community at large that the Teamsters were trying to use and to control the Chicanos rather than to help them. Although this feeling stemmed in part from the firing of Mayor Cornejo as business agent for the union in 1964, it was increased by the Teamsters' reluctance to stand up for Chicanos when their jobs and rights were repeatedly being violated.[94]

An incident in the fall of 1969 raised further questions in the minds of the community's Mexican Americans about the Teamsters union. Moses Falcón, the business agent for the union since the firing of Juan Cornejo, was found dead in a hotel in Ohio.[95] Although at the time of his death he was only thirty-five years old, and according to his doctor had been in excellent health, the coroner ruled that he had died of an acute heart attack. His family and many others suspected foul play, but no autopsy was performed and the mysteries surrounding his death were never answered. Coincidentally, at the time of his death Falcón had apparently become interested in trying to disaffiliate the union from the Teamsters and in joining with others to work for a local union.[96] Thus, in the face of such opposition by local Mexicans, the union had moved full circle by 1970 into being dependent upon management, not workers, for support and encouragement. The management was encouraging, even pressuring, workers to join the union, while the workers themselves were engaging in efforts to decertify the Teamsters and form a local Chicano union.[97]

the spring elections

Besides school policies and questions of economic domination which were now being raised in the community, political offices were soon also involved in this broad movement to unite and bring self-determination to the Chicano community. Building upon their successes, the strike organizers engaged in a massive voter-registration drive that produced a record number of registered voters. They then proceeded after another MAYO goal, the formation of La Raza Unida party.[98] Luz Gutiérrez, José Angel's wife, became the head of the party for Zavala County, and others active in the movement registered as members. School-board and city-council candidates filed not only in Crystal City, but in the neighboring counties of Dimmit and La Salle, where organizing efforts were also taking place. With school policies so much in the forefront of political concern, mere Mexican representation on the board became totally inadequate. Control of the school system and redirection toward Chicano needs became the goal, and Gutiérrez headed a slate running for the three positions falling vacant on the seven-man board.

Finding candidates was still a difficulty, however. Although Gutiérrez was independent of the local economic structure because of his funds from outside the community, few others in the town could afford to be quite so independent. In particular, school teachers sympathetic to the movement were afraid to run for fear of not having their contracts renewed. Selected to run with Gutiérrez, then, were Mike Pérez, a popular dance-hall operator, and Arturo Gonzales, a twenty-one-year-old gas-station attendant. Pérez was a fairly well-off businessman who could not be much affected by Anglo boycotts. Gonzales was young, single, and in the words of one of his friends, "didn't give a damn" about the possibility of Anglo reprisals.

A sweep of the city council was of course no longer possible because of the charter change adopted the year before. This change in the political set-up had been made explicitly to discourage a repeat of the 1963 disaster. For the spring elections in 1970 only two of the five council seats were up for election. Pablo Puente, operator of an auto-parts store, who had been fired from his job with the city by the CASAA forces in 1965, and Ventura Gonzales, a worker at the Del Monte cannery, became the two council candidates. Both these men, however, became the victims of Anglo reprisal. They were fired from their jobs within the year.

As it turned out, La Raza Unida party was extremely lucky to have even these two candidates running. Discouraging impoverished candidates, the city charter still included a requirement that any candidate for the council must be a property owner. Shortly before the commencement of absentee voting, the city attorney and city manager disqualified Pablo Puente, one of the two Raza Unida candidates, because he did not own property.[99] With help from the Mexican-American Legal Defense Fund the question was immediately taken to court. As the Anglo city fathers had no doubt expected, the Fourth Court of Civil Appeals ruled that the question of putting Puente's name on the ballot was moot because balloting had already started. Appealing the case to the federal courts, attorney Jesse Gámez of the Legal Defense Fund claimed that such a decision by the Court opened the door to fraud. Any community, he argued, could wait until just before the start of absentee balloting to deny a candidate a place on the ballot for any of a number of clearly unconstitutional practices and could do so successfully because the question would immediately become moot. With Puente agreeing to forfeit the absentee ballots, the Federal Judge ordered Puente's name placed on the ballot barely in time for the election.[100]

The anti-La Raza Unida coalition, although demoralized by the school strike, fought vigorously. For the council, the two incumbents, one Anglo and one Mexican American, chose to run for re-election. For the school board, significantly, the three incumbents (including Urbano Esquivel) chose to resign. Their position in being opposed to the Chicano demands and yet capitulating had left them in a peculiarly vulnerable position from both sides. Nominated to take their places by the anti-strike coalition were two Mexican Americans and one candidate of partly Mexican heritage. This in itself was a further move toward accommodation of Mexican Americans by the Anglo community, but again as in 1965 the Anglos had decided to run a slate with a preponderance of Mexican Americans only after an explosive issue had mushroomed in the community, and they had chosen the Mexicans they wanted.

Facing the threat of Gutiérrez and his supporters taking over the school board and the city council, and having tried intransigence and failed, the school board tried desperately to head off a further defeat. They were aided in this endeavor by appointing a new superintendent. The current one, John Billings, had been bitterly attacked by the Anglos for starting all the trouble because he had compromised with the students in the previous spring. He therefore resigned, effective in June. John Briggs, a former school superintendent who had more recently been working in Corpus Christi at an Educational Service Center, was hired as assistant superintendent in early March, until Billings officially resigned in June. The board also hired Briggs to be superintendent under a three-year contract beginning in July, 1970. Briggs and his wife had two adopted Mexican children, and thus could hardly be accused of having racial hatred for Mexicans. Briggs, however, was willing to work closely with the Anglo board to try to head off the militants. The new Anglo strategy was to work quickly and efficiently to try to implement the reforms that were forced on the district by the strike.[101] The school board thus refused to renew the contract of the junior-high-school principal, and the high-school principal resigned to become a full-time teacher. There was only a short time in which to work before the April elections, but it seems clear that Anglo board members wanted to bring about many of the inevitable changes in the school system as painlessly as possible, with themselves in control of the changes. The difficulty of this strategy as a means of heading off Gutiérrez, however, was that the board had clearly not acted on these reforms until it was forced to do so by the Chicanos, and until after the Chicanos had built up a powerful organization mobilizing their people for the election. Because of this, the board had a credibility problem when it claimed that it was concerned about improving the education of the Mexicans in the district.

The reaction of the local paper throughout the election campaign was also indicative of greater accommodation. Whereas from 1963 to 1969 the *Sentinel* editor had run front-page editorials warning of community disaster should nonbusiness, unqualified candidates win, in the 1970 election, the *Sentinel* had only a short, perfunctory editorial in the last issue before the election.[102] Because the owner, Dale Barker, had long been identified with the ruling Anglo group, it was apparently felt that to have run editorials again would have been counterproductive. Increasingly in the community, far more so than in 1965, it was felt that Mexicans themselves would have to tackle the militants. More than ever before, Anglos had to work behind the scenes and through Mexicans who were sympathetic to their cause.

Yet in terms of campaign rhetoric in support of the Anglo-Mexican coalition, little appeared to have changed between 1963 and 1970. The coalition continued to talk about the need for responsible, business-oriented candidates who would not inject racism and hatred into the community. Although a small advertisement appeared in Spanish for the council candidates mentioning some of the economic improvements the council had tried to make in the last year, by far the largest advertisement intoned that Crystal City needed "Responsible Men for Responsible Jobs." Said the ad:

> Education and City Government are big businesses that need proper management by competent and responsible people.
>   It is important that you vote for men who offer business and professional experience and the willingness to devote their time to representing the best interests of all citizens. [103]

Thus, according to the ideology represented in this advertisement, poor migrant workers should not look for people to run the school system who particularly understood their problems and difficulties. They should instead have big businessmen, or "qualified" men with "an understanding of the business community" be their leaders. Constant references by Anglos to the need for this sort of leadership throughout the decade of struggle revealed their continued conservatism. Although their candidates' racial origins might have changed, their basic philosophical ideas remained conservative.

In case it was not obvious why poor migrant workers needed big businessmen to run their children's schools, the town's industrial establishment also placed large advertisements in the local paper, in English and Spanish. These tended to emphasize further this business domination of the Anglo-Mexican coalition. The advertisements began by noting that in order to improve the economic welfare of the town, industry was vitally needed. This was something which nearly all residents could agree upon, but the ad went on to say:

> Industry officials seek a community with harmonious relations and a stable government. They avoid areas where there is agitation by militant groups which could hinder their progress. The working people of Crystal City hurt themselves when they vote for candidates for the school board and city council who are associated with militant groups that are unfriendly to industry.[104]

By this ideology, the poor of Crystal City were caught in an inescapable bind. If they won, they lost. In trying to limit agricultural and business domination over the community, the city's poor would only be hurting themselves. According to this dominant Anglo ideology, then, Crystal City Mexicans should be careful to be "responsible, and trustworthy." Otherwise they would get no jobs.

This advertisement represented an economic reality that was a powerful force which had always limited the degree to which changes could occur in the community. It was also probably the most important reason why radical changes in the relationships between Mexican Americans and Anglos throughout the area were so rare. The Mexicans might be a majority of the population, even a voting majority. But, as the advertisement noted, the Anglos in the end held the cards. The Mexicans had come to Crystal City basically for economic reasons. And the Anglos still controlled the economic structure of the community. If the Mexicans got out of line and tried to limit the economically powerful, the Anglos would, and did, first try to fire them and prevent them from getting any other jobs.[105]   But if the Mexicans became too powerful and too well organized, then the Anglos might leave. And with no jobs available, the community would die. In 1963 after Los Cinco Mexicanos won office, one of the packing sheds in the city moved to a nearby town. Now word was being spread by Anglos that the huge Del Monte plant might close down if the city tried to make it pay any taxes. While this was in the end untrue, no one knew how far Del Monte would be willing to go before it carried out its ultimate threat.[106]

The successful school strike had revealed, however, that even if arrangements in the area did represent this ultimate truth—that the Anglos in the end could devastate the economy of the town—there was still room in the community for maneuver within the system. How much, no one knew.

As the campaign progressed, Gutiérrez became the most visible of all the candidates. Although he was hated like perhaps no other figure in South Texas politics, his opposition could not use many of the personal arguments they had levied against Cornejo and the 1963 revolution. As a native boy well known in the community, Gutiérrez could not be called an outside agitator or labelled a puppet of anyone. Charges that he was inexperienced could hardly be made after the masterfully executed strike. Charges that he was uneducated and unqualified could not easily be made against his eighteen years of formal education and his two degrees. Instead the opposition centered their attack around the claim that Gutiérrez and the ideas of La Raza Unida were "un-American." He was a dangerous radical, a vicious exploiter of his own people, and in fact a communist and an atheist. He was even called a murderer by some, in reference to one of his previous statements as president of MAYO that if all other means failed, it would be necessary to "kill the gringo."[107]

Gutiérrez, however, did not present the image of a wild-eyed radical. Instead he concentrated on being considered as a person able and willing to devote himself to the poor Chicanos, those that had been exploited by the "gringos." To counter some of the charges the Anglos were bringing against him during the campaign, Gutiérrez showed at his rallies such things as autographed photographs from Ted Kennedy and George McGovern, and his invitation to the Nixon-Agnew inauguration.[108] By mocking the Anglo charges of his being a fire-breathing devil, Gutiérrez succeeded in minimizing their effect while entertaining his supporters and giving them confidence. But his major issues were those that related to the school strike, the MAYO goals of self-determination, and all that the community had experienced in the last year.

In terms of campaign organizations and get-out-the-vote drives, both sides were extremely well prepared. The Anglos controlled the voting procedure, and had done their best to make sure that many voted by absentee ballot. As an indication of voter interest and community mobilization, the turnout was considerably higher than in the 1968 presidential election.

Election day was tense. Both sides feared spies, and sabotage, and fraud. Each wondered what a loss would mean and what the future would bring. John Ziller, a student present in the town for the election, described the process:

> The poll was located at the high school ... and the Anglos and the Mexicans had both taken sides early in the day. La Raza Unida had set up a table on the school grounds and had staffed it with high school people. .... It was all intended for the purpose of voter education to insure that all voters were informed about the ballots and the poll itself. The Anglos collected on the opposite side of the street checking off voters from a list of the same that they had. The Anglos would occasionally venture across the street to take pictures of "outsiders" like myself, the VISTA lawyer, and Richard Avena [chairman of the State Advisory Commission on Civil Rights]. It was a pathetic scenario of polarization. ...[109]

Texas Rangers, however, were not around. The Anglos had apparently decided by now that calling in the Rangers would do them more harm than good.

When the results were announced, Gutiérrez and his running mates had captured fifty-five percent of the vote. Three days later Ventura Gonzales and Pablo Puente, his name now on the ballot, smashed to victory in the city-council elections with over sixty percent of the vote. As in 1963, the greater number of Anglos in the school district than in the city itself resulted in La Raza Unida candidates running better for city-council places than for the school board. The vote totals were as follows: [110]

School Board Election		City Council Election	
José Angel Gutiérrez	1,344	Ventura Gonzales	1,341
Mike Pérez	1,397	Pablo Puente	1,306
Arturo Gonzales	1,344		
E. W. Ritchie	1,119	Emmett Sevilla	835
Rafael Tovar	1,090	Charlie Crawford	820
Luz Arcos	1,081		

In nearby Carrizo Springs and Cotulla, the results of La Raza Unida work also produced victories in city-council and school-board races. These victories were perhaps even more remarkable because neither town had ever gone through the political mobilization and trauma which Crystal City had known. Such victories in nearby towns confirmed the belief that the second revolt was based upon strategies far more exportable to other South Texas communities, but the degree of success in these other communities was not yet clear.

At the electoral level, at any rate, La Raza Unida had been stunningly successful in the whole Winter Garden Area. Its greater organizational sophistication and clearer ideology had led to remarkable successes. In Crystal City the second revolt had been based considerably more upon local talent and involvement than had been the first. But although the local Chicano community had played a much larger role, financial support from outside the community and the help of such organizations as the Mexican-American Legal Defense Fund may have been almost as instrumental in *sustaining* (if not in organizing) the revolt as the Teamsters and PASO had been in 1963. Not only were nearly all the leadership at least partially supported by money from outside the community, but the aid of the Mexican-American Legal Defense Fund had proved important in getting Puente's name restored to the ballot, in defending the four students who were originally charged with obstruction of Anglo businesses, and in getting one of the high-school students readmitted to school after she had been expelled for distributing unauthorized pamphlets. And their presence during the boycott may have served to deter the

Anglos from bringing charges against the students during any of their marches.

With a solid local base of Mexican Americans buttressed by help from outside, Crystal City again stood on a threshold. Chicanos had achieved unquestioned electoral success, and their intellectual competence and expertise were in marked contrast to the first election of Mexicans in 1963. But it was still not clear how successful La Raza Unida would be in trying to govern the deeply divided community. Nor was it clear how many changes they would be able to bring about.

6 la raza unida and the first year of rule

In beginning their period of office, La Raza Unida faced a number of problems. The first and foremost was that of assembling a majority coalition. The institutional set-up by 1970, it should be recalled, was such that only a minority of the school-board places and city-council seats were up for election that year. Thus the victorious Raza Unida candidates were in a minority. On both boards, however, a critical swing vote was provided which allowed them to gain control of the governing bodies. How this occurred was further indication of the superior organization of Raza Unida and of the mobilization and polarization in the community.

On the school board, the critical swing vote was provided by Eddie Treviño. Although he had been appointed three years previously by the Anglos on the board, Treviño had gradually evolved into a quiet, one-man opposition. Treviño related that he had been appointed to the board just because he was a Mexican American, and that at first he had been completely in the dark about how the board operated and about what it was doing. As surprised as anyone at his appointment, Treviño related that the board president told him that they had chosen him because he was a "better-off Mexican American" and would "set a good example for the community" since he had a

good job and was a family man.[1] At first Treviño had thought
that the Anglos wanted to open the door to him and to the
Mexicans in the community, but gradually he became convinced
that the Anglos were not seriously interested in helping the
Mexicans.

His first shock came in observing the other Mexican on the
board, Urbano Esquivel.[2] Esquivel maintained that he did not
believe there was any serious discrimination in the schools, and
on policy matters he often showed himself to be more conservative than some of the Anglos. An example of this came when
the school district discussed its policy on free lunches. Their
policy had generally been that only children without fathers
could be eligible. When one of the Anglo farmers on the board
mentioned that the wages he paid could not support a man with
very many children and that therefore the policy should be
broadened to include more children in the free-lunch program,
Esquivel joined other Anglos in voting against liberalizing the
program. This was done under the philosophy that it wouldn't
be good to give too many because then everybody would want
free lunches. Through observing the board's attitudes toward
poverty programs and federal guidelines in general, Treviño
became convinced that the board was not really interested in
helping the poor Mexicans of the community. Anglos often
argued against "give-away" programs. Child-care centers and
even kindergartens were opposed, because, as one board member reportedly said, "All the mamas will have babies since
somebody'll take care of them."[3]

Although upset at these attitudes, Treviño was reluctant to
say anything throughout these discussions because he was worried about his job at Del Monte, and knew that his supervisor,
who was also on the board, was watching all his actions. On the
question of faculty selection of student favorites, however,
Treviño became a minority of one by voting against having the
faculty choose student leaders. When the superintendent and
other board members asked him why he had voted against
them, Treviño told them that "some of the teachers discriminate." At this the rest of the board badgered him to give an
example of discrimination. When Treviño did name one teacher,
the board's reaction was, surprisingly, one of concurrence. They
all realized that this teacher discriminated, but as one Anglo
told him, "Well, one teacher doesn't make any difference."[4]

The Anglos on the board thus seem to have recognized that there were teachers in the schools that were anti-Mexican; yet they continued to renew their contracts year after year.

As students became restive with school policies, Treviño himself began to become more outspoken. His opposition became even clearer when at the November, 1969, board meeting he had made a motion to move the meeting to a larger room so that more of the protesting parents could follow the proceedings. The motion died for lack of a second. And in December Treviño had been the only member of the board who voted against rejecting the students' demands.

Because of all this the Anglos knew that Treviño was lost to the Raza Unida opposition, barring a miracle. The Anglos, however, were desperately searching for that miracle, and were willing to do almost anything to keep Gutiérrez from becoming president of the school board. The board presidency was obviously the position Gutiérrez wanted and expected, having masterminded the school strike and the spring campaign. Hoping to split the Mexican membership on the board in any way possible to prevent Gutiérrez from assuming leadership, the Anglos employed their incoming school superintendent, John Briggs, to approach Treviño about making him, rather than Gutiérrez, president of the board with the support of the Anglos. Treviño told Briggs, however, that he was not interested in being president of the board, and he refused to go along with this Anglo strategy. After this tactic failed for the Anglos, Briggs was again employed to seek out Mike Pérez, the top vote-getter on the Raza Unida ticket. Briggs entreated Pérez to accept the board presidency, with the support of the three Anglos. Pérez also refused to deny Gutiérrez the presidency.[5]

When the time came for swearing in of the new members and for the election of the board president, however, the Anglos weren't through. Briggs presided over the election of the president, and he recognized first an Anglo member who proceeded to nominate Pérez for the presidency. This was seconded by another Anglo. Although Pérez protested that he did not feel he was well-enough qualified to serve and that his businesses required too much of his time, the Anglos insisted that they thought Pérez could handle the job. They refused to withdraw their motion. A vote was thus taken on naming Pérez to be president, with the three Anglos voting in favor and Pérez and the other Mexican Americans all voting against. After this action, Gutiérrez was then nominated and elected president, on a similar four to three vote.[6] La Raza Unida was thus able to form a majority on the school board in spite of the desperate tactics of the Anglos. These tactics of trying to divide them had resulted rather in solidifying the four Mexicans.[7]

Regarding control of the city council, La Raza Unida again gained a crucial swing vote which allowed them to become the governing majority. Although chosen by the Anglos to run for the council in 1969, Francisco Benavides had never been closely associated with the Anglo ruling group. He had been offended when the council refused to name him mayor even though he had outpolled all the other candidates in the election. When Benavides asked the other councilmen why they had not chosen him mayor, he was told that it had "been indicated" by the Anglos that Paul Mata should be mayor. This remark indicated that the Mexican councilmen were something less than free agents. It also meant that Francisco Benavides was to be passed over for the job because Paul Mata was deemed a safer, more trustworthy person by the town's politicos.[8] With this background, Benavides was an obvious target in La Raza Unida's drive to gain control, and his support for La Raza Unida provided them with a three to two majority. Thus the recently approved institutional procedure of staggered terms for the council, which were designed by the Anglos to prevent another takeover, failed.

Although these developments concerning Benavides and Treviño could be considered strokes of luck, they were clearly more than that. In the aftermath of the strike there was considerable pressure being brought to bear by members of La Raza Unida on the entire Mexican community. Benavides, as the owner of a grocery store, could not have been unaware of the consequences which might have followed from his refusal to join forces with La Raza Unida. The example of the successful boycott of Jesús Rodríguez's grocery after Rodríguez became a CASAA partisan was still clear in everyone's mind. The loss of Treviño and Benavides to the opposition, in marked contrast to what happened in 1963 when Mario Hernández abandoned Los Cinco, demonstrated how much more powerful the second revolt was in its local organizational base. Mexicans no longer had to fear only Anglo reprisals if they sided with the revolt;

they also had to recognize that the Chicanos themselves were sufficiently well organized to provide considerable counter pressure.

These defections also emphasized problems Crystal City Anglos faced in trying to coopt Mexican Americans into their leadership. If Anglos picked Mexicans that were absolutely trustworthy, they could also be absolutely sure that such Mexicans would carry little weight in the Chicano community. If they picked men who were independent and respected in the Chicano community, then Anglos would not be able to rely on them in critical situations. This presented a strategic dilemma for the Anglos for which there was no easy solution.

La Raza Unida thus surmounted its first hurdle, gaining a workable majority on both councils. But the lame-duck council and the school board had both done their best to tie the hands of the incoming officials. The city council had quickly voted to grant the Del Monte Corporation a seven-year reprieve on being annexed into the city so that the company, which had a yearly payroll of over two million dollars, could continue to pay no city taxes. This, it was estimated by the city manager, represented a loss to the city of about $13,000 a year.[9] To try to void this lame-duck action, the new city government brought suit. Charging conflict of interest was involved, they noted that Charlie Crawford, one of the members of the council, was salaried by Del Monte at the time the contract was approved, and that R. A. Taylor, the city attorney at the time of the contract, also happened to be the attorney for Del Monte.[10] The company, however, remained adamant in not wanting to be annexed. The head manager at the plant, Gilbert Brook, explained that the plant felt it should not have to pay taxes because the city had not done anything for the plant. It was rather the plant, through money and jobs, that had helped the city.[11]

The school board had also taken preventive measures by hiring under a three-year contract a new school superintendent, John Briggs. They did this, of course, in full knowledge that they were likely to lose the spring elections. In the hopes that La Raza Unida, if successful, would last only one year, the school board also gave all Anglo principals and administrators two-year contracts. Raza Unida tried working with the new superintendent until August. At that time, after it was discovered that Briggs had been keeping files on the four Mexican board members, and had in general been trying to divide Mexican unity on the board in order "to create harmony" between the Anglos and Mexicans in the community, Briggs was reassigned. After a public hearing on these charges, he was fired.[12]

In dismissing Briggs, La Raza Unida was taking a very bold action, for Briggs had worked to implement many of the new policies, to recruit more Mexican-American teachers and administrators, and had been from the beginning one of the more moderate Anglos in the community. But in accepting the appointment by the Anglo board when the Raza Unida takeover appeared imminent, Briggs had seriously compromised his claim to impartiality in the school district. And in his desire to work to heal the wounds in the community, to bring together the two races, and to depolarize (and depoliticize?) the community, Briggs' goals were fundamentally against those of La Raza Unida. For when Briggs spoke of creating harmony between the races, La Raza Unida interpreted this as a synonym for splitting the Mexican community.

By firing Briggs, La Raza Unida immediately involved itself in a legal dispute, with the Texas State Teachers Association, the Texas Classroom Teachers Association, and the Texas Education Agency all siding with the ousted superintendent either openly or tacitly. The out-going board had also given contracts to many teachers whom La Raza Unida would have preferred to fire. When one of these school teachers began passing out John Birch Society literature to her classes which stated that La Raza Unida personnel were communists, the new board violated her contract as well by firing her. This brought another suit against the board.[13]

the legal system and the november elections

In fact as the months progressed, the newly elected Raza Unida officials became more and more embroiled in legal controversies. In working to bring broad changes to the community, the legal system began to assume a larger and larger role. At times it provided them with crucial victories; at other times its intervention meant defeats.

The extent to which the legal system was crucial to determining the degree of change in the community was no more clearly illustrated than in the contest to take control of the county in November, 1970. In January of that year, as has been noted, La Raza Unida was organized as a third political party. This did not affect the city elections, which were nonpartisan, but for county offices Raza Unida candidates could be placed on the ballot only if the party itself was accepted on the ballot. If La Raza Unida candidates had chosen to run as Democrats, as earlier insurgents had done, they would have had to pay expensive filing fees and would have had to run in May, when many of the migrants had already gone north. By running as a third party in the November elections, La Raza Unida hoped to avoid both these procedural problems. But there were ideological as well as practical reasons for forming a third party. The Raza Unida leadership had little love for the Democratic party. The party had, after all, been the dominant party throughout South Texas and thus to them had been the main instrument of repression in the area. And the Republicans had been a nearly totally Anglo party in the community from the beginning. Gutiérrez argued that by forming a third party, Raza Unida supporters could participate in their own institution, one that valued rather than exploited them. In their own party conventions in May, candidates were selected in open participation, with Spanish as well as English used. Through these procedures, Gutiérrez argued that the Chicano community—including the lowliest farm worker and laborer—could more easily feel that politics was his business, not just a matter for rich Anglo businessmen and landowners.[14]

Realizing that La Raza Unida would give them their most serious challenge in the history of the county, the Anglos might have been expected to seek out and run as many acceptable Mexican candidates as possible for these county positions, as they had done in the school board and council races. Since one of their main charges against La Raza Unida was that it was racist, one might have expected the Anglos to be proving their interest in racial harmony and integration by backing Mexicans as well as Anglos. Instead, not only were all the county-commissioner candidates Anglos, but so also were their candidates for county judge, county clerk, and county treasurer. The Anglos were not backing a single Mexican for county office. This fact indicated a failure even to try cooptation.[15]   To

Chicanos it offered further evidence that Anglos were interested in sharing power only after Mexicans had taken everything over.

The most important county race quickly shaped up to be that of county judge, since it is generally considered the most powerful county position in Texas. Irl Taylor, the incumbent, was running for re-election. Taylor was a retired businessman with no background in law.[16] The Raza Unida candidate, Julian Salas, had been a justice of the peace since 1965. He, like Taylor, had had no legal training. Salas had also had very little experience as a justice of the peace, because no cases were ever brought before his court. Highway patrolmen, it seemed, preferred other justices of the peace.[17]

In a newspaper interview in May, 1970, Irl Taylor had commented that it would be a disaster if Raza Unida won because "the economy of Crystal City is all Anglo." Taylor noted that there was a distinct possibility that property taxes would be raised if the Raza Unida candidates were elected. But he consoled himself with the thought that even if Raza Unida were successful, "they won't be able to run the county" because they aren't qualified. Further, he observed, "the better thinking Mexican Americans are not going to let" Gutiérrez take over the county.[18]

To strengthen his position, Taylor sent out a confidential letter to all Anglo voters in the county. This letter noted that only 1,450 out of 3,996 voters in the county were Anglos. Said Taylor, "Every single one of these 1,450 should be a committee of one to be sure and vote...." He continued:

> Of these 2,546 registrants who bear a Spanish surname, I cannot beleive (sic) that all of them are "chicanos." I proudly claim many Mexican-Americans as my friends. And I know many of those people do not go along with this "kill the gringo," "squash the gringo like a beetle" philosophy that is so freely preached by this small, militant group for their own glory and financial personal gain.
>
> I also know each of you have many friends among the same people. So why include them when we bad-mouth these people? It would be better and we would feel better, if we would think twice and refer only to the individual militants. We need these clear thinking progressive people in our communities and they need us. With them we can win in November. . . .

The cold facts: we must have 600 Mexican-Americans added to the 1400 Anglos to win, and they live among us. Why not work with them and show them they are appreciated? After all they are responsible American citizens.[19]

Judge Taylor and the other county officials up for re-election also sent out to the voters, Anglo and Mexican, a list in English and in Spanish of the accomplishments which had occurred during their four years in office. In particular, they noted the building of the new courthouse and jail, the surplus-commodity program, and road-improvement and welfare services which were done in cooperation with state officials. La Raza Unida, however, was quick to dispute these accomplishments. They noted, for example, that the county might have had a new courthouse much sooner, since in 1963 the county had abruptly pulled out of a joint city-county building complex which would have cost considerably less money than the courthouse that was eventually built. The county had pulled out of this joint endeavor, they reminded people, shortly after Los Cinco gained control of the city government.

On the question of surplus commodities, La Raza Unida argued that the Mexican Americans of the community seemed overwhelmingly to desire food stamps rather than surplus commodities.[20] Such a program would cost much less in administrative and storage facilities. Besides resenting having to stand in a long line each month to pick up their peanut butter and other surplus commodities, the Mexicans wished to be on food stamps because they would have much more control over what they ate, and from whom they bought their merchandise. For apparently these same reasons, however, the county had refused to allow food stamps to be used.[21]

As it turned out, all this campaign literature and organizing of each Anglo into a "committee of one to be sure and vote" turned out to be less necessary than feared. Although La Raza Unida conventions were held and slates of candidates were nominated for county offices in Zavala, Dimmit, and La Salle counties, institutional procedures worked to make their getting on the ballot much more difficult than they had expected. The Texas election code, it turned out, was unclear at best, and misleading or contradictory at worst, on what procedures a third party had to use to get on the ballot in a specific county.[22] Given these circumstances, the Anglo county officials in all three counties refused to place the names of La Raza Unida candidates on the ballot. Although the party filed suit, after an enormous amount of legal maneuvering and appeals, the party still could not get on the ballot.

The only action left was for the party to conduct a write-in campaign. Owing to the nature of the procedures for write-in votes under Texas law, such a campaign had little chance of success. Stickers could not be used; names had to be written in. In a community where many of the voters in the Chicano community were functional illiterates, getting them to write all their candidates' names correctly and in the proper place became an insuperable task. Although the courts did rule that election officials could help illiterates vote if requested, the Anglo election officials refused to do so since they were not required to.[23]

Although the Anglos had probably insured the defeat of La Raza Unida in denying Raza Unida a place on the ballot and in refusing to help illiterates vote, they continued to conduct an extremely high-powered campaign. The county had always been the preserve of Anglo power, especially throughout the years of turmoil in the city. Thus every effort was made to insure that the county would continue to be a bulwark against the militants. Many Mexicans reported that certain Anglos threatened to take them off welfare rolls and off surplus commodities if they voted for La Raza Unida. *La Verdad*, the newspaper of La Raza Unida, charged that the county head of the state welfare agency, Ben Ivey, went with Mrs. Irl Taylor to visit certain welfare recipients, telling them that voting for Irl Taylor was a prerequisite for an increase in welfare payments.[24] All this activity created some fear and confusion because at the very least the Anglos could launch careful investigations into the income of the Mexicans on welfare and surplus commodities, and perhaps they could find in the process either legal or illegal means of disqualifying them.[25] Also, "the Puppets" were out in force, taking unrequested absentee ballots to sick and elderly Mexicans, getting them to sign their names, and then voting the ballots for them.

Being fully in control of all the county-election machinery, the Anglos also moved the polling places to locations which would make the Mexicans more uncomfortable. In particular, the voting place for northeastern Crystal City was moved from the high school, with its large area for voting, to the all-Anglo Methodist Church.[26] Moving to the cramped quarters of the church meant that voting could be much more carefully observed, all the more easily since Texas law did not require small towns to provide any voting booths. The move also meant that in order to vote, Mexicans would have to enter surroundings which were certain to be unfamiliar to them, and where they could be sure they would not be wanted. In these circumstances, trying to remember how and where to write all the Raza Unida party names on the ballot was taxing indeed. The time taken to do this, as well as the lack of voting booths, meant that Anglos could easily tell how everyone had voted.[27] Amidst all this activity, the FBI was sent into Crystal City to investigate the absentee voting and election procedures. Although statements were taken from a number of people, the FBI did not file any charges.[28]

When the results of the election were announced, all the Raza Unida candidates had lost, although in several cases the write-in candidates had captured more than forty percent of the vote. Considering that the Mexicans comprised only slightly over sixty percent of the county electorate, doing this well under these circumstances was to many a symbolic victory.[29] But the incumbent county commissioners and county judge, all Anglo, were re-elected. Because terms were for four years, La Raza Unida could not hope to gain control of the county for at least another four years.

Thus in spite of all the activity, mobilization, and involvement in the Chicano community, all county commissioners and the county judge remained Anglo in a county which was three-quarters Chicano. County policy would continue as before. In terms of tax rates, police policy, and welfare policies, the county might have been important in upgrading Chicano life. Instead it stayed steadfastly opposed to the Chicano activists, just as it had in 1963. Although control of the county was not crucial to the success of Crystal City radicals in the city and in the schools, their failure here did keep them from expanding their power, from instituting certain changes that could only be implemented through the county, and from ousting Crystal City Anglos from all governmental offices.

Without control of the county, one of La Raza Unida's most difficult but most important goals would remain impossible: that of land redistribution. At present almost all the land in the county belonged to Anglo farmers, ranchers, or absentee land-lords. Several important Texas politicians, such as John Connally, were important absentee owners in the county. Only through high taxation could the Chicano community hope to get any of this land, or at least get money for improved services. The defeat of La Raza Unida also meant that attempts to tax more heavily the oil companies in the county would have to be postponed.[30] It had recently been revealed that oil companies in Texas were drilling wells and then capping them. By capping them, the companies were able to pay little or no taxes because the wells were not being used. Yet at the same time the oil companies were using these wells as collateral for bank loans and financial transactions.[31] La Raza Unida wanted to challenge this whole setup, saying that if the companies could use these wells as collateral for hugh financial transactions, then they should be taxed at this rate. Under the Anglos, however, the oil companies were sure to be safe from such a challenge.

changes: the schools

In spite of this defeat at the county level, and in spite of the institutional and legal restrictions which were preventing La Raza Unida from bringing about greater changes, in both the city government and in the schools the Raza Unida leadership was managing to institute a number of changes. In matters affecting the schools in particular, the system continued to feel the effect of the successful strike. The school attorney, R. A. Taylor, was fired, and Jesse Gámez, a young San Antonio lawyer who had grown up in Crystal City, was hired in his place. The faculty and administration also changed considerably after the strike. After resignations, the firing of Briggs, and the ending of some of the lame-duck board's contracts the following spring, the schools changed even more. By the fall of 1970, for the first time nearly forty percent of the faculty was Mexican American. And many of the new teachers, both Anglo and Mexican, were quite different from their predecessors in outlook. Because the Crystal City school district was establishing itself as a beachhead for Chicano power, or as Gutiérrez had said, "for extending education to the Chicano," the teachers

accepting appointment tended to be more or less sympathetic
to the aims of La Raza Unida.

Besides important changes in the composition of the faculty,
the number of teacher aides was greatly expanded, and many
Chicano mothers were able to find employment and help the
school system at the same time. Similarly, the number of
cafeteria workers was increased, with Chicanos becoming the
new employees. The Raza Unida administration was thus making full use of the school system to employ many of its
supporters. This could be done since the schools were one of
the biggest employers in the county. Money that had always
gone to Anglos now began shifting dramatically to Mexican-
American members of the community. This could happen,
however, only with the dismissal of some Anglos who had
worked in the school system for many years. By acting in this
fashion, La Raza Unida leadership wielded the school system
into a buffer against Anglo economic intimidation. As an example, when one of the city councilmen, Ventura Gonzales, was
fired from his job at Del Monte, he was immediately hired to
work for the school administration.[32] The degree of change in
school personnel in the year after Raza Unida gained control is
indicated in the table that is found below.[33] Stated in other
terms, forty-one of the sixty-eight new teachers and administrators hired during the 1970-1971 school year were Mexican
Americans. Of salaries which totaled over $40,000 monthly for
these new employees, over $25,000, or almost two-thirds, was
going into Chicano hands.

Personnel Category	1969-1970	1970-1971
Anglo Administrators	11	4
Chicano Administrators	0	9
Anglo Teachers	91	78
Chicano Teachers	27	50
Negro Teachers	0	4
Anglo Teacher Aids	13	3
Chicano Teacher Aids	11	64
Anglo Cafeteria Workers	12	4
Chicano Cafeteria Workers	4	21

As all these statistics indicate, tremendous changes in personnel in the school system occurred within the first year, in spite of the efforts of the lame-duck Anglo school board to provide "continuity" in the school system.

Changes in curriculum and in policy within the school district were at least as important. Bilingual education was started in the early grades, and courses in Mexican-American history and culture begun. Besides these new courses, the content of other courses began to change. The school administration encouraged teachers to use new methods and new materials to reach the Chicano children and to try to stem the enormous dropout rate. Especially in civics, history, Spanish, English, and journalism courses, changes were being made.[34] Some teachers of English began to use more contemporary materials, including Chicano poetry and literature which had been written in English. The underground presses were studied and used. In journalism, questions of news slanting and biases in the press were studied and explored. Spanish classes began utilizing much Chicano literature and current events.[35] History courses began emphasizing aspects of history which bore on Mexican and Anglo settlement of the Southwest. In this they emphasized aspects which had earlier been neglected, such as the terms of the Treaty of Guadalupe-Hidalgo in 1848 and the ways it had subsequently been violated. The focus of the agricultural program was changed from an emphasis upon such problems as cattle raising, which was useful mainly for farmers and ranchers, to questions facing migrant workers. Such problems as labor contracts, unionization, and mechanization were being read about and discussed.

The library as well began to reflect the change in emphasis within the school. Although before the school boycott the library had almost no literature on Chicanos, within the first year after the boycott over $350 in Chicano books and materials had been acquired.[36] The schools also instituted a program called "Youth Tutoring Youth," whereby slow learners from the upper grades were paid to tutor slow learners from lower grades. In addition to hiring a Mexican-American counselor to advise high-school students of career opportunities, the school district took a much greater interest in scholarships for Chicano students. Their most dramatic success occurred when the University of California at Los Angeles awarded four-year, $14,000 scholarships to two Chicano high-school students.[37]

School programs aimed at the health and welfare of the community were also instituted and expanded. A free-breakfast program for school children was initiated, and the free-lunch program greatly expanded. As this indicates, the district was also more aware of and more willing to accept federal aid. In this first year of Raza Unida control, federal funds increased from $417,000 in the 1969-1970 school year to $720,000 in the 1970-1971 school year.[38] When it was discovered that the previous school administration had returned $20,000 in unused federal funds, Gutiérrez commented: "This is tantamount to a crime."[39] A Title IV grant was accepted for the purpose of facilitating integration and increasing faculty sensitivity to problems Chicano children faced in the school system. Hired as the director of this program was Erasmo Andrade, a Chicano activist who had twice run unsuccessfully for the state senate against John Connally's brother, Wayne Connally. Because of Andrade's previous activities, John Briggs, who was still superintendent at this time, actively opposed his appointment, thinking it a disaster to appoint a militant to such a sensitive spot. Andrade, however, was a close friend of Gutiérrez's, and he was hired over the superintendent's objections.

The school district also refused to allow army recruiters onto school premises or to permit any employee from serving as registrar for the Selective Service System. This had been common practice in the school district, and it continued in the rest of South Texas.[40] Further emphasizing their antimilitary policy, the school board employed Erasmo Andrade (who had received training with the American Friends Service Committee) as their draft counselor. In support of the César Chávez lettuce strike, the school board refused to allow non-farm-workers-union lettuce to be served in the school cafeteria.

Besides these changes in personnel and policies in the district, important changes also occurred in extracurricular activities connected with the school. Because of the changed procedure for the selection of cheerleaders following the school strike, five of the six cheerleaders elected were Mexican Americans. When the one Anglo resigned rather than be the only Anglo cheerleader, another Mexican was selected. Diana Palacios, the girl who

Mayor Juan Cornejo. Courtesy *San Antonio Light.*

José Angel Gutiérrez. Copyright © Express Publishing Co.; printed with permission.

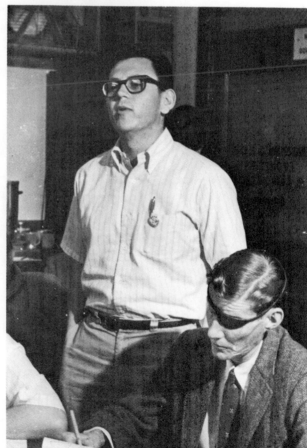

Students in front of Crystal City High School during the school boycott, December, 1969. Courtesy *San Antonio Light.*

Thanksgiving songfest in 1971 at the new Crystal City Community School. The children were dressed in red, white, and blue, and sang a medley of patriotic songs. Courtesy *The Zavala County Sentinel.*

had been denied selection as cheerleader by the faculty in the spring of 1969, became the head cheerleader. This symbolized the victory of the Chicano students perhaps more clearly than any other action.

It was, however, changes in the high-school band that surprised and upset the Anglos most. After the old band director resigned after the boycott, the new band director, Elpidio Lizcano, began making a number of changes. A new fight song, "Jalisco," was added to the band repertoire, and the band learned how to spell "RAZA" on the football field. This to the Anglos was an outrageous example of racism. But the Anglos were at least as offended by another practice which Mr. Lizcano instituted. At halftime he began translating his English announcements into Spanish. When this first happened, many Anglos began screaming and shouting obscenities from the stands as he spoke Spanish. After the game, rumors quickly spread that if Lizcano spoke Spanish at the next football game, a fight would break out. Extra police were on hand for the next football game, and everyone—Anglo and Mexican—waited tensely to see what would happen. At halftime, after speaking in English, Lizcano again translated into Spanish. There was, however, no fight afterwards. But nearly all the Anglos quit the band.[41] With cheerleaders and the band clearly dominated by Chicanos, football games no longer were a bastion of Anglo control.

The Crystal City schools were thus abruptly, consciously, being transformed into agents of "Chicanismo." As this transformation outraged the Anglos, so support for and interest in the schools grew in the Mexican-American community. Over two hundred Chicano dropouts returned to school voluntarily within the first year under the new administration, and school-board meetings (now held in the high-school auditorium so as to allow plenty of room for interested persons) regularly attracted hundreds of people to their weekly meetings. With Gutiérrez presiding, and the four Mexican-American members arrayed against the three Anglos, the struggle between the two groups was visible for all to see. The board meetings in fact demonstrated that the community continued to be as polarized as ever. Anglo board members would occasionally lose their tempers, but Gutiérrez always remained firmly in control, to the delight of the Mexicans in the audience. Gutiérrez would also translate the board proceedings into Spanish whenever he thought it necessary.

These changes in the school system not only had an impact on the citizens of Crystal City; their impact on the rest of the region soon became apparent. In the first year of Raza Unida control, a number of Anglo parents in Crystal City (although a distinct minority) had their children commute to nearby towns or enroll in private schools in San Antonio rather than continue to send their children to the public schools in Crystal City. In a reverse action, however, nearly forty Mexican-American students from the nearby town of Asherton journeyed to Crystal City daily in order to attend the school. In the spring of 1970 Chicano students in the nearby town of Uvalde launched a boycott, hoping to repeat the experience of Crystal City. The boycott was precipitated when one of the few Mexican-American teachers in the Uvalde school system found that his contract had not been renewed following his attempt to run for political office. Although this boycott had significant support in the Chicano community, it ended in nearly total defeat, with all of the several hundred Mexican-American children participating in the strike being flunked.[42] The Crystal City school system, however, did what it could to help the students. It offered to enroll those strikers who could afford to come, and Crystal City hired the Mexican-American teacher who had been fired from the Uvalde schools.

As further evidence of impact of the Crystal City revolt on South Texas, Mexican-American parents in Lockhart, Texas, who were upset over the school district's hiring of Crystal City's former superintendent, John Billings, conducted their first successful protest. Charging that Billings was "a disruptive element in our community," the Mexican-American parents forced Billings to resign.[43]

The experiences in Crystal City schools thus served to influence a number of other school districts in the area, bringing hope to Chicano students and their parents, and bringing fear and outrage to Anglos. The Crystal City school district was clearly serving as a beachhead and training center for Chicano activists and educators who hoped to be able to gain control of many other school districts in South Texas in the near future.

By raising issues and ideas concerning the schools which had long been either ignored or suppressed, the Crystal City schools, by their very existence, were subversive to the authorities governing other communities in South Texas.[44]

As earlier remarks have indicated, however, these changes did not occur smoothly or without significant problems and opposition. The whole system of inducements and punishments which had been central to the Anglo method of control, and which the school system had always reflected, was being overthrown. Values Anglos had tried to instill into Mexicans, and acculturation patterns which had been prerequisites to success and achievement, were being discarded. New values—those emphasizing pride in being Chicanos and in retaining their cultural heritage—were rapidly being substituted for the old Anglo values. Spanish was no longer frowned upon. Chicano symbols went up in the school cafeteria. All this not only brought confusion and disillusionment to the Anglos, who had always considered the schools a pillar of their authority; it also tormented those Mexicans who had made a serious effort to adapt to Anglo values. Instead of being pointed to as "good examples" for other Mexicans to follow, and of being able to consider themselves as leaders, the anti-Raza Unida Mexicans now found themselves mocked and scorned by a Mexican leadership they considered illegitimate and disgraceful. Yet these people were in many ways most in agony over the changes occurring because they were caught in the middle, not quite a part of either group. Said one sadly, "We are the ones that have a bad time. They [La Raza Unida supporters] don't bother you white people. They take it out on us!"[45]

Throughout the school year incidents of one sort or another occurred. When the school held its first assembly marking Mexican Independence Day, most of the Anglos refused to attend or to hear the invited speaker, State Senator Joe Bernal of San Antonio. Another time many Anglos walked out of a school assembly when a prayer was said in Spanish. Reaction among the Anglo teachers was also severe. Very few of them were willing to alter their teaching methods or the substance of their courses, and in the first year under La Raza Unida only about one-quarter of the teachers were reordering their courses in the direction the new school authorities encouraged. At the

end of the first semester several teachers quit, among them Mrs.
John Briggs, the wife of the ousted school superintendent. Mrs.
Briggs stated in her reasons for leaving:

> The atmosphere produced by [the] people who are sup-
> posedly trained administrators and educators does not make
> teaching enjoyable, a pleasure, nor a challenge to those of us
> that are professional teachers and have the successful experi-
> ence, degrees, and certification to back this claim.
> I personally cannot support some of the recent policies
> and actions of the majority of the board members, especially
> those concerning the teaching of students how to evade the
> draft, the boycotting of certain food items, the encourage-
> ment of civil disobedience, and the condoning of revolution-
> ary signs and symbols being displayed in classrooms by mili-
> tant, so-called teachers.[46]

One of the most articulate statements expressing Anglo anger
and frustration over the Raza Unida-dominated school system
came from Miss Judy Perkins, a school teacher who also resigned after one semester under the new leadership. Part of her
long letter of resignation, which summed up much of the Anglo
feeling toward the whole Chicano movement, stated:

> Three years ago I came to Crystal City to teach and make
> my home. At that time, it was a peaceful town where a
> person could feel like a part and belong, but the past three
> years have brought many changes which have disrupted the
> lives of all the citizens of this community, especially the
> children.
> . . . I believe in better education for all people, not just a
> few, and I always tried to be fair to all of my students,
> regardless of race or creed.
> I still possess this fine belief; however, I now feel dread
> and fear when I face the students in my classes. The class-
> room situation in the Crystal City school has become almost
> intolerable to me. I feel as if I am constantly under pressure,
> without freedom of speech or right to be an individual.
> . . . Teaching, to me, is a way of life, and I have felt
> dedicated to that way of life until now, but that dedication is
> slipping away or rather being taken away from me by stu-
> dents who do not respond to me as a teacher and friend
> simply because my skin is white.
> I say this because many of these same students were under

my instruction before a radical leader came and told them that the Anglo had infringed upon their rights and had discriminated against them.

Before Angel Gutierrez came back to Crystal City, friendship, response and learning existed in the school. This is no longer true because these students have been brainwashed into turning against the Anglo.

True enough, there has definitely been discrimination against the Mexican-American in Crystal City, but only to those who wanted to be discriminated against. How can they blame others for what they do not have? I have had to work for everything I have. I worked for my education, which was not given to me because I was Anglo, but because I was willing to work for it.

Everyone has the same opportunity regardless of race. The same public school that was open to me was open to my brown and black neighbor. The same college loans and work programs were also open to them.

The same opportunity is still open today, only to those who can see opportunity and accept a challenge. I am proud to be a part of a country where I can work for what I want and then be able to keep it.

In Communist countries this is not possible and that is exactly what is happening here in Crystal City, individual honors being taken away and given to those who do not work to accomplish those honors.

Yes, there is discrimination, but now against the Anglo and the Mexican-American who have taken advantage of opportunities and have accepted challenges.

... employees are being hired according to political beliefs, which to me coincides with communistic societies. I do not agree with the policies of our Raza Unida administration and do not want the good citizens of Crystal City to think that I am proud and honored to be working in the schools where bad conditions and relations exist. By continuing my work here, I feel that I am advocating their policies.[47]

As Miss Perkins' statement indicated, the philosophy behind the changes in the schools struck at the core of the dominant, conservative ideology which Anglos had enforced upon the region. But the Anglos were not really aware of their strong ideological position until the Chicano movement confronted them. To understand this deeply sincere shock and outrage, Calvin Trillin has said that it is necessary to realize that many

Anglos had "always regarded the status quo as nonpolitical and the traditional arrangement of control by race as nonracist." [48]

Substantial resistance to the new board policies thus came from the Anglo teachers, who were still a majority in the school system, and from the Anglo students. But there were other difficulties facing La Raza Unida school policies. The district remained severely limited in its financial resources, and the problem was compounded because some Anglos in the community began engaging in their own form of disobedience by withholding their school taxes. By the end of December, 1970, the school district was $42,000 behind its tax collections for the previous year. And by spring seventy-six individuals or businesses, all but one of them Anglo or Anglo-owned, were still refusing to pay their taxes. [49] Among others, the local Baptist Minister, Rev. Bruce Stovall, backed this "boycott" by arguing,

> ... some of the persons who are supposed to be educational leaders have turned out to be political pawns, lacking in principles and ethics. ...
> If all it takes to run a school is a few militant teachers and some 16-year-old kids with a direct line to the Gutierrista headquarters, then why should we as taxpayers maintain a bunch of highly paid, incompetent, gutless, so-called educators? The funds may as well be spent on some other worthless cause. [50]

Although nearly all the major businesses in the school district, such as Del Monte, were reluctant to join the boycott, the boycott nonetheless was an added burden to the already impoverished school district.

In coming at a time when the board was trying to institute new policies on a broad front, the boycott placed further limits on what the board could do. For example, textbooks not recommended by the state adoption committee had to be paid for by the local district. In trying to counteract the traditional Anglo story of Texas history told in textbooks, and in trying to bring new books for Spanish and for bicultural courses, the board found itself without the money for any extensive book buying. [51] Again owing to limited financial resources, building facilities remained overcrowded and inadequate. Any new building program would require the use of bonds, yet this could be a difficult and time consuming process, as the school district was to find out. As of the spring of 1971 the board still had not been able to inaugurate a program designed to bring into the schools the estimated ten percent of Chicanos who were legally of school age but who were not in school.[52]

With the board employing so many new ideas and new personnel with limited resources, many disruptions of normal school activities occurred, even concerning such questions as where and when classes would be meeting. Federal and state agencies also began taking a close look at many of the school-district's innovations. An investigation in the fall of 1970 by the Texas Education Agency, at the request of local Anglos, found numerous deficiencies in the implementation of and the facilities for the migrant program.[53] The Texas Education Agency further criticized several aspects of the school system in general, such as the absence of the teaching of patriotism in the schools, the method of purchasing some equipment, and the lack of adequate planning periods for teachers. An anonymous "Crystal City Citizens Committee" formed to serve as a watchdog on the school district. It immediately began writing streams of letters to the local newspaper, and to state and federal authorities, arguing that violations of state and federal laws were occurring. The goal of the Citizens Committee seemed to be to get the Texas Education Agency to revoke accreditation to the district. This move would have had a shattering effect upon the schools, among other things denying them federal and state funds. If this were to happen, Anglos with sympathetic Mexicans might have been able to oust the incumbent board members.

Although denying accreditation to the school system would have been most unlikely, partly because it would have been such a drastic step, the school board and administration continued to run into pressure from local and statewide organizations which were concerned about changes being made in the schools. Statewide educational organizations were aghast at some of the changes. They were particularly horrified at the use of the school to create and maintain a radical Chicano organization in the community. Even many moderate-to-liberal professional educators were deeply concerned about the tide of events in the schools. Trained to view the schools as "apolitical," or at least as not in open conflict with the economic, social, and political structures of the area, these officials were upset at the obvious and deliberate injection of politics into the schools. To them the school leadership seemed to be going out of its way to continue the tensions in the community. The Crystal City school district, for example, even held commemorative exercises on the anniversary of the school walkout.

Officials in the state whose job was to facilitate integration were likewise upset with the deliberate polarization La Raza Unida officials were engaging in. Officials in the Texas Education Desegregation Technical Assistance Center (TEDTAC) were generally worried over the "excesses" among various Raza Unida educators.[54] In the fall of 1970 they sent down a trouble-shooting team to try to foster integration and cultural awareness, and to bring greater harmony to the community. In particular, they were horrified at the bitter hatred which flared up constantly in the public meetings of the school board. Because of the extreme polarization on the board, TEDTAC thought it best to begin with a "softer" program than their normal one. When the Anglos began to like the program, however, Erasmo Andrade, who, as director of Title IV funds, was in on the meeting, began to criticize the whole format, questioning their decision to use this program rather than a more hard-hitting one. When this happened, other members of La Raza Unida also began to criticize the effort, and the meeting ended in a disaster.

This experience was particularly bitter for TEDTAC, and the officials lamented over the fact that these Chicanos could not show more understanding and charity toward Anglos. These people were against meeting hatred with hatred, and they were hoping and expecting that Chicanos would treat Anglos in ways that Anglos had only rarely treated Chicanos. Their disappointment over the continued exacerbation of racial tensions in the schools led them to conclude that the militants did not really "have the school children at the center of their thinking." Said one official, "The children are being used."[55] This feeling was similar to ideas voiced by John Briggs, the ousted school superintendent. He had felt that events following the boycott were designed more for political purposes than to further education. He had said, "If they had been interested in education, they would have been interested in cooperation." He also had felt that he had been demoted and fired because he was "stealing the thunder" from Raza Unida people by working to implement their reforms in a quiet, inconspicuous way.[56]

There was, in many ways, a great deal of accuracy in all these charges. From a professional educator's point of view, the children were being "used," and to use school children as the focal point of struggle between racial groups was to them horrible. It put tremendous strain upon the children and meant that political name-calling and scuffles were common even among young children. Yet La Raza Unida, as we have noted, was premised upon fighting the dominant Anglo economic, social, and political institutions of the society, all of which they considered racist and colonialistic. And their manner for doing this was in uniting the Chicano community through the family structure; and the children, often the best educated and least vulnerable members of the family, were crucial participants in the process. They were also the future leaders of the community, and thus were prized at least as heavily by the Chicano militants as by anyone else in the town. The professional educators and integration trouble-shooters, however, viewed racial conflict as something which needed to be resolved by mutual accommodation. Hence they wanted to bring the school-board members together, help them see and understand each other's views, and get them all to compromise their differences.

These professional educators, however, did not see or understand the possible functions of continued polarization and racial conflict.[57] La Raza Unida was not interested in bringing about "harmony" in the community: they were interested in acting upon ancient grievances and in letting the Anglos know that things would never be the same again. Flaunting power and watching the "gringos" squirm was an integral part of their strategy, for it served to unite the Chicano community, to help them overcome their feelings of inferiority, and also to radicalize Mexican Americans by "exposing" the tactics Anglos would use in reaction. All this was part of the strategy of "recognizing the enemy in all their involvements of policies, roles, and power manipulations."[58] It meant that the Chicanos had no real interest in people who wanted "reconciliation" now, or even integration in the usual sense of the word, because they felt certain that any reconciliation would mean acceptance of what to them was the dominant Anglo colonial structure of South Texas. They thus had a fear of "coming to terms with their environment" before they had changed it.[59]

All of this meant that the school system, while undergoing considerable changes in personnel and policies, was consistently wracked by tension because of the changes and the reactions these innovations produced.

changes: the city

In the city government important changes were also taking place. Shortly after the spring victory, the Raza Unida councilmen hired as city manager Bill Richey, a former VISTA worker in nearby Cotulla and a close friend of Gutiérrez.[60] In Richey the city had an educated, efficient administrator and a tireless worker for La Raza Unida. Richey's Anglo background made him an anomaly in Crystal City and yet made charges of "reverse racism" against La Raza Unida less credible.

Although Richey was faced with a number of problems, these were nothing compared to the ones Ozuna had confronted. The local talent he could rely on was much stronger, and although there were some resignations, these were not of the magnitude of those Ozuna had faced. Also, Richey and the council majority were both anxious to avoid the debilitating struggle which had brought down the first Mexican government. Although Richey worked closely with the councilmen, they were aware of the prerogatives of the city manager. And Richey's being a close friend and graduate-student colleague of Gutiérrez, his previous work in community organization in Cotulla and in Crystal City, and his obvious energy and dedication, made him respected by the local Mexican population.

Upon taking office, the new city government began improving the quality of the city's staff and police force and hiring and training Chicanos to the extent that soon Chicanos were holding positions they had never held in the city bureaucracy before. In being much more willing to develop and use Mexican-American talent, Richey was aided by the resignation of several Anglos from the city government. Teresa Flores became the new city clerk. She had served the city for many years as secretary, but had never been promoted to city clerk. The new public accountant for the city was a Mexican American, Juan Ramirez of San Francisco.[61] José Garza became assistant city manager, and Ramón García became the first Chicano ever to be utilities supervisor for the city.[62] R. A. Taylor, who had returned to being city attorney after George Ozuna was fired in 1965 and who had been the attorney for the schools and for Del Monte for many years, resigned in the face of an imminent dismissal. Taylor was succeeded by Jesse Gámez, who was also being employed as the attorney for the school board. New and old employees began receiving additional training to increase their expertise and efficiency. At the same time more Mexicans were appointed to city boards and commissions, often replacing Anglos. As in the years from 1963 to 1965 under Los Cinco, the city's Mexican community became more familiar with the workings of the city government in all its aspects.

Along with these changes in personnel, the city also undertook several policy changes. Within two months of taking office, the city council passed a resolution to try to prevent the State Department of Public Safety from allowing highway patrolmen to patrol within the city without explicit city requests for assistance. This action was taken, City Manager Richey explained, because "citizens had complained about Highway Patrolmen patrolling in the barrios and La Placita during meetings."[63] Richey was reported in the local paper to have said that "the Highway Patrol had no business out in the barrios and that their . . . business was out on the highways."[64] Richey added that "the resolution was made necessary by the public antipathy to the Highway Patrol and Texas Rangers." He then noted that the city itself would need to meet its responsibilities now that the highway patrol would not be around, and that to do this "more policemen, better trained policemen, and better equipped policemen will have to be provided." He then commented in an obvious jab at protesting Anglos that "the city should have done this long ago."[65]

This rebuke to the highway patrol (and by implication the Texas Rangers) upset the local Anglos and the Department of Public Safety. Colonel Wilson Speir, Director of the Department, commented that he didn't "know of any other city in Texas that had passed such a resolution."[66] This action by the new city government symbolized the contempt La Raza Unida had for state police practices. The resolution also revealed their self-confidence. A short time later another resolution, equally loaded with symbolism, was passed proclaiming the week of

September 12-18 as "Semana de la Raza" (week of La Raza). This coincided with the Mexican national independence day, September 16th.

In other actions, the city also increased health-insurance benefits for all city employees and increased their salaries by ten percent. The council also annexed a poor, all-Mexican area north of Del Monte. This area, known as "Camposanto" because it was adjacent to the Mexican cemetery, had been requesting annexation and city water for several years without success. With the annexation, plans were quickly made to extend water to the area. The city also bought a paving machine, hoping to help extend pavement to that half of the town which still did not have paved streets. With the aid of the city's urban renewal program, lights were installed in municipal parks, more trees were planted, and drainage lines were extended. On its own the city also worked to improve the park and recreational areas in the Mexican sections of town which were still not covered by urban renewal. Playground equipment and basketball goals were installed, and "La Placita," the open-air plaza for rallies and meetings in the Mexican community, was similarly improved. All these changes provided clear material and symbolic evidence that the city government of Crystal City was sympathetic to the Mexican community.

The new city government, however, also faced serious problems in its first year in office. Their ability to annex the large Del Monte plant on the edge of town remained unresolved, and until this legal battle was decided the city would be losing about $13,000 a year in taxes from the company.[67] More than the loss of this money concerned city officials. Unless the plant could be annexed, it would remain under the jurisdiction of county and state police rather than under the city police. In the event of a strike at the plant, which seemed distinctly possible because of the rising power of the local Mexican community, the difference between city police and county and state law enforcement might be crucial to the outcome of the strike.[68]

In attempting to change policy in the huge urban renewal project, the new city officials also ran into legal difficulties. The massive urban renewal and public housing program had by the end of 1970 poured $14,000,000 into Crystal City.[69] Over half the city was under the urban renewal program, which was generally considered by Housing and Urban Development officials to be one of the outstanding programs in the country.[70] In terms of acquisitions, demolitions, relocations, and contracting, the project was one of the biggest businesses in the community.[71] Through its existence since 1958 the program had been run by Sam Anderson, a former realtor. Although Anderson was an able director willing to use the numerous funds from the federal agency, he was resented by the Chicano militants for his close ties to the Anglo business world and for his reluctance to employ Chicanos in important positions.[72] Chicanos charged that the contractors for the program were always Anglos, and that Mexican-American businesses tended to be bought out by urban renewal while Anglo businesses were relocated into new, more attractive quarters.[73] There was also the belief that important Anglo landowners and money lenders had made considerable money off the program.

La Raza Unida spokesman also noted that the most important Mexican American on Anderson's staff, Fidel Rodríguez, could hardly be considered sympathetic to the ideas of many of the Mexicans in the community. Rodríguez had stated, for example, that although he had been a migrant worker, he had been able to work his way up successfully and that others in the community could have done the same if they had had more ambition.[74] That Anderson's most important Mexican assistant should hold this view indicated perhaps the philosophy behind the urban renewal program in Crystal City and the kind of Mexicans Anderson was most interested in helping. The program was also criticized by many Mexicans who were aware that, along with the progress, the program had also uprooted people and forced some families to move into other slums. "Camposanto," the Mexican slum without water north of town, had, for example, grown considerably as urban renewal had affected more and more areas within the city.[75]

How much all these problems were the fault of the director, and how much they were more the fault of the program itself, was more difficult to determine. It should also be pointed out that Anderson had had to work under a variety of city administrations, and that if he had tried to incorporate many of the ideas that Raza Unida supporters were now wanting, he most likely would have been dismissed long ago by any of the Anglo administrations. Nevertheless, as a step towards gaining control of the massive program and of ousting Anderson as director, the

Raza Unida council majority tried to appoint two new commissioners to the urban renewal board. These two nominees were no
less than José Angel Gutiérrez himself and Rodolfo Palomo, a
close friend of Gutiérrez who had graduated from Moorhead
State College in Minnesota and had returned to be active in
community betterment activities such as the Head Start Program.[76] Mayor Paulino Mata, who was a holdover from before
the spring election, refused to appoint the new members even
though it was the wish of a majority of the council.[77] The Raza
Unida majority therefore ousted Mata as mayor and named
Francisco Benavides as the new mayor. Benavides then proceeded to appoint Gutiérrez and Palomo to the Urban Renewal
Commission.

Because the ousting of Mata appeared at first to be of
questionable legality, with Mata charging that the meeting in
which he was ousted was illegal, federal authorities used this
action as reason to intervene to protect the director, Sam
Anderson.[78] Finnis Jolly, director of the San Antonio Housing
and Urban Development Area Office, announced that because
of the action of La Raza Unida councilmen, the entire urban
renewal program for the city would come to a halt, except for
the salaries of Anderson and his staff.

In order for the city to continue to receive urban renewal
funds, the Raza Unida leadership had to accept a compromise
worked out with the federal authorities whereby both the
holdover urban renewal commissioners and the new Raza Unida
appointees were placed on the commission and all actions had
to be taken by unanimous vote.[79] They were forced to accept
this compromise even though Mata in the end filed no suit and
the whole question of the ousting of Mata and the appointment
of Gutiérrez and Palomo to the board therefore appeared to
have been legal. The compromise prevented Raza Unida from
having a majority on the board. Although this provision of
unanimity might have been viewed as a compromise to prevent
the Raza Unida sympathizers from being denied a voice, to
Gutiérrez it was an attempt by Anderson and the federal authorities to protect themselves from charges made by Raza
Unida.[80] By requiring unanimity, the urban renewal authorities
would be able to reply to criticism by noting that Raza Unida
supporters had also supported their actions. The agreement,
however, was considered a temporary one, to last until the April

city-council elections settled the question of who was rightfully mayor. Nevertheless, the rapid intervention of federal authorities when it seemed possible that Anderson might be fired could not have been lost on the Raza Unida activists. It was a clear example of another constraint within which they had to work.[81]

In attempting to attract industry to Crystal City, the city administration was also trying to pursue new policies; yet again it was facing certain important constraints. The Raza Unida leadership claimed that the Crystal City Industrial Foundation and other business groups had been interested in attracting only certain kinds of industries, those wanting cheap and nonunion labor such as textiles.[82] There was even some indication that farmers and ranchers, as well as the large Del Monte plant, had not been particularly enthusiastic about attracting new industries because it would compete with their surplus labor supply.[83] The new government, however, immediately began searching for new ways to attract jobs. It tried to get government contracts, especially through provision of the Small Business Administration which were supposed to allow for minority group businesses to get contracts even if their bids were not competitive.[84] Noting the large amount of federal military spending in San Antonio, the leadership also hoped to attract some of these jobs to Crystal City. These efforts, however, were not successful.

Attracting industry and jobs thus remained a critical problem for the city and was compounded by the lack of opportunities for migrant workers in the north. Owing to conditions in the area, particularly concerning the lack of skills and of water in the area, the Raza Unida leadership realized that they could not get industry "in the normal sense" to locate in Crystal City.[85] Yet they were still very much in search of jobs. Hoping to stem the departure of the jobless from Crystal City to the urban ghettos, Richey noted, "We've got to get industry or repeat the saga of the Blacks migrating to the cities."[86]

Although the Raza Unida leadership was aware of the critical nature of the problem and was engaging in new steps to try to attract jobs to the area, their ultimate success or failure would depend upon far more than the community's willingness to try new approaches. It would also depend upon such factors as industrial attitudes, the kinds of federal programs that were available, and developments within Mexico itself. A new program launched in the last decade by the Mexican government, the Border Development Program, was designed to attract American industry into Mexican communities bordering the United States. These companies entering Mexico could import machinery, raw materials, and key personnel free of restrictions as long as their entire production was exported. A study done for the Economic Development Administration (EDA) of the U.S. Department of Commerce concluded that "literally hundreds of industries, such as toys, garments, electronic and mechanical sub-assemblies, have located or are locating on the Mexican side of the border."[87]

What this program meant for the development of industries on the American side of the border, however, was more ambiguous. The report noted that the program "is opposed by organized labor and others in the United States as encouraging runaway industry." It then added that "the real problem is whether it represents exploitation of labor."[88] Although the report indicated hopes that Mexico's Border Development Program might stimulate industrial development on the United States side also, people in Crystal City seemed to think that the program would be yet another reason why industry would prefer to locate in places other than Crystal City.

Since the industries on the Mexican side of the border would of course be paying wages much lower than the American minimum wage, both Anglos and Mexicans in Crystal City recognized that the only hope of attracting this sort of industry to Crystal City would be through low wages and tax write-offs.[89] Although many Anglos were willing to do this, the Raza Unida leadership was reluctant to encourage the kind of industry which to them would merely continue the economic exploitation of Mexicans in the area. The report for EDA recognized this dilemma when it noted that "the only remote hope for bringing medium and large industry to the border is to provide subsidies to attract them. Such subsidies can take many forms—tax incentives, freight subventions, wage allowances, government contract preferences, etc."[90] Although noting the need for outside stimulation, the report concluded that in truth "progress will most probably come through the expansion of existing industries and services in response to increasing incomes from moderate growth of population and improved capabilities

of the people."[91] The situation in Crystal City at the beginning
of the 1970's, however, was one of losing population, not of
moderate growth. Thus the community would clearly be dependent upon outside forces in its efforts to attract industry, to
upgrade the skills of its people, and to stem the flow of people
to other areas with greater opportunities.

The fragility of the condition in Crystal City was further
emphasized in a study on the relative merits of attracting
industry versus encouraging relocation. Niles Hansen and William Gruben noted that

> Despite the efforts of the Economic Development Adminis-
> tration and other government agencies to attract more firms
> to South Texas, it is difficult to imagine that enough growth
> can be generated to increase significantly the employment
> opportunities of the Mexican Americans residing there. Re-
> moteness from the major centers of economic activity, poor
> natural resources, underdeveloped human resources and pres-
> sures from Mexico are negative factors which are not offset
> by attractive factors—other than low wages—that the region
> might offer to private firms.[92]

Based upon the results of their interviews with people who had
left South Texas for other areas of Texas and the nation, the
authors concluded that "in general, our findings suggest that
comprehensive relocation assistance would be more efficient in
increasing income and employment opportunities for Mexican
Americans of South Texas than efforts to attract industry to
the region."[93] This report thus further emphasized the precarious economic foundation upon which the town rested, and
this weakness seriously hampered efforts by the city to upgrade
opportunities for the Chicano population of the town.

changes: community organization

Besides these changes and attempted changes in the city and
the schools, La Raza Unida had also been able to strengthen
itself organizationally with their year in office. Not only was
the school system being used to employ many Mexicans as
teacher aids, in the cafeteria, in the business office, or as
teachers, but a broad community organization was being per-
fected. Ciudadanos Unidos [United Citizens], the organization
of parents which had arisen out of the school boycott, gradually

evolved into a broad-based, multifunctional organization to direct and to serve the Mexican community. Organized at the level of family membership, with several different suborganizations designed to meet the needs and interests of youth, women, workers, and teachers, Ciudadanos Unidos began to assume the position of a comprehensive community organization. In building such an organization, La Raza Unida seemed to be further implementing the strategy of community-organization activists and scholars such as Saul Alinsky and Miguel Tirado.[94] By the spring of 1971 over two hundred families were members.[95] Membership, however, was selective rather than open. This restrictive requirement was to try to prevent spies in the organization and to try to insure that all the families were dedicated to improving the Mexican community in a manner in sympathy with La Raza Unida goals.

The organization was composed of three major committees. One focused on political action, and thus was in charge of recruiting candidates and of getting people registered to vote. A second was in charge of finances for the organization and its projects, and a third was concerned with social action, and engaged in organizing a voluntary day-care center, a credit union, and various self-help measures. From these three committees a board of directors for the entire organization was selected. Gutiérrez was on the board, but he was by no means the leader of the organization or the leader of its committees. Instead, in following an Alinsky model and in attempting to avoid what Tirado has called the tendency toward dictatorship, Gutiérrez seemed concerned to develop as much local organizational talent as possible. As a result, he was but one of several important leaders in the organization, and the chairman of the board of directors was José Serna, father of one of the high-school activists, the owner of a filling station, and the Raza Unida candidate for county commissioner of precinct three in the November, 1970, elections.[96]

The dispersal of leadership in the Ciudadanos Unidos organization, and their attempt to build overlapping organizations as a recognition of the diversity of membership within the Mexican-American community, also reflected the view that the organization should contain a heavy dose of participatory democracy. According to several members within Ciudadanos Unidos, the leadership of the organization exercised that rare quality of "recognizing the need to develop a consensus among the membership before acting."[97] Together the members of Ciudadanos Unidos organized projects which were dear to the membership as much as to the leadership. There were projects to care for the area around the Mexican cemetery and to work to get a cheaper funeral agency into the town. There were also raffles, bingo games, and dances.[98]

The development of Ciudadanos Unidos in the community meant that during the first year of La Raza Unida rule the Mexican community continued amazingly well organized and well informed, in marked contrast to the period under Cornejo and to much that has been written about Mexican-American political behavior.[99] To many Mexicans of the community, the organization served as a further example of Raza Unida concern for the people. Scholarships were given to students, and help was procured in finding and in providing social services. Since several of those most active in the organization were demoted or fired from their jobs, one of the organization's most important functions was to try to find work for all its members.

Besides organizing Ciudadanos Unidos, La Raza Unida further strengthened themselves organizationally by taking over control of the Mexican Chamber of Commerce, ousting its moderate, coalition-minded leadership. The Chamber, which had evolved into a social and drinking club, was not firmly restricted to businessmen. It was thus possible for La Raza Unida partisans to become members of the club and thereby gain control of the organization. Historically, the Mexican Chamber of Commerce had been the one organization which the middle-class Mexicans had controlled. Their loss of the organization to La Raza Unida meant that the Mexican community was becoming even more united under the new militant leadership.[100]

the anglo reaction and the spring elections

All these changes and developments in the community had their impact on the elections in the spring of 1971. The campaign for the school-board and city-council elections quickly shaped up to be as heated as the campaign in 1970, and on both the city council and the school board, control was at stake. Eddie Treviño, the Mexican-American who had provided the crucial fourth vote for La Raza Unida, and Malcolm (Buddy) Maedgen, a wealthy rancher, were up for re-election on the school board. For the city council, Mayor Frank Benavides, the holdover councilman who had provided the crucial vote for the Raza Unida majority, was up for re-election with the two "CASAA" holdovers: former mayor Paulino Mata and his friend and fellow school-teacher, Santos Nieto.

The campaign provided interesting contrasts and elaborations upon earlier campaigns in the city. In particular, the battle emphasized that the Anglos had made some important changes in tactics, if not in substance, this year they had been locked out of power. No counterpart to CASAA had been created. As the Anglos realized, José Angel Gutiérrez would have been eager to confront a rival organization. [101] He could quickly have weakened any such counterorganization through ridicule and through "exposing" the Mexican-American "vendidos," or "sell-outs." The general strategy Anglos thus tried to follow once La Raza Unida assumed control was to maintain a yet lower profile, working more than ever with and through Mexicans. [102] But this required unusual restraint and forebearance at the very time Mexicans were most provocative, and thus the strategy was never universally agreed upon or followed by the Anglo population.

Even in this lower profile, Anglos did not withdraw from politics; they lived and breathed it like everyone else in the community. But they talked only among their friends and tried to encourage Mexicans to assume a greater role in opposing the "Gutierristas." [103] Since counter-racism or reactive cultural nationalism had mushroomed in the Chicano community, Anglos realized they needed to be more careful. At the same time, those Mexicans who had contacts with Anglos and who sympathized with the Anglo opposition were quickly considered as "sell-outs" and "traitors" to their own people.

Given the development of racial polarization, it was difficult for the Anglos to know how to react. Emotionally many wanted to fight with everything they had against what they considered to be "un-American" and "communistic." They were all accustomed to their ethnic group running the community, whether in the open or behind the scenes, and the Anglo community had become very politically oriented and active since the 1963 revolt. Yet strategically Anglos had to face the uncomfortable fact that they were a small minority of the community and that, with the rise of race consciousness and resentment against the "gringo," their political activity and support could easily be turned into a "kiss of death." The consequences of these unpleasant options—being pulled one way emotionally and another way tactically—meant that Anglos in the community often reacted in a confused manner that tended to cancel out separate actions.

Although some Anglo activities were kept covert, there were also a few activities very much in the open. For some Anglos there was comic relief in the organization of a German-American Parents Association (GAPA), modeled to ridicule the Mexican-American Parents Association which had been organized in Uvalde during their unsuccessful strike. GAPA duplicated many of the Chicano complaints, substituting the word "German" for "Mexican." In the fall of 1970 it confronted the school board with a long list of demands.[104] Besides demanding such things as that Gutiérrez apologize for his racist statements and resign, that the American flag be displayed in every classroom, that the pledge of allegiance be said every morning in classrooms, that teachers speak English at all times (or, "if this is not possible we demand them to speak German to the students"), GAPA also contained a hefty dose of ideology. The organization stated that it wished to call attention to the fact that

> No ethnic minority has any special lease on poverty. People of all national origins have had to overcome some special problems arising from their ethnic backgrounds. The color of a person's skin, their last name, religious beliefs, the language of their forefathers, or any other phony alibi should not be used as an excuse of failure.
>
> We believe that the responsibility for success or failure lies squarely on the individual; if they are willing to pay the price that is demanded by life, they will succeed. [105]

The number of Anglos who were members of the organization ranged in estimate from around ten to around sixty, but it was never meant to be a serious alternative to the Raza Unida organization, or to perform the functions that CASAA had been able to do.

Within the high school, the Anglo students began to withdraw from extracurricular activities and school-sponsored events as Raza Unida children took them over. Some students who were opposed to La Raza Unida organized a group calling itself Concerned Young Americans. Their main activity during the year was to present the Mexican-American band director with a petition requesting that football halftimes be conducted exclusively in English. [106]

A third activity which was neither anonymous nor of low profile was the attempt by fired superintendent John Briggs to win reinstatement. A public hearing was held in Crystal City over La Raza Unida's actions against him, and the legal battle and the involvement of various statewide teacher organizations on Briggs' behalf meant that all people continued to be aware of Briggs' status. This activity, as well as the organization of GAPA and related efforts, violated the general Anglo attempt to maintain a low profile, but in general the tactics used by the Anglo community in opposing La Raza Unida were different in important respects from the period of CASAA activity in response to Cornejo. Since to increasing numbers of Mexicans, the long years of Anglo rule were interpreted as years of exploitation, of control, and of using the Mexican people, all but the most careful and covert Anglo political activity ran the strong risk of being counterproductive. Most Anglos therefore tried to remain calm and not play into Raza Unida hands.

Since many Anglo activities were more circumspect than in previous years, it was more difficult to follow their political activity. There did seem to be definite indications, however, that a new group of Anglos was working hard to develop ties with moderate, anti-Raza Unida Mexicans. [107] A group of younger Anglos, who were often relatively new to the community, and who were clearly not anti-Mexican in a strictly racial sense, seemed to become more and more important as the older Anglo leadership seemed to withdraw in pain, disgust, and impotence. Some in this new leadership were willing to admit confidentially that many of the Anglos in Crystal City were racists and that these people were the worst enemies of moderate Anglos. Almost assuredly because of the influence of these moderate Anglos, no Anglos ran for either the school board or the city council in the spring elections of 1971. La Raza Unida officials were thus opposed only by other Mexicans in the community. Buddy Maedgen, the incumbent Anglo school-board member, chose not to run for re-election. His decision to resign deprived La Raza Unida of one of their favorite opponents.

Although the Anglos decided to run no candidates, they seem to have played an important part in the selection of the "anti-Gutierrista" candidates. With Maedgen not running, the two Mexicans selected to run for the school board were Teodoro Muñoz and Alfredo Ramón. Muñoz was the stepfather of Ramón, and both of them, along with Mrs. Teodoro Muñoz, were well known for their opposition to La Raza Unida. They had been opposed to the school boycott, and Muñoz's grocery store had even been boycotted by Raza Unida militants. [108] In reacting to these two opposition candidates, allied under a "For Better Government" coalition, one top Raza Unida spokesman said, "I couldn't have done better if I'd picked their candidates myself!"

For the city council, the three anti-Raza Unida candidates chosen were incumbents Mata and Nieto, along with Gilberto Salazar, the owner of a bakery located in the same building as Muñoz's grocery. [109] These men were considered by Raza Unida supporters as the "gringo" candidates because of their opposition to La Raza Unida and their opposition or neutrality in the school boycott. They were also unable to answer La Raza Unida questions concerning how they had been selected to run. This question became more important because the Raza Unida candidates were claiming to be "community selected," through having been chosen by the Ciudadanos Unidos organization. None of the anti-Raza Unida candidates seems to have made any effort to establish an independent, moderate position. None of them risked angering any of their Anglo supporters. In fact, Buddy Maedgen publicly endorsed the anti-Raza Unida candidates for the school board. [110] Because of their refusal to develop a position independent from the general Anglo charges against La Raza Unida, they were made to seem dependent upon the Anglos for support. As the campaign progressed and Anglos became more publicly involved, it became clear that the Anglos were dominating the anti-Raza Unida candidates, both financially and in terms of voter support.

Yet an important reason the anti-Raza Unida Mexican candidates appeared to be under the control of the Anglos seems to be traceable to developments in the Mexican community under Raza Unida rule. It appears possible that a number of the moderate Anglos might have preferred different Mexican candidates. These few people in the community most likely realized that La Raza Unida could not be defeated without independent, respected Mexican candidates who were willing to risk alienating some Anglo support. But at the crucial level of candidate selection, no Mexicans who might have served as a fulcrum for a moderate counterattack were willing to run. One Anglo lamented about these leadership problems by saying of the Mexicans, "We've had them financed, but they are not interested."[111]

This dearth of powerful, respected opposition candidates seemed to be an outcome of La Raza Unida activities while in office, for in their first year of rule they had managed to solidify their position in the Mexican community. Their changes in the schools and the city, their concern for helping the poor and the migrants of the community, had meant that many Mexicans who were uncomfortable with some of the activities of the Raza Unida leadership nonetheless preferred them to what had existed before. Or, even if they didn't prefer La Raza Unida, these Mexicans realized that La Raza Unida had undertaken enormously popular reforms and that to run against them could only be done with extensive Anglo support. They also knew that to rely on Anglo support was to risk exposing themselves and their families to bitter personal attacks by Raza Unida supporters who would accuse them of being traitors, "vendidos," and men *sin pantalones*. [112] Thus the anti-Raza Unida coalition in the city was beset with serious organizational and leadership problems.

In contrast, the Chicano community was even better organized for the upcoming election than it had been in the months immediately following the school strike. The selection of candidates by Ciudadanos Unidos was an indication of their greater strength. Chosen to run for the school board with Eddie Treviño, who was up for re-election, was Rodolfo Palomo, the college-educated poverty worker who had also been appointed to the Urban Renewal Commission earlier in the year. Rudi Palomo was, like Gutiérrez, a local boy who had done well. Also like Gutiérrez, he was in his middle twenties, married, and the father of two small children. For the city-council position, Ciudadanos Unidos selected Roberto Gámez and José Talamántez to run with Francisco Benavides, who was seeking re-election. Both Gámez and Talamántez were local boys who had graduated from Crystal City high school, had received a college education, and were now teachers in the school system. [113] Talamántez also had worked with migrants in Wisconsin, had been active in adult education programs in Crystal City, and was a scout-master. Gámez had been active in the National Guard, and since 1968 had been working during the summer in various projects to help migrants in the Midwest. Gámez had also been active as a scout leader and had been elected secretary of the Mexican Chamber of Commerce when La Raza Unida won control of the organization from more conservative businessmen earlier in the year. Both Gámez and Talamántez were in their early thirties, were family men, and had worked in a number of activities designed to help the Mexicans of the community.

The selection of Talamántez and Gámez signified that Raza Unida was now able to draw upon the talent in the school system. As one member had noted, "We have had good people tied up in the school system for years, afraid to do anything because they knew they'd be fired." [114] With Raza Unida now in control of the schools, teachers who had long wanted substantial changes in the approach to Mexican children were able to act. Concomitant with these developments, teachers in the schools who supported the aims of La Raza Unida had organized an Educators in Action Committee, which was headed by council-candidate José Talamántez. Around 125 teachers, administrators, and school personnel were members of the group. Interestingly, the group included several of the new Anglo teachers that had been hired since the school strike. [115]

The Raza Unida candidates for the 1971 elections were thus considerably more experienced in school matters than were the Raza Unida candidates who had run with Gutiérrez in 1970. At the same time the men chosen were young family men who had been born and raised in Crystal City and had, like Gutiérrez, gone on to receive a college education. They were thus men who could serve as examples to school children and to the rest of the community that it was possible to escape the poverty cycle. They were not threatening types who seemed extremist or irresponsible to the majority of Mexican Americans in the community, old and young. They were not long-haired "Castroites" who dressed in fatigues, as some of the MAYO organization people elsewhere in the state did. They were, instead, reassuring family men who had done well. Because of this, the charges that the anti-La Raza Unida forces in the community were making concerning communist and alien influences seemed less credible. [116]

From the beginning the campaign was well organized on both sides. [117] Voter registration was at an all-time high and it was obvious that after a year of so many changes in the city and schools the turnout would be heavy. The anti-Raza Unida candidates moved further in the direction of acknowledging their ethnicity by taking out full-page Spanish advertisements in the *Zavala County Sentinel.* They pledged, with the help of God, to provide honest, businesslike leadership that would work for the betterment of all in the community and that would not discriminate against any segment of the community. But as everyone knew, regardless of all the Spanish ads, they were the candidates of the Anglos. At times it seemed that the Crystal City Citizens Committee, the anonymous group opposed to La Raza Unida, provided more thrust to the opposition than the candidates themselves. This watchdog group charged during the campaign that several thousand dollars was mysteriously missing from the school cafeteria fund, that the students coming from Asherton were illegally postponing their tuition payments to the school, that the school library contained pornographic literature, that the school had bungled on its payments of insurance premiums for the teachers, and that there was a serious discipline problem in the schools. The school authorities replied that cafeteria funds were missing because the federal funds were late in coming and that the school district had made its insurance payments in time to prevent the policies from lapsing. But these charges over administrative mismanagement and their answers were essentially peripheral to the much broader question of who would control the school, and for what purposes.

As for the "For Better Government" candidates themselves, it was not very clear where they stood—which changes in the schools they approved (if any), or what changes they would want to make in the city or schools if elected. An event late in the campaign emphasized their vulnerability to the charges of being dominated by Anglos and of being unwilling to discuss the issues confronting the schools. The Educators in Action

Committee, the group supporting La Raza Unida, announced that they would be holding a forum at the high school for all school-board candidates. Interested citizens were invited to come and hear all the candidates speak and to question them on their ideas for the schools. The two "For Better Government" candidates, however, never showed up for the meeting. To have gone would have forced them to confront La Raza Unida partisans, but at the same time their failure to show up allowed La Raza Unida to portray them as being both cowardly and uninterested in problems facing the schools. [118]

The last school-board meeting also proved to be both entertaining and beneficial to La Raza Unida. At this meeting Gutiérrez goaded Buddy Maedgen into a confrontation by announcing to the audience that Maedgen was one of those boycotting the payment of his school taxes and that he owed the school district $715.80. Gutiérrez then said that Maedgen was guilty of malfeasance in office and told Maedgen, "I'm not going to count your vote." This infuriated Maedgen, who stated that his tax status was none of Gutiérrez's business and demanded that his votes be recorded. At one point when Maedgen was speaking, however, a Mexican-American lady in the audience stood up and shouted, "Go ahead and pay your taxes and then you talk!" This whole episode delighted the Raza Unida partisans in the audience, and left the Anglos furious and even more embittered. They noted that Gutiérrez had recorded Maedgen's votes in executive sessions without any trouble, and charged that he was merely making a "show for the audience." [119] Further playing into La Raza Unida hands, Maedgen later read a prepared statement attacking the policies of the school board and endorsing the anti-La Raza Unida candidates.

Maedgen's outbursts and his participation in the tax boycott had already discredited him in the Mexican community. [120] But La Raza Unida further discredited him by obtaining Department of Agriculture statistics on farm subsidies in Zavala County. There they found that Maedgen had received $26,000 in farm subsidies in the previous year alone. Labeling this money "Gringo Welfare," La Raza Unida succeeded in embarrassing the Anglos and outraging them at the same time by equating farm subsidies to welfare. Not only was the tactic sound because the agricultur.l-subsidy program was based precisely upon the con-

cept of "getting something for nothing"; it was also uncomfortable to the Anglos because they had so often railed against
"welfare" and the "gimme philosophy."[121]

The Anglos, however, managed to create their own excitement as the election approached. Less than two weeks before
the election, the *Sentinel* editor ran the headline, "School Loses
Accreditation."[122]   At a glance it appeared that the worst fears
of the Chicanos had been realized and that charges by the
"Citizens Committee" had been vindicated. It appeared that the
school would no longer be accredited by the state of Texas and
that high-school graduates would be faced with severe handicaps
in trying to enter colleges. By reading the article carefully,
however, one could see that the school had lost its accreditation
with the Southern Association of Schools and Colleges, not
with the Texas Education Agency. And it had lost its accreditation not because of inadequacies or mismanagement of the
schools, but only because the district had not bothered to fill
out the forms necessary for continuing to be a member of the
association. Nevertheless, a flurry of activity was necessary to
explain the *Sentinel* story, every word of which was correct.
Superintendent Gonzales sent home with each school child a
letter of explanation accusing Dale Barker, the editor of the
Sentinel, and Wayne Hamilton, the school-board member who
had reported the loss of accreditation, of an "enormous dis-
service" to the community. [123]   Gonzales pointed out that the
Southern Association of Schools and Colleges had never done
anything for Crystal City, that it did not determine whether or
not a student could be admitted to college, and that less than
half of all high schools in the state of Texas were members of
the organization. The new administration had therefore decided
to let their membership in the organization drop rather than
continue to pay dues. Gonzales then explained that the school
system was still accredited by the Texas Education Agency, and
that this accreditation was important.

The greatest excitement of the campaign, however, occurred
as a result of the school-district's announcement in early March
that twenty-three teachers, all of them Anglos, would not have
their contracts renewed. [124]   This was approximately one-third of
all the Anglo teachers in the schools. A majority of these were
leaving under the board's new retirement policy which affected
teachers over sixty. But also included among the twenty-three

were several teachers not of retirement age who had been for years heartily disliked by many of the Mexican students and who were now vociferous in their opposition to La Raza Unida. Immediately this action became the central focus of the campaign. The Texas Classroom Teachers Association (TCTA), an organization of 45,000 teachers, acted so swiftly that their activity was clearly premised upon the upcoming school-board elections. Saying that several local members of their organization had requested an investigation, they immediately sent down a team of investigators from their Professional Rights and Responsibilities Committee. Whether they notified the superintendent before they arrived in Crystal City on March 29, five days before the election, is still a matter of dispute. Superintendent Gonzales claimed he was denied the "common courtesy" of being notified of their visit, but TCTA responded that Gonzales knew they were coming. [125] The investigating team talked to members of their local TCTA chapter and to some of the fired teachers and some students, but according to Gutiérrez, they "did not speak to Mexican-American school-board members, administrators, teachers, or students." [126]

Two days after their visit to Crystal City, the investigating team announced that they were recommending sanctions against the district because of "numerous deficiencies" and deplorable conditions existing in the district. [127] Thus on Thursday, April 1, two days before the school-board election, news of the TCTA action hit the papers. The *San Antonio Light* trumpeted in headline, "Schools Lashed in Crystal City." [128] At first La Raza Unida appeared surprised by the action and seemed unsure of what effect it would have on their campaign. As word began to spread of the manner in which the investigation had been conducted, however, Mexican Americans around the state began to flock to the defense of the Crystal City district, and blistering attacks were made upon the TCTA for their hasty, politically inspired visit. The head of the Mexican-American Legal Defense Fund in San Antonio, Ed Idar, sent a stinging letter to TCTA reminding them that for some time he had been urging an investigation of conditions in Karnes City, Texas. There over three hundred parents had signed a petition concerning harassment and intimidation of Mexican-American and Negro students by officials, administrators, and teachers, and had charged that the district was failing to employ Mexican-

American and Negro administrators, officials, teachers, and counselors. Idar noted that the Karnes City petition by parents represented conditions which, if true, would be clearly unconstitutional and would be far worse than that which had been alleged in Crystal City. Said Idar:

> . . . it would seem that the situation in Karnes City would also merit sanctions by TCTA. I am sure you agree with me in the old saying that what is sauce for the goose is also sauce for the gander.
>
> Accordingly, I hereby request that TCTA conduct an investigation of the Karnes City School System in the same spirit and with the same zeal that it has shown toward the Crystal City School District. . . .
>
> I am sure that TCTA does not desire to appear one-sided or to be in a position of singling-out only those districts where political developments have placed control of a school district in the hands of the Mexican-American.[129]

At the same time the president of Texans for the Educational Advancement of Mexican-Americans (TEAM), Josue González, charged that "the arbitrary and speedy action by the TCTA and its preoccupation with acquiring news coverage is an obvious attempt to influence the results of this Saturday's school-board elections."[130] The president of TEAM stated that his organization would "ask the Justice Department to review the racist-inspired harassment of Crystal City's elected officials and school administration."

The election-eve rally for La Raza Unida included the Lieutenant Governor of New Mexico, the highest-ranking Mexican American in state government in the country. Gutiérrez pointed out to the crowd that it was no accident that several notables were present for the rally, and that César Chávez had come to Crystal City in February. This had happened, he said, because Crystal City "was a symbol of La Raza."[131] Gutiérrez spoke in his usual cool, clear manner; but others in the crowd gave more typical harangues. Towards the end of the emotionally charged meeting there was a plea for no violence or trouble on election day, and the crowd was reminded that "the gringos" killed President Kennedy, Robert Kennedy, and Martin Luther King. "Who are the violent ones?" asked the master of ceremonies. The crowd shouted, "The gringos!"

On election day there was no violence and the voting went

smoothly. With La Raza Unida in control of the voting machinery, there appeared to be no attempt to impede the voting process. Ironically, Gutiérrez spent most of the day on duty in the army reserves. [132] Close to 3,000 people voted, which was far more than had ever voted in a presidential election and around 400 votes more than had voted in the 1970 election. With this even greater turnout, La Raza Unida candidates were swept into office with an increased margin. Three days later, La Raza Unida candidates won the city-council positions in another record turnout. They also increased their margin of victory, winning nearly two-to-one over the all-Mexican, Anglo-supported slate. As a further indication of the intense mobilization and polarization in the community, the three independent candidates drew hardly any votes at all. [133]

School Board		*City Council*	
Eddie Treviño	1,668	Francisco Benavides	1,649
Rodolfo Palomo	1,657	Roberto Gámez	1,626
		José Talamántez	1,622
Teodoro Muñoz	1,236		
Alfredo Ramón	1,218	Paulino Mata	911
		Santos Nieto	891
		Gilberto Salazar	890
		Roberto Cornejo	40
		Ralph García	14
		Mariana García	4

After a year in office, La Raza Unida thus solidified its control. It now had total control of the city council, and a five-to-two majority on the school board. This meant that for both the city and the schools, control would remain in their hands for at least two more years. More so now than ever, what had traditionally been considered an apathetic, powerless Mexican community was being transformed into an organized, mobilized majority fully in control of the political institutions of the city. Faced with the clear possibility of changes in the structure of the community and the schools, and then given the opportunity to pass judgment on these changes, Crystal City's Mexican community had turned out in phenomenal numbers to register approval.

7 chicano control and the future

The strengthening of La Raza Unida's control after a year in office was in marked contrast with the Cornejo years. Mexicans had been able to run the community without the aid of the local Anglos and without the degree of chaos and confusion that had followed the Cornejo victory. The election thus seemed to vindicate those Mexicans who had argued against the idea that a coalition with the Anglos was the only way Mexicans could improve their condition in the town.

For the same reason the election results were a bitter blow to the Anglos, in several ways more painful than the preceding year's disaster. After the school strike, many Anglos had realized that Gutiérrez and his radical band had been strengthened, but they consoled themselves with the belief that once the "Gutierristas" gained control, the resulting incompetence would be so obvious that a successful reaction would set in similar to the reaction against Cornejo in 1965. Through trying to remain relatively quiet and by allowing the "Gutierristas" to "dig their own grave," the Anglos had generally hoped that racial polarization in the town would subside and "responsible" Mexicans would rise up and (with Anglo help) throw out the irresponsible radicals.[1]

With the turmoil in the city and schools during the year of La

Raza Unida rule, as evidenced by numerous court suits and investigations and by the rebuke from the Texas Classroom Teachers Association, most Anglos in the community had remained guardedly optimistic that La Raza Unida could be thrown out of office. The Anglos were also encouraged by the response to the firing of the twenty-three Anglo teachers, which seemed to further unite all those people opposed to La Raza Unida.

Their hopes for a return to moderate rule were thus rudely shattered by the election results, and it was extremely hard for them to understand what had happened. Said one of the Anglos, "After all the turmoil in the school, obvious to even the densest of minds, you would think a fair number of voters would have been switched during the year. . . ." This Anglo then elaborated:

> So it continues to be a source of wonder why so many people will deliberately set about destroying the schools and the economy of their town. Of course there is the circumstance of continual harassment and intimidation, and many of these former peons will revert to type. Many voters are no doubt accounted for by that. Also they are known to vote aliens. It is not considered nice to demand proof of nationality in registering voters any more, and lists of aliens are not available. So it is easy enough to vote Mexican citizens. The balance is the inscrutables--the fairly well-to-do, fairly intelligent, educated people who persist in supporting the radicals.

Most Anglos in the community just could not believe that the changes being made in the schools and city were changes which the majority of citizens in the community urgently wanted. It was impossible for most Anglos to believe that, when contrasted with the decades of Anglo rule, the citizens preferred the new leadership and the changes. The Anglos appear instead to have persisted in believing only those things which would not radically overthrow their own belief structures. Thus they tended to believe that the Mexicans had been bought or had been intimidated, which was something they knew from their own experience was a way to win an election. To explain the phenomenal voter turnouts, one Anglo commented that La Raza Unida had "high-school students racing along the streets knocking on doors and persuading the occupants to go to the polls in transportation provided while studying a marked ballot." This was an accurate observation, as La Raza Unida did indeed have a very comprehensive network for getting people to the polls. But from this fact this same Anglo concluded, "They simply overwhelm the people, many of whom might not have the least interest in voting until pressured into it." Another cried, "They had them hypnotized!"

It was indeed ironic for Anglos to claim that Raza Unida was voting people who might have had no interest in voting, particularly after CASAA had so magnificently developed their own absentee-voting system for sick, elderly, and dependent Mexicans. This Anglo explanation again imputed to the opposition characteristics which Anglos had used in the past, and which seemed to be the only ones Anglos could understand and accept. *La Verdad*, the Spanish newspaper for Crystal City which was begun by Gutiérrez, commented on the Anglo feelings after the election:

> It is not possible to dispute the results of the elections, which were honest and open. La Raza Unida has obtained political control of this city through the democratic process of free elections, and this is what hurts the gringo like a kick in the ---, that the system which he has proudly presented as the best in the world has been used with success to destroy his tyranny.
>
> And if they fear what Chicano control means, it is because they have guilty consciences over the injustices which they have perpetrated on Chicanos for so many years.[2]

La Verdad also noted that "it seems that the gringos are incapable of losing political control without losing at the same time all sense of fair play and decency. . . .We know of at least six cases in which Chicanos who have supported La Raza Unida have had their salaries cut, have been demoted, or have been fired."*

Whatever the reasons for their crushing defeat, Crystal City Anglos now had to face the fact that La Raza Unida would be in control of the city and the schools for at least two more years. This led them to some painful and difficult choices, as

---

* These Anglo tactics emphasize the extent to which Crystal City seems to offer evidence that the "pluralist" model of politics and political competition is not applicable, at least to areas like Crystal City and much of South Texas.[3]

they realized that "the reputation of the town as an undesirable place to live [will keep] out those with enough energy and ambition to benefit the community." There was also an increased sense of isolation and bitterness among Anglos, and a resentment over the role federal programs were playing in the new government. It seemed as if their own government were abandoning them through providing support and jobs to the opposition. But many Anglos also continued to believe—much as United States policy makers seem to have believed about the Viet Cong—that the Mexicans couldn't go on like this forever, that they were bound in the end to be conquered by the superior might and intellectual skills of the Anglos, and that this was so because of the Mexican's inherent incapacity to rule without Anglo guidance. Said one Anglo in the wake of the defeat, "The city is bound to be on the brink of a crisis, if not complete collapse."[4] The city simply *had* to be in this condition after a year of "irresponsible" Mexican rule.

Conditions in the town thus produced continued polarization, with Anglos increasingly aware that their methods of regaining control were not working, and with the Mexicans more and more successful in establishing Crystal City as a beachhead and model for Chicano power in the Southwest.

Following the spring elections of 1971, most Anglos withdrew their children from the Crystal City schools and sent them to nearby communities or to a newly established private school, "open to all races and religious groups" and "free of politics and harassment by La Raza."[5] By the fall of 1971 less than twenty Anglos remained in the public-school system.

At the same time, relations between the school district and state educational authorities became more strained. In May the State Board of Education upheld Education Commissioner Edgar's decision to nullify the ousting of Briggs and demanded that the district pay him the $60,000 guaranteed him by the Anglo board in 1970.[6] Resentment and anger over the Texas Classroom Teacher Association's sanctions against the district resulted in a court suit by the board against the TCTA. At the same time the board realized that the organization was doing all it could to hurt the district, through sending out notices to teacher placement organizations and others to tell them of the "deplorable conditions" in Crystal City. Gutiérrez was quoted as saying that the sanctions would hurt the Crystal City public-school system in retaining and recruiting qualified teachers and that the bad publicity could also affect funding of certain federal assistance programs. "We cannot escape getting smeared by all this stuff," he commented, and added that "some teachers will wait until the last minute to move out."[7]

On another legal front the city was stymied in its attempt to annex and tax the huge Del Monte Corporation. At first it seemed likely that the city would win at least a partial victory, because the 1970 agreement between the lame-duck city council and Del Monte over not annexing the plant involved what to Raza Unida was a clear conflict of interest. The city attorney and a city councilman at the time of the agreement were both being salaried by Del Monte. But after three years of legal appeals, a federal jury ruled that the city did not have the right to annex and tax the corporation.[8] Thus it seemed likely that the huge Del Monte corporation would continue to pay no city taxes, at least until the seven-year contract expires in 1977.

The city also found itself stymied in its attempt to move against the all-Anglo country club, which was leasing property from the city. In 1971 the city padlocked the premises, claiming that the club was in violation of Title IV of the Civil Rights Act of 1964 since the club had admitted no Mexican Americans or Negroes to membership. The country club, however, launched a suit against the city to recover its property, and the city followed with a counter-suit. This battle again was drawn out, but the city seemed to be losing its fight to have the lease declared invalid.[9]

In spite of these legal restrictions on Raza Unida activity, changes in city and school personnel continued. At the end of April City Manager Richey resigned his post to make preparations for attending Harvard Law School. Although he stated that he expected to return after Law School, few Raza Unida supporters doubted that his energy and organization skills would be missed. Richey was replaced by Francisco Rodríguez, a former Crystal City native who had attended college in Wisconsin and had been Richey's assistant for several months. [10]

In other personnel changes La Raza Unida moved to solidify its control over the city. When new members sympathetic to La Raza Unida were appointed by the council to the Housing Authority Board, the Housing Director—a Mexican American widely respected by Anglos because she had "pulled herself up

by her own bootstraps"—was ousted. The council selected as
the new director Eddie Treviño, who had been demoted by Del
Monte and was on the edge of being fired ever since he sided
with La Raza Unida in April of 1970.[11] The city's corporation
court judge, Salvador Galván, who had been a city councilman
on the Holsomback ticket that was defeated by Cornejo in
1963, was also ousted. Julian Salas, the unsuccessful candidate
for county judge in 1970, was appointed in Galván's place.[12]
The city also launched an investigation of their volunteer fire
department, amid charges that the all-Anglo firemen had refused to admit several Chicanos who had applied to join the
force.[13]

The 1971 elections also cleared the way for La Raza Unida to
appoint its members to the Urban Renewal Commission. Thus
the compromise with federal authorities following the attempt
to appoint Raza Unida members in December of the preceding
year ended. But La Raza Unida, although it ousted Elvira
Galván as Housing Director for the city, made no similar move
against Sam Anderson. Although they clearly had the legal right
to oust him, they remained fearful of federal reaction should
they oust the powerful and widely respected urban renewal
director. They were particularly fearful that the Nixon Administration, already looking for areas to cut back on urban-renewal
and federal-housing projects, might use the firing of Anderson
as another pretext to stop the urban renewal program.[14] But
with control of the Urban Renewal Commission, they did begin
to limit Anderson's authority over hirings and firings in the
agency. And when this happened, Anderson and eleven of the
thirteen members of his staff resigned. As his replacement, La
Raza Unida hired Juan Cotera, a Chicano activist who had
received his education at the University of Texas in architecture
and urban planning.[15]

What long-term effect the resignation of Anderson — who
took nearly all his staff with him to the South Texas community of Alice — would have on the future of the urban renewal
program in Crystal City was unclear. But Cotera did proceed to
reorient the program in light of criticisms leveled against urban
renewal by La Raza Unida, although he had to be careful to
work with federal authorities.[16] Contracts began going to local
Chicano construction firms, which were formed in response to
the Raza Unida takeover.

The city and school elections of the spring of 1972 were less
heated than the previous races, as control of either unit was not
at stake because of staggered terms. La Raza Unida, however,
won by the greatest margins yet, electing all its candidates by
over two-to-one margins.[17] The previous autumn the party had
made the decision to run candidates statewide, and thus much
of their political effort was spent developing the party elsewhere.[18] In September, 1972, the party hosted its first national
convention. Delegates from around the state and from over a
dozen other states met in El Paso, organized the party struc-
turally, and formed a *Congreso de Aztlán* to serve as the party's
main body. José Angel Gutiérrez served as the party's temporary
chairman, and was later elected director of the *Congreso*. In
organizing and leading such a national movement, Gutiérrez was
clearly hoping to expand the impact and size of the party far
beyond Crystal City and the Winter Garden area.

Although La Raza Unida and José Angel Gutiérrez received
their greatest national attention through this meeting, much of
the press was merely interested in how the movement would
relate to the presidential election between McGovern and Nixon. When La Raza Unida voted not to endorse either candidate,
it was considered a victory for Nixon. Shortly thereafter rumors
circulated that Raza Unida had earlier reached an understanding
with the Nixon Administration that they would urge their
followers not to vote Democratic in return for administration
support of federal-aid measures in Raza Unida controlled areas.
Whatever the truth of the rumors—and it seems quite likely that
there was at least some kind of understanding reached—they
proved an ironic answer to those who had argued that Raza
Unida as a third party would have no bargaining power with the
established interests running the two major parties.[19]

Although Raza Unida candidates ran in other states in the
November elections, the party was most successful in Texas,
where Ramsey Muñiz, the party's candidate for governor, drew
more than six percent of the votes cast (over 200,000) and very
nearly caused the Republican candidate, Henry Grover, to be
elected.[20] The other statewide Raza Unida candidates, however, did considerably worse.[21] Altogether La Raza Unida had
forty-nine candidates running in the state, with most seeking
county office. Seven were successful: two in La Salle County
(Cotulla), and five in Zavala County. In fact, in Zavala County

the party was finally able to crack the Anglo domination of the county, in one of the toughest and most bitter battles to date.[22] Unlike the 1970 county elections, where the party had been unable to get on the ballot, in 1972 Raza Unida narrowly elected Rey Pérez county attorney, defeating long-time Anglo leader R. A. Taylor. And Sheriff C. L. Sweeten was at last beaten, falling to José Serna by a larger margin. The sole Democratic victory in county elections was that of a Mexican American, Martha Cruz, who defeated Raza Unida's nominee Armando Bermea for Tax Assessor-Collector.[23]

The county elections represented an expansion of Raza Unida strength, but the party still did not have control of the county. That could not come before 1974, when County Judge Irl Taylor and two other commissioners would be up for re-election. The closeness of the vote surprised many in the party who had hoped Raza Unida would win bigger victories. The fact that Anglos controlled the election machinery, and that there was perhaps growing resentment among some Chicanos over the role of Ciudadanos Unidos and the party leadership, together seem to have accounted for the close outcome. Two disputes within the party had left serious scars. Mike Pérez, a school-board member, became the first Raza Unida elected official to break with the party, charging that the leadership was becoming too powerful. Shortly thereafter his dance hall in Carrizo Springs burned down under mysterious circumstances. And in the month before the November election, five of the seven-man police force quit over the decision by the city council, operating on a recommendation by Ciudadanos Unidos, to suspend one policeman for alleged misconduct involving excessive brutality. The police force charged that this was political interference in the running of the department.[24]

Expansion of La Raza Unida's base beyond Crystal City was slow and tedious, as even gaining a foothold in the county required enormous mobilization. Shortly thereafter, however, the school administration decided to coordinate its bilingual and bicultural program, and to move toward the concept of teaching Mexican-American children to read and write Spanish before they learned to read and write English. There were several educational theories to support this method, even from the stand-point of learning *English* more thoroughly, but the proposals quickly became controversial.[25] Many parents in the com-

munity were fearful that their children would never learn to
speak, read, or write English, and although the school authorities and Raza Unida officials tried to assure them that this
would not be the case, the officials' failure to set a definite time
for when children would switch from Spanish to English caused
many parents to continue to be deeply disturbed.[26] The spring
1973 school-board elections consequently became another tor-
rid affair. Significantly, all the incumbents on the city council
and school board, including Gutiérrez, chose not to seek re-
election. Their stated reason was to allow others in the community a chance to serve, and thus avoid the habit, so prevalent
among South Texas Anglos, of staying in office for decades.
The results showed that La Raza Unida had lost considerable
ground since the 1972 election, although they again emerged
victorious.[27] Rudy Palomo, an old friend of Gutiérrez, was
elected the new school-board president, and Ventura Gonzales
became the new mayor.

As this discussion of electoral struggles and victories by Raza
Unida during 1972 and 1973 indicates, changes continued with
La Raza Unida in control. By the school year 1972-1973, about
two-thirds of the school faculty and the entire administration
were Chicano.[28] Of the 119 members of the 1973 graduating
class, 116 were Chicanos. With the almost complete withdrawal
of local Anglos, the public schools had thus become an even
more powerful bastion of "chicanismo," and numerous grants
from both public and private groups, including a Carnegie Grant
to develop Chicano administrators, kept the district expanding.
With the dismissal in 1973 of a suit against the issuance of
bonds to finance new school buildings, the district was also set
to launch a massive building program.

There were undercurrents of resentment, however, among
some of the school teachers and others in the community over
the salaries being drawn by those administering many of the
new programs. And still others felt that these administrative
positions, which went rather consistently to the Raza Unida
leadership (both husbands and wives), should be dispersed to
more people in the community.

The schools also had to face the question of how much
discipline and how much freedom to allow. Many of the children had taken the school strike to mean an end to punishment
and discipline, and most of the Raza Unida teachers and admin-

istrators wished to allow the students greater freedom. But where to draw the line proved difficult, and teachers, students, and parents found themselves divided over this question. After several years in control of the schools it seemed that the board, administrators, and teachers were gradually moving toward a more traditional policy regarding educational freedom and discipline.[29]

Even with the special educational programs, enormous problems remained. Some migrant and nonmigrant children, for example, continued to suffer from the economic pressure to work when there were jobs.[30] Improvement and the continuation of problems thus coexisted in the schools.

The Supreme Court decision in the *Rodriguez* case on school financing, which was brought by the Chicano-controlled Edgewood school district in San Antonio, was a blow to Crystal City, just as it was a blow to all poverty-stricken areas of the country.[31] Although a statewide protest was organized to try to force the legislature to restructure school financing anyway, so that poor areas and areas with low tax bases could get greater state support, the legislature did not respond.

Attempts to develop a massive health clinic, treating both physical and mental illnesses, proved to be arduous. Although important steps were taken, the health-clinic proposal ran into opposition from the state governor and from many doctors. After the 1972 election, the Nixon administration wished to disband the Office of Economic Opportunity and cut back on social services generally, and the funding and development of the clinic continued to be a source of worry. The goal, however, was not only to improve health services and facilities in the area—which were in dire need of improvement—but to provide needed jobs for many and to use the program as a further source for training Raza Unida leaders.[32]

The question of a health clinic, and other federal and foundation aid, took on greater importance as the city continued to be unable to attract industry. With unemployment continuing as a severe problem, the community found itself enormously dependent on outside aid for improvement. The precariousness of the local economy thus continued unchanged.

Nevertheless, a series of disparate, yet related, events underscored the power of the Chicanos and La Raza Unida in Crystal City. In the fall of 1971 the local Catholic priest, who had been

critical of La Raza Unida, was replaced by one far more in
sympathy with "la causa." In January, 1972, a "huelga" occurred when one of the local packing sheds lowered wages from
$1.60 to $1.30 an hour.[33] Many people from the community
and schools (including the new Catholic priest) journeyed to the
fields to picket, and the strike ended successfully when the
owner agreed to restore wages. Another important event occurred in 1972 when President Luis Echevarría of Mexico gave
Crystal City a bust of Benito Juárez, which was dedicated with
much fanfare. Next to Juárez were inscribed the words, "El
respeto al derecho ageno es la paz."[34]

Episodes such as these—involving both great symbolism and
clear evidence of political power—emphasized the transition
that had occurred in the town.[35] The city was changing from
the "Spinach Capital of the World" to the "Chicano Capital."

an assessment of the anglo failure

All these changes and developments emphasized again that
the Anglos had, temporarily if not permanently, completely lost
control of the politics of the town. The polarization of the races
in Crystal City and the strength of the reactive cultural nationalism in the Mexican community had bewildered nearly all the
Anglos in the town.[36] Like colonizers, most Crystal City Anglos had grown up assuming that their culture was superior and
had taken for granted their right to rule. And like colonizers,
they ended up being amazed that the numerically dominant
"natives" should question the superiority of Anglo rule. But in
defense of the Crystal City Anglo it is important to realize that
what they had assumed and tried to implement in Crystal City,
particularly concerning making rewards to the Mexican population dependent upon acculturation, was in many ways the
essence of what the dominant groups in American society seem
to have done for centuries.

Although there were several important differences between
the Crystal City Anglo and the American Anglo-Saxon, perhaps
the greatest is simply that the American Anglo-Saxon won
whereas the Crystal City Anglo failed. It should not be forgotten that, as Sheldon Wolin has commented, history has been
written by the victors; thus what the Anglo-Saxon in America
has done—in teaching everyone to speak English and to give up

his native language, in integrating and acculturating to a large extent the various white ethnic groups which came to America—is either accepted as *fait accompli* or commended as an example of nation-building for others to emulate.[37] But the failure of the Anglos in Crystal City has made it easy for them to be condemned for trying to do many of the things which seem to constitute much of the essence of the American system.

In truth, the differences between the Crystal City Anglo and the American Anglo-Saxon were probably not so great as the differences in the population with which each had to work. The size and tenacity of the local Mexican population made them different from the millions of European immigrants who voluntarily left their countries to come to the New World. One might argue that the Anglos of Crystal City set up more barriers for the Mexican population than did Anglos elsewhere in the country, but many Mexicans also did not want to be "Anglicized," and they were buttressed in their cultural orientations by having Mexico just across the river and by viewing this area of Texas as being historically their own.

Bearing these points in mind, it seems that Crystal City Anglos have been subjected to unusual and certainly multifaceted attacks, often by people who to them must seem hypocrites in their criticism. Some of the most damaging criticisms of Crystal City Anglos have come from outside newspapers. These papers are usually quite conservative on hometown matters, but they seem to find it much easier to be "liberals" when it comes to other towns. The *San Antonio Express*, in an editorial entitled "Crystal City Mexican-Americans Making an Inevitable Change," commented that "other South Texas communities made the transition from tradition-[al] . . . Mexican-American majorities who accepted Anglo-American domination as the way it was. Crystal City is late making the change."[38] To Crystal City Anglos, if the *San Antonio Express* had really wanted to criticize people who refused to acknowledge the rightful place of Mexicans in American society, the paper could very easily have looked at a number of other towns in South Texas. There they would have found some towns with "no racial problems" at all, but only because the Mexicans were without the resources to fight or because they constituted a permanent minority of the town's population.

Crystal City Anglos have argued forcefully that many surrounding towns have done far less to speed racial integration, to
find and attract Mexican candidates and supporters, than did
Crystal City Anglos after the 1963 revolt. Yet because Crystal
City revolts have occurred and have succeeded, Crystal City has
received far more attention than these other communities that
are both more stable and more despotic. One Crystal City Anglo
noted that upon meeting other Anglos in South Texas, these
Anglos express amazement at how conditions in Crystal City
could be so bad. He charged, however, that these outside Anglos
have never bothered to notice that conditions in their own
home towns might be far worse and that Mexicans might
encounter far more discrimination there than in Crystal City. In
his report on the school boycott, the Reverend Kenneth Newcomer noted:

> In conversations with people of other communities, I sense
> an enormous feeling of relief on their part that all of this
> conflict has taken place in my town and not theirs. And I
> marvel that this conflict has gone on for three months—and
> yet I see no evidence that other school boards, other adminis-
> trations, and other concerned citizens have related these
> painful experiences of ours to themselves to the point of
> implementing constructive planning regarding the issues
> raised here.[39]

In further defense of the Crystal City Anglo, it seems necessary to point out that the Anglos and the Mexicans of Crystal
City met under very unequal circumstances and that their
inequalities had existed long before the town was ever founded.
That is, Crystal City Anglos did not *cause* the inequalities
between the two groups, inequalities that stemmed from two
cultures widely different in levels of technology and moderniza-
tion. Crystal City Anglos were there to profit from conditions
of inequality which already existed. It is also clear that before
either of the revolts in Crystal City occurred, the Mexican
population had been making some improvement, both in absolute terms and in relation to the Anglo minority. How much
this improvement occurred because of or in spite of the Anglos
is a matter of dispute, but the improvement should not be
forgotten. This obvious betterment has meant that Anglos have
been all the more bewildered by the polarization that has

occurred in the community. To them there had been obvious signs of improvement in race relations in the community and of an increase in Anglo tolerance toward Mexicans, at least toward those who were becoming more like the Anglos. Yet in their view, their own increasing tolerance was met by increasing intolerance in the Mexican community.

Their ultimate failure led them to much soul-searching and bitterness, and in this process it became clear that many local Anglos either did not understand some of the basic tenets of democracy, or that if they did, they rejected the concept. Said one Anglo matron, "Something is wrong with the government when we allow them to overthrow the government."[40] She seemed unable to recognize the distinction between personnel in office and the offices themselves, and that being able to "overthrow" the personnel in office is one of the essential features of democracy. But after the many years of rule by Anglos in Crystal City, this confusion was perhaps understandable. Another Anglo was more aware of what was happening and its relation to democracy. Commenting on the striking students, she said, "What they're complaining about is the selections based on grades or ability. . . . Well, if you're outnumbered, as we are, that's the only way you can stand a chance. If everything went by student vote, we wouldn't have a chance in the world. . . . They'd be chosen by the majority."[41]

Another Anglo, more sophisticated than many, commented:

> We've got to change tactics to fit these unscrupulous people. We've got to be as unscrupulous as they are! The weakness of democracy is that it allows communistically-oriented groups to work their way into the system. And some in the Chicano movement are communist, like Castro in Cuba. . . . Gutiérrez is the same kind of personality as Castro. He knows that armed rebellion won't work here, but another way for them to succeed is to tax people out of existence. They can make the system work for them. . . . I'm tired of democracy. We need a benevolent dictator. This experience is making us all move to the right.[42]

This same person commented bitterly about the role of the federal government in the Crystal City revolts and was particularly furious at the Department of Justice and the FBI, which he claimed had done nothing when Anglos were fired from their jobs because "they aren't Brown enough." He then commented, "As it turns out through the Justice Department, only Gutierristas have civil rights."[43]

There was thus among the Anglo community of Crystal City tremendous alienation from their own system of government, both local and national. Those who didn't understand what democracy involved tended to think the whole Raza Unida movement was antidemocratic. Those who did understand what democracy involved tended to *be* antidemocratic. Many social scientists have argued that the masses don't understand what democracy involves and that in important ways they are antidemocratic.[44] In Crystal City, however, many of the Anglos seemed to be fundamentally antidemocratic because of the experiences they had endured and because they had always been a privileged minority.

Not only did alienation from local and national government, pessimism, and bitterness flourish in the Anglo community; Crystal City Anglos also had to suffer from having failed so obviously. All the Anglos in the town and in the area became "Monday-morning quarterbacks," and this led to great divisiveness within the Anglo community over who or what to blame.

Although hindsight does reveal that the Anglos committed some glaring blunders, it does not show that their errors were foolish ones, obviously destined to fail. We have argued from the beginning that much of the reason for the explosive situation in Crystal City lay more in the history of the community than in what any one Anglo or group of Anglos did at the time of the revolts. The history of settlement of the community—the economic base in agriculture and its concomitant land use—led to a heavy preponderance of poor Mexican Americans in the community. This economic base (more specifically the seasonal nature of agriculture in the area) produced migrant workers who could be more easily mobilized for radical politics than permanent residents of the community.* And the introduction

---

* The reasons for this seem to relate to what S. M. Lipset and William Kornhauser have observed in the socioeconomic basis for radical politics.[45] The isolation and geographic mobility of migrant farm workers means that they have few ties to the existing order. Thus once organized, they tend to be radical. Their suffering from recurrent unemployment and underemployment may have further radicalized them, as Maurice Zeitlin found in the case of Cuban workers in similar situations.[46]

of outside capital and management through the Del Monte plant (and especially its decision to allow unionization of its packing plant) changed the balance of resources between the Anglos and Mexicans in the community. The combined set of factors produced a community in South Texas which was more nearly unique than general.

But unquestionably there were Anglo mistakes which allowed the Chicanos to capitalize on this potentially explosive situation. Given these conditions which affected the town, and with the benefit of hindsight, the main mistake the Anglo community made was in not seeking out and recruiting more Mexican Americans for leadership. If they had done this, they might have developed a stable middle class which would have served as a buffer against the migrants. By waiting until after the Mexicans had already been mobilized to begin serious efforts to develop Mexican leadership, the Anglo activity could not produce the gratitude and indebtedness among Mexicans which most likely would have been the result had the Anglos begun these efforts more earnestly before the Mexicans became organized. Because their activity in trying to develop a "responsible" Mexican leadership occurred in concert with an equally strong effort to prevent the rise of more militant Mexicans, the Anglos created the impression that they were more interested in holding the Mexican down than in helping him. And their activities led to the conclusion that Mexicans could gain more by working against the Anglo than with him. This political situation proved fertile for the strong community organization which was premised upon the belief that Anglos would give in only through pressure, not through moral suasion or an appeal to reason.

Although hindsight leads us to this conclusion, it seems clear that very powerful arguments could have been (and indeed may have been) raised by Anglos against engaging in activities to develop a solid Mexican leadership. Crystal City Anglos, like South African whites, have numbered slightly less than twenty

---

Migrant workers can be contrasted with those Mexican Americans who are tied to a particular piece of land which their *jefe* or *patrón* would own. Tenants and sharecroppers would be far more susceptible to control, as indeed those in the outlying parts of Zavala County were. Ozzie Simmons has noted this distinction in South Texas, as did Eric Wolf generally.[47]

percent of the population and from the beginning have been a highly privileged minority. If the community's Anglos had engaged in compromises and intermarriage with the Mexican elements of the community at the outset, as Anglos had done in older towns along the border, then a policy of trying to reach out and develop Mexican leadership would probably not have led to uncontrollable results. But to be in the situation of a Crystal City Anglo was to find oneself, like a South African white, surrounded by a racial majority of semiliterate, politically inexperienced people. To begin to make political contact with this group, to begin to give them entrance into the workings of the society, would under any circumstances have been highly risky. And it would have meant that, even if the best possible results had occurred, the Anglos would almost surely have eventually had to relinquish control of the community. Given this situation, one cannot say that it was irrational for Crystal City Anglos to be more interested in retrenchment than in compromise, for the stakes from the beginning were extremely high, involving very nearly the Anglo's whole way of life.

One might argue that after the first revolt in 1963 the Anglos should have realized that they could no longer rule as they had before, and that they should have worked to defuse and depoliticize any development which threatened to get out of hand. But the Anglos thought they had done this in the years since 1963. Race relations seemed to be improving, Mexicans were being consulted on more and more matters, and by 1969 the community seemed more stable than at any time since 1963. Thus after all the concessions that the Anglos felt they had made, by the spring and summer of 1969 it seemed to them impossible that the Mexican-American community could be repoliticized.

Not only should these points be borne in mind; we should also recall that both revolts occurred at times which were difficult to predict. That is, in neither instance did it appear that the Anglos could have had clear and incontrovertible evidence that a successful revolt was about to occur. The Anglos could not have been prepared for the unprecedented Teamster and PASO involvement in community politics, and in the spring and summer of 1969 it was not obvious that denying the students their demands was playing into the hands of the radicals. By negating the concessions and by issuing a strong statement on what would happen if any further attempts at agitation were to occur in the schools, the board thought it was handling the situation in the best possible way. It seems to have been a very reasonable gamble to try to crush the incipient organization through intransigence. This had worked before, as for example when some of the protests over the poverty program had ended in failure, when high-school students had protested over discrimination in the high school in the late fifties, and even when Diana Palacios and her supporters had protested the discriminatory nature of cheerleader selection the year before. And this intransigence has continued to work in many other places in South Texas.

The logic behind this intransigence has been explained clearly by Michael Parenti in his examination of the successful defeat of an attempt to build a community organization in Newark, New Jersey. In noting that the incipient ghetto community organization was defeated even on the most reasonable of demands, such as on the demand for a traffic light at a corner where several people had been injured, Parenti concluded that the political officials' "unwillingness to make tangible allocations is due less to any consideration of immediate political expenditure than to their concern that present protests are but a prelude to more challenging and more costly demands."[48] He noted that a victory even on some things as reasonable as a traffic light "might have strengthened precisely the kind of oppositional activity that Newark officials wanted to discourage."[49] Instead he noted that the ghetto residents' defeat reinforced the status quo by leading them to conclude once again that there was no use trying to better their condition since they saw no opportunity for effective protest.[50]

The decision by the school board to nullify the superintendent's April, 1969, agreement with the students was without doubt prefaced in large part on the hope that through sternness the students and their supporters would return to apathy. The board also feared that by giving in on these points, authorities would merely be whetting the appetites of the students. Only with the return of Gutiérrez and his conscious attempt to lay the foundations of a community organization did the balance of power between the two groups appear to shift. Thus even with these explosive preconditions in Crystal City, it seems likely that the Anglos could have maintained power had it not been for extremely sophisticated and astute leadership within the

Chicano community. And even had the Anglos had the foresight to realize quickly that mass mobilization under astute leadership was occurring, it would most likely be demanding too much of any people to argue that they should have capitulated as quickly and as painlessly as possible. Most Anglos were so emotionally involved in the situation that even if they could have been convinced that a showdown would lead to their defeat they would still have preferred martyrdom to compromise. After all, they could quickly have argued, was the Alamo really a defeat or a victory?

The result of this policy of intransigence, however, meant that in the end their capitulation was all the more crushing, and their authority and legitimacy as the community's rulers were destroyed during the two-week school boycott.

"containment" of crystal city

The example of Uvalde, Texas, a community only forty miles north of Crystal City, proved a few months later that intransigence in the face of organized opposition can in different circumstances be an extremely successful tactic against the Chicano movement. In the aftermath of the Chicano victory in Crystal City, euphoria set in over much of South Texas, with Chicanos elsewhere wanting to duplicate the feats of "Cristal." Thus when the Uvalde school board refused to renew the contract of a Mexican-American teacher who had run for office, students launched a boycott.[51] While organizing around the firing of this Mexican-American teacher, the Chicano students demanded many of the things the students in Crystal City had wanted. Although the Chicano community of Uvalde united to an extent never before known in the town, and although several hundred students participated in a school strike which lasted longer than the Crystal City strike, their protest ended in disaster. The board refused to give in, and all the striking students were flunked.[52]

There were several important differences between the two strikes. Crystal City's occurred at a tactically stronger time of the year, near the Christmas holidays rather than near the end of the school year. Second, and at least as important, the Chicano community in Uvalde constituted slightly less than one-half of the voting population of the town. Thus Chicanos alone could not take control of the community, even though in the school system they constituted slightly over sixty per-cent.[53] Also, the Uvalde community apparently did not under-go the preparation in terms of community organization and parent-student cohesion which the Crystal City Chicano com-munity had received.[54] This latter point, however, may have been less important than the second point, which was that the Anglo community knew they could continue to rule indefinite-ly so long as they remained united; they did not, in other words, need any Mexican support in order to stay in office.

The Anglo victory in Uvalde was not without certain conse-quences, however. Racial polarization in the community in-creased and Chicanos became more and more resentful because they were not able to crack the system. Because of the strike activity, the federal government also became involved. In Sep-tember of 1970 the Department of Health, Education, and Welfare issued a report which was strongly in sympathy with the Mexican-American community's demands.[55] But the board continued to refuse to negotiate with the students or with the parents, and conditions remained at a deadlock, with the Anglos on top and the Mexicans on the bottom. At the first school-board election following the strike, one of the leaders of the Mexican-American movement ran for the board. She was beaten nearly ten to one in a turnout which saw very few Mexicans go to the polls. The Mexican community apparently realized they were a minority (albeit one constituting over forty percent of the voters of the community), and knew that her race was doomed to failure. Her defeat, however, allowed Anglos to claim that the protest movement had been crushed and that their own intransigence had proved to be the wisest policy in discrediting the Mexican leadership which had arisen during the school crisis.

The example of Uvalde thus indicates that intransigence can be a very successful strategy for Anglo communities to continue to use in much of South Texas. It failed in Crystal City ultimately because of the different demographic ratio of Anglos to Mexicans. That is, the potential for a Mexican-American victory, defined here in sheer numerical strength, had always existed in Crystal City. But it does not exist in most places in South Texas.

All this, and examples elsewhere—including the Winter Gar-

den towns of Carrizo Springs and Cotulla—would seem to indicate that Anglos have many options open to them, depending
upon their own abilities, the abilities of the Mexicans, and the
skill and sagacity of the local Mexican leadership.

the uniqueness of crystal city

The foregoing thus indicates that it does not seem inevitable
that La Raza Unida or militant Chicanos will take over South
Texas. On the contrary, the results so far seem to indicate that
the success story of Crystal City, in both 1963 and 1969, was
dependent upon characteristics which have not been at all
common to South Texas: a homogeneous (and largely migrant)
Mexican-American community lacking "upper-class Spanish"
leaders; an Anglo community accustomed to running the town
almost completely on their own; a history of settlement which
led to a heavy numerical preponderance of Mexican Americans
over Anglos; the presence of an international union; and lastly
the development of extremely intelligent, politically-astute
Mexican leadership. All these characteristics which were involved in one or both of the Crystal City revolts do not seem to
be present in great quantities across South Texas. Where many
of the characteristics are present—as in the towns of Carrizo
Springs and Cotulla and in the new towns of the Valley—it
seems that the lack of any one of them, such as the presence of
politically-astute leadership, can frustrate the entire movement.

As we noted earlier, in most areas of South Texas, including
the large cities of San Antonio, El Paso, and Corpus Christi,
Mexican Americans do not constitute even a slight majority of
the voting population. And in those areas, such as Brownsville
and Rio Grande City, where Mexican Americans do constitute
an overwhelming numerical majority, we have noted that, rather
than a homogeneous Mexican-American community, there have
tended to be a few old, established Mexican families who have
played important parts in governing. In these communities
Anglos have been accustomed to ruling in concert with upper-
class Mexicans rather than ruling completely on their own.

We also noted the scarcity of unions in South Texas and the
rather dismal prospect for unionization in South Texas. This
further reinforces the uniqueness of Crystal City. The most
serious attempt at unionization was the attempt by the United

Farm Workers to organize workers in the Rio Grande Valley in 1967-1968.[56] This ended in failure when Mexico permitted strikebreakers to cross over to work the fields and when the Texas Rangers and local law officials had most of the strike leadership put in jail.[57]

Franklin Garcia, a labor organizer for the Meat Cutters Union in San Antonio, has been successful in organizing unions in several small communities in South Texas and in getting his union men elected to office, but his struggle has been bitter and constant.[58] He has spent several months in jails and has often had to battle for years to achieve union recognition. On the prospects for bringing changes to South Texas, he has commented, "I don't see any solution." In noting the amount of finances and the toughness it takes to conduct a successful strike in South Texas, Garcia has remarked that in this extremely hostile area an international union is a "necessary evil" because of the need for outside resources. He has also noted that for the same amount of resources "unions can get ten times as many people organized in New York or California as they can get in South Texas" and that for his union in particular, the men he has been able to get organized in his years of work will never be able to repay what the International Meat Cutters has already put into organizing efforts in South Texas.

Ray Shafer of the Teamsters in San Antonio, and Ray Marshall, a professor of Labor Economics at the University of Texas, seemed equally skeptical of the possibility for a strong union movement in South Texas.[59] And of course, even if the union movement were to spread in South Texas, the possibility would remain that the unions might side with management rather than with Chicanos, as the Teamsters have recently done in Crystal City. Thus, as Franklin Garcia noted, "Crystal City is a rarity."

Only in the development of politically astute leadership would the future for South Texas Mexican Americans seem to augur well. With the gradual educational upgrading of the Mexican-American population, Chicanos are becoming increasingly self-confident and knowledgeable and are developing tactics of community organization. Concerning this important characteristic of the second Crystal City revolt, then, it seems that this necessary but not sufficient condition for the revolt will spread to other communities in South Texas.

Even on this condition, however, the development of political leadership would not occur without a serious effort and much opposition. The Raza Unida mayor of Cotulla, for example, found himself unemployed and unable to find work after his election, even though he was qualified to be a teacher.[60] The basic problem facing those who wish to expand the Chicano movement in South Texas was noted by Albert Peña, the former Bexar County Commissioner (representing the West Side of San Antonio), who of all big-city Mexican-American leaders in Texas sympathized most with the Raza Unida movement. Peña remarked, "It is so difficult for leadership to stay in these small towns" even if they are local, indigenous leaders, because they cannot find jobs. Referring to Anglo tactics, he commented, "They cut off your leadership."[61] Given this political, social, and economic situation of tremendous inequality between Anglo and Mexican American, the need for outside funds to support and protect community organizers while they are in the field would thus appear absolutely essential. For even in Crystal City (which has had a base far more favorable to organization than most other communities), the Teamsters Union and PASO, and later the outside support given to Gutiérrez and his organization, all seemed to be critical for starting in motion the process of organization and for preventing it from being derailed by the greater resources and greater skills of the Anglos.

There is a further problem facing the development of leadership among the Mexican-American people of South Texas. The younger, better-educated, and more radical leadership that are likely to spearhead the Chicano movement are separated from the mass of Mexican Americans by their education and by their greater affluence, much as the colonial intellectuals were separated from their native populations.[62] The gap between the leadership and the masses is essential for any other successes in South Texas because the history of the first revolt in Crystal City indicates that leadership truly *of* the people, truly representative of the Mexican-American population of South Texas, simply cannot survive in the economic, social, and political structures of South Texas. Yet as a corollary, for the movement to win more successes ways must be devised to bridge the gulf between the leadership and the masses. Otherwise, it seems the masses will retreat into apathy or despair, or will be resentful of the "success" of the leadership. And the leadership can always be tempted by inducements the Anglos are able to offer.[63]

As examples of surrounding communities seem to indicate, even in areas where Chicanos are numerically dominant the movement can be deflected either through the lack of mass participation and mass mobilization or through cooptation of the leadership. And in areas where Chicanos form a significant portion of the population, but less than half of the voting population, the movement could fail even as it mobilizes and politicizes the Chicano community.[64] It seems, then, that a sharp distinction should be made between the development of Chicano consciousness and their assumption of political and economic power. It is possible that the Chicano community in most of Texas could become radicalized, embittered, and basically excluded from the political process as a consistently losing minority. Since the Chicano is a minority in nearly all of Texas and the Southwest, his radicalization would not occur without reactions from the dominant Anglos. It is also quite possible that the rhetoric of some in the Chicano community, particularly the use of the word "gringo" and the goal of at least partial separatism, would mean that Anglo communities might react with increasing distrust of Mexican Americans. Already some Anglo politicians in South Texas seem to be trying to forge Anglos into a countermonolith by citing the example of the takeover in Crystal City.[65] Those Mexican Americans who are elected to office with Anglo support might be forced to abandon basic desires and goals of many in the Mexican-American community or risk political extinction.[66]

While retrenchment could be the basic direction Anglos will choose to follow, it is also possible that the radicalism of the young leadership in Mexican-American barrios across South Texas would cause officials to work to defuse the situation by acting on some of the demands, coopting some of the leadership, or trying to create their own kind of moderate Mexican leadership. It is possible that in this manner gradual amelioration of the tremendous economic, social, and political disparity between Mexican Americans and Anglos would take place. That is, the radicals might increase the parameters of politics and might in this way broaden the area within which politicians, businessmen, educators, and others would all be willing to act. But the example of Crystal City from 1965 to 1969 should

220 CHICANO REVOLT IN A TEXAS TOWN

remind us of the danger of losing perspective on the degree and importance of changes that have occurred, as indeed should the radicalization of the Black movement in America at the very time when many whites preferred to think that civil-rights questions had been settled.

It is of course possible that something less than a complete Chicano revolt of the sort that Crystal City has known might be possible in circumstances where conditions were not quite so favorable. That is, a coalition of Mexicans and Blacks, or of Mexicans, Blacks, Labor, and Anglo liberals might be possible which would constitute a revolt capable of implementing a number of similar changes. In Karnes City, Texas, for example, a coalition of Mexicans and Blacks has organized to protest discrimination against both groups in the school system.

A revolt which represents a broader-based coalition thus might be possible in a number of communities. Such a revolt would incorporate the Chicano community but would not be composed solely of them.

Whatever does happen in the future concerning Chicano politics, it does seem that an important distinction should be made between the development of political awareness and the assumption of power. That Mexican Americans will increasingly desire change and will in the process move toward greater interest and activity in political, social, and economic spheres seems very likely. But that they will also move toward greater power, or greater control over their own destiny does not necessarily follow. Crystal City has been an exception, and in the end it is likely to remain an exception.

the future of crystal city

As for the town of Crystal City itself, it seems likely that La Raza Unida will continue to dominate the politics of the community. With the exodus of Anglos, the opposition was further depleted in their resources to fight Raza Unida, and the Mexican community was increasing its already overwhelming numerical dominance in the town. Only loss of contact with the masses or a split in leadership similar to that which occurred under Juan Cornejo would appear capable of bringing in a regime more in sympathy with Anglo and business interests in the town. There clearly have been tensions along these lines, as the desertion by Mike Pérez and the firing and resignation of two police chiefs indicated. But so far the movement has stayed united enough to keep political control, and its activities have been enough in line with the majority of the town's thinking to keep winning elections. Although Gutiérrez's term of office on the school board was over in 1973, and he decided to resign from the board and instead oversee the Carnegie Institute grant to train Chicano administrators, it is not clear what effect this will have on the unity and style of the movement.

At any rate, it seems clear that how long the community migrants and uneducated masses will continue to allow themselves to be led by outside educators and local boys who in making good have removed themselves somewhat from the plight of the migrants will depend to a great extent upon the sensitivity of the leaders to the continued sufferings of the migrants and on the degree to which they will be able to upgrade the still extremely impoverished and disadvantaged community. A leader as brilliant as Gutiérrez, who continued to spend part of his summers traveling north with the migrants to found and teach in migrant schools, might be able to hold together such a coalition indefinitely. And the development of Ciudadanos Unidos, which under the present leadership had allowed the Mexican community a say in the development of programs and ideas for the community, was another essential bridge between the leaders and the masses.

Yet the demands on the time of the leadership, particularly on José Angel Gutiérrez, meant that important decisions concerning priorities had to be made. From the beginning of his involvement in Crystal City, Gutiérrez accepted speaking tours around the nation. The growth in the Chicano movement also meant an increase in conferences, which Gutiérrez often attended or keynoted. Gutiérrez also began teaching courses on the history and politics of Mexican Americans, and expressed a desire to finish his doctorate in political science at the University of Texas. And of course journalists and researchers were constantly after him for interviews. All this meant that his time in Crystal City itself was limited, and some Mexican Americans complained of this. They argued that Gutiérrez and the leadership should have been spending more time helping and encouraging the people of Crystal City.

One who was a supporter of La Raza Unida added that the

leadership should be putting more emphasis on teaching the Mexicans responsibility and competition, and should spend less time teaching them bitterness. Others argued that more time should be spent teaching illiterates, although this is a taxing and heavily time-consuming job. And there was some local resentment at the number of outside leaders and teachers. Said one Mexican, "Students can't look up to [outside leaders] because they don't know them. They should build indigenous leaders. Students feel deflated when they see people passed over that have tried."[67] Said another, echoing the same idea, "You've got to train the peon. If you don't the gap will always exist." Speaking of the Mexican-American people, he then added ominously, "They'll hold it against you unless you start helping them." Another criticized the heavy emphasis on the political side of community betterment, saying that more help should be given to writing wills, being made aware of social-security benefits, learning about property and homestead laws, and so forth.

Gutiérrez was no doubt aware of these problems, and through Ciudadanos Unidos the regime showed a willingness to work not just to win elections but to change things after being in office. Yet the demands on the leadership were enormous, and if anything, they seemed to increase as the mass of poor Mexican Americans responded to the rhetoric of fundamental change. Adding to all these difficulties, however, was the clear fact that many Mexican Americans of the community, although as of now a distinct minority, disapproved of the "gringo-baiting" and "chicanismo" ideology and tactics of the Raza Unida leadership. These Mexican Americans, often better-off and more established than the majority, will continue to oppose La Raza Unida, and their long-term impact on the movement is uncertain but cannot be ignored.

The importance of Anglo machinations in preventing the Raza Unida leadership from disintegrating should also not be forgotten. But policy decisions on how far to press the Anglos, how many teachers to fire, which court suits to bring, which issues to press, and how to balance their limited resources between statewide and national work and fund raising versus help to the local Mexican Americans continue to strain the movement, as it would strain any movement which was committed to so many changes. As long as the Anglos remain actively involved in trying to overthrow La Raza Unida, there will probably be much less chance for division of the Mexican community in Crystal City, since bitter polarization has already been accomplished. But should the Anglos ever simply give up and/or leave in great numbers, then the strains within the Mexican-American community would most likely become greater. Questions over who should do the leading and how far the movement should go would then assume even greater importance as the need to unite in the face of hostility abated. And how La Raza Unida will change as a result of years in power is the subject of intense speculation. Will it gradually "come to terms with its environment," or will it continue to try to change drastically the opportunities and resources of Chicanos in the area?

At the same time, with the opportunities for migrants drying up rapidly, and with the community having already lost population between 1960 and 1970, it is apparent that the future of the community rests upon more than the community's willingness to try new approaches to bring in industry and to upgrade the skills and education of the community. The future also depends, as we noted earlier, upon decisions Anglos will make regarding the community. They are the ones who hold the capital. There is little doubt, for example, that a decision by Del Monte to leave the community would be devastating. Both the Raza Unida leadership and the Del Monte management itself are aware of this fact.[68] Yet the community is not dependent only upon Anglo business. Important national developments have aided the Chicano activists, particularly the increase in federal funds. A corollary of this, however, is that a drying up of these funds would devastate the community. These programs have not only poured money into the community; they have also been an important source of income for the leadership.

In the years since the Cornejo failure other changes in national attitudes and policies toward Mexican Americans and the poor have also occurred. Foundations and churches are more aware of problems of poverty and discrimination, and they are willing to help out in Crystal City in both public and confidential ways. These changes made the leadership less vulnerable to local economic intimidation than was the leadership in 1963, but these national organizations were at times concerned about the militancy, the direction, and the rhetoric of the leadership.[69] At any rate, the need for funding of programs and for technical expertise in developing and manning the numerous programs which would have to be launched in Crystal City if the migrants are to be upgraded and the community developed will no doubt continue to grow. To what extent the community can find resources to meet these needs remains unclear.

conclusion

We see then that any assessment of the success of La Raza Unida in Crystal City, or its applicability to the rest of South Texas and the Southwest, must be qualified. In comparison with the first Chicano takeover in 1963, the current regime showed important differences. Their goals were clearer and more unified. Their leadership was more confident and experienced. The community now had more resources available to it because of the greater political consciousness of the local Mexican community. La Raza Unida had produced a political situation where the community's Anglos, long accustomed to governing, were now locked out of the local government. And in their victory over the Anglos, they also discredited Mexican Americans who had worked closely with or identified with the local Anglos.[70]

This was a situation unprecedented elsewhere in South Texas. But even in their victory over Anglos, and more conservative Mexican Americans, tremendous tasks still faced the new regime. How to attract and keep outside help while not slighting or overlooking indigenous leadership and manpower would continue to require careful balancing and sensitivity. Second-level leadership in the Chicano community remained weak, although it was improving in experience. The egalitarian spirit of the revolution and the common struggle in the Chicano community had as by-products introduced women and young people into the leadership councils of the movement. Tapping both these resources already strengthened the leadership, but steering a steady course between the twin pitfalls of ideological purity at the expense of the desires of the indigenous population, or coming to terms with the many forces that opposed them in a manner that deflated the people, would continue to be difficult. Federal programs and national foundations were helpful, but they carried with them serious constraints in being designed much more for incremental change than radical innovation. And

the threatened Nixon Administration cutbacks again emphasized the precariousness of the Crystal City economy.

Owing to these and to further institutional constraints which
have been placed upon protest organizations, such as the need
for funds, the need to attract and then hold together divergent
interests within their coalition, and the difficulty of overcoming
biases found in the setup of political institutions they sought to
control, La Raza Unida was thwarted in important ways even as
it won astounding victories. Perhaps in gaining control of the
county they would be able to acquire considerably greater
revenues through taxing the large Anglo landholders, but until
this happened they would continue very much in need of
outside funds.

And finally, it should also be remembered that in Crystal
City there were peculiarly auspicious circumstances for revolt.
Thus, to say that the Raza Unida revolt was achieving unqualified victories or that its successes in Crystal City could be
duplicated elsewhere would be both naive and adventuristic. In
communities such as the old border towns, where Mexican
Americans have always had an important role in governance
even as their substantive policies have been oppressive, race and
class lines do not clearly merge. It is thus difficult to see how
the Crystal City strategy could work without important
changes. In communities where a majority of the population is
Anglo, not only must the strategy be modified in important
ways, but the impact of the rhetoric of Crystal City militants
might easily damage those Chicanos who must work in coali-
tions, either with Blacks or with labor and liberal Anglos.

Also, even though the goals of La Raza Unida have been far
more carefully constructed than were those of Los Cinco Mexicanos, the regime will eventually be faced either through success
or through failure with deciding upon what the whole policy of
self-determination for the Chicano community really means.
Just how to relate to Anglo cultural domination, whether and
how to blend with it or fight it or isolate themselves from it, are
questions which remain unresolved. How much the Chicano
movement should be one of separate cultural nationalism, and
how much it should be one which would eventually prepare
Chicanos for integration with Anglos as equals, remains unclear.
How this basic question is answered will have important consequences upon the relationship of Mexican Americans to Mexico

itself. Gutiérrez has said, for example, that "the Rio Grande never has separated us and never will."[71] But if this is true, does it follow that an upgrading of the Mexicans of the United States can only occur as Mexico itself develops? As long as there is an inexhaustible supply of cheap labor just across the border, eager to enter the United States to find work, how much can Mexican-American communities uplift themselves as they are constantly influenced by and replenished by Mexicans from Mexico? How can the problems facing Mexican Americans be disassociated from problems facing Mexicans on the other side of the border? How this question is answered will depend in great part upon the attitudes of Mexican Americans and Mexicans of Mexico themselves. These questions of identity are not unique to Chicanos of Crystal City, or of the Southwest. They involve fundamental questions of identity facing all cultural minorities and all disadvantaged peoples. In fact they involve all human beings, who must in the end decide as individuals what their identity and what their goals should be.

But in facing these problems and difficulties, which at times may seem overwhelming, the Chicano community can call upon the very resources which have been opened up by their struggle in Crystal City: the confidence, the pride, the experience, and the feeling of community. Their successes have brought a feeling of control over their own destiny that is simply not measured in terms of dollars spent, legal suits filed, or theoretical and practical problems which must be resolved. The stereotype of a fatalistic Juan Tortilla, a loyal servant happiest when he is stooped in the fields picking spinach for the Anglo, has been shattered for both Anglos and Chicanos alike. As the Chicano community goes about trying to overcome the enormous problems they must face, this faith in themselves may be their most valuable possession. It will mean that the choice will be theirs to a greater extent than it ever has been before.

appendix one

A. TOTAL NUMBER OF WEEKS WORKED
BY LABOR FORCE
IN ZAVALA COUNTY, 1959*

Total Weeks Worked	Number Who Worked
50-52	1,561
48-49	285
40-47	511
27-39	780
14-26	774
13 or less	810

*Model Cities Application by the Crystal City Urban Renewal Agency to the Department of Housing and Urban Development, 1967.

B. FAMILY INCOME IN CRYSTAL CITY, 1959*

| | Number of Families: | |
Income	Anglo**	Spanish-surnamed***
Under $1,000	27	361
$1,000 -1,999	60	367
$2,000 -2,999	47	309
$3,000 -3,999	69	110
$4,000 -4,999	58	61
$5,000 -5,999	45	25
$6,000 -6,999	51	19
$7,000 -7,999	21	3
$8,000 -8,999	35	4
$9,000 -9,999	29	0
$10,000 plus	51	13

*U.S. Bureau of the Census, "Special Table PH-6" for Zavala County, Texas, 1960, unpublished table.

**Computed by the author from subtracting the Spanish-surnamed families from the total family census. It thus includes the few Negro families in the city.

***Families who spoke Spanish in the home but who had Anglo surnames were included in with Anglo families. Note that this is different from the 1969 income, which includes Spanish-language and Spanish-surnamed families.

C. FAMILY INCOME IN ZAVALA COUNTY, 1969*

Number of Families:

Income	Anglo**	Spanish-surnamed & Sp. language
Under $1,000	21	82
$1,000 -1,999	28	289
$2,000 -2,999	35	260
$3,000 -3,999	20	280
$4,000 -4,999	22	165
$5,000 -5,999	59	167
$6,000 -6,999	28	192
$7,000 -7,999	54	154
$8,000 -8,999	57	83
$9,000 -9,999	44	25
$10,000-11,999	65	71
$12,000-14,999	65	20
$15,000-24,999	49	19
$25,000-49,999	10	6
$50,000 plus	27	0

*Taken from the U.S. Bureau of the Census, Census of Population: 1970, *General Social and Economic Characteristics*, Final Report PC(1)-C45-Texas, Washington, D.C.: U.S. Government Printing Office, 1972, pp. 1037 and 1165.

**Computed by the author from subtracting the Spanish-surnamed and Spanish-language families from the total family census. It thus includes the few Negro families in the county.

appendix two

GUTIÉRREZ PRESS CONFERENCE*
APRIL, 1969, SAN ANTONIO, TEXAS

MAYO has found that both federal and religious programs aimed at social change do not meet the needs of the Mexicans of this state.

Further, we find that the vicious cultural genocide being inflicted upon La Raza by gringos and their institutions not only severely damages our human dignity, but also make it impossible for La Raza to develop its right of self-determination.

For these reasons, top priority is given to identifying and exposing the gringo. We also promote the social welfare of Mexicanos through education designed to enlarge the capabilities of indigenous leaders.

We hope to secure our human and civil rights, to eliminate bigotry and racism, to lessen the tensions in our barrios and combat the deterioration of our communities.

Our organization, largely comprised of youth, is committed to effecting meaningful social change. Social change that will enable La Raza to become masters of their own destiny, owners

*Source: *The Congressional Record*, April 15, 1969, p. 9059.

of their resources, both human and natural, and a culturally and spiritually separate people from the gringo.

Only through this program, we of MAYO see the possibility of surviving this century as a free and complete family of Mexicanos. We will not try to assimilate into this gringo society in Texas nor will we encourage anybody else to do so.

Rather, MAYO once again asks of friends here and across the nation to assist us in our efforts. We intend to become free as a people in order to enjoy the abundance of our country and share it with those less fortunate.

MAYO will not engage in controversy with fellow Mexicanos regardless of how unfounded and vindictive their accusations may be. We realize that the effects of cultural genocide takes many forms—some Mexicanos will become psychologically castrated, others will become demagogues and gringos as well, and others will come together, resist and eliminate the gringo. We will be with the latter.

[Asked his definition of gringo]

A person or an institution that has a certain policy or program or attitudes that reflect bigotry, racism, discord, and prejudice and violence.

[Asked if a majority of Anglo-Americans were gringos]

According to the Kerner report we could say yes to that answer.

[Asked if he could say that some of his best friends are Anglos]

That's a racist statement. I wouldn't be that derogatory or condescending. . . . I would say that a lot of people are friends of mine and some of them are Anglos.

[Asked what he meant by "eliminate the gringo"]

You can eliminate an individual in various ways. You can certainly kill him but that is not our intent at this moment. You can remove the base of support that he operates from, be it economic, political, or social. That is what we intend to do.

appendix three

A. HIGH SCHOOL STUDENT DEMANDS, SPRING, 1969

1. No punishment for students involved in demonstrations for better education.

2. Teachers should stop taking political sides and preaching them to students.

3. Twirlers should be elected by band members, instead of faculty.

4. Students should select most popular, most beautiful and handsome, etc., boy and girl, and cheerleaders, instead of faculty.

5. The school should have bilingual and bicultural programs, recognizing that Spanish is just as good as English.

6. Pave the school parking lot.

7. Provide the band with new uniforms.

B. SETTLEMENT REACHED WITH SUPERINTENDENT

JOHN BILLINGS, SPRING, 1969, AND NULLIFIED IN THE SUMMER BY THE SCHOOL BOARD

1. Any infractions must be dealt with by school officials.

2. Teachers should not be derogatory about Mexican-American achievements, and teachers have been ordered to treat all students equally.

3. The selection of twirlers should follow the general rule of most schools in the area.

4. Concerning the election of class favorites, there should be a Spanish-surnamed student and Anglo student selected for each position, and two more Mexican-American cheerleaders should be selected.

5. Teaching in classrooms could not be in Spanish, however, the librarian has been instructed to order as many books as possible on Mexican culture.

6. and 7. Fiscal limitations were the reasons for the unpaved parking lot and old band uniforms.

C. HIGH SCHOOL STUDENT PETITION TO SCHOOL BOARD, NOVEMBER 1969 (Reproduced Exactly as Written)

1. Homecoming Queen Regulation done away with. Regulation: (Girl eligible only if one of her parents graduated from high school. We do not want Homecoming Queen to be presented before game or announced.

2. Elections of Cheerleaders held by the Student Body.
   (1) Twirlers by (Band)
   (2) Most Handsome & Beautiful
   (3) Most Representatives

3. Same regulations applied to Fly Jr. High School in the elections of cheerleaders.

4. Mr. Harbin retire as principal because he is unfair and discriminates.

5. Teachers should not call students names like, animals, stupid idiots, ignorants,

6. Teachers should not discrimination and if they do they should not be allowed to teach.

7. Have Sept. 16, recognized as a Mexican-American holiday. (We don't mind going to school one more day.

8. Have a Mexican-American counselor a long with Mr. Moore. A Mexican-American will understand us better.

9. Have Bilingual education. Have Texas History books revised. We want new textbooks with the history of Los Mexicanos. (A course with the history of the Mexicanos and be valued as one credit.

10. Students not punished for organizing peacefully and demanding what is right.

11. Have a student organization within school. Goal is to help people within our community that need help in clothing, money and food.

12. Publish a newspaper and sell it at noon hour. Everybody will have a say in this newspapers.

13. Dress-Code - Pants can be worn by girls during the cold weather.

14. Showers to be put in girls and boys dressing room.

D. REVISED PETITION PRESENTED BY HIGH SCHOOL STUDENTS TO THE SCHOOL BOARD, DECEMBER, 1969 (Reproduced Exactly As Written)

1. That all elections concerning the school be conducted by the Student Body such as:

    a. Class Representatives

        1. The qualifications such as personality, leadership, and grades be abolished. These factors do not determine whether the student is capable of representing the student body. The students are capable of voting for their own represenatives. The represenatives are representing the students, not the faculty. All nominating must be done by the student body, and the election should be decided by majority vote.

      b. Cheerleaders should be elected by the Student Body not judges from out of town.

      c. Twirlers should be elected by the BAND MEMBERS.

      d. The present method of electing Most Handsome, Beautiful, Most Popular, and Most Represenative is done by the faculty. This is not fair. The method of cummulative voting is unfair.

      e. National Honor Society— The grades of the students eligible must be posted on the bulletin board well in advance of selection. The teachers should not have anything to do with electing the students.

      f. No other favorites should be authorized by School School Administrators or Board Members unless sumitted to the Student Body in a referendum; for example; Homecoming Queen, Who's Who, and Mr. and Miss CCHS.

2. We want immediate steps taken to implement bilingual and Bi-cultural education for Mexican-Americans. We also want the school books revised to reflect the contributions of Mexicans and Mexican-Americans to the U. S. society, and to make us aware of the injustices that we, Mexican-Americans, as a people have suffered in an "Anglo" dominant society. We want a Mexican-American course with the value of one credit. These are some books which will be educational;;;;;;;;;

      1. *NORTH FROM MEXICO* by Carey McWilleiams First printed in 1948.

      2. *LATIN AMERICANS in TEXAS* by Pauline R. Kibbe. First printed in 1946.

      3. *AN AMERICAN-MEXICAN FRONTIER* by Dr. Paul S. Tayor. First printed in 1934.

      4. *CONQUISTADORS in NORTH AMERICAN HISTORY* Paul Horgan Printed in 1963.

A list of many other books may be accquired by writing the DEPARTMENT of SOCIAL RELATIONS, University of Texas, Austin. and asking for the ANNOTATED BIBLIOGRAPHY ON THE MEXICAN-American which they compiled.

3. We want any member of the school system who displays prejucide or fails to recognize, understand, and appreciate us Mexican Americans, our culture, or our heritage removed from Crystal City's schools. TEACHERS SHALL NOT CALL STUDENTS ANY NAMES.

1. Mr. Ruthledge, a civics teacher, calls students animals, carpetbaggers, aliens bananas, fruits, and vegetables.

   a. Lydia Maltos was told last week not to speak SPANISH during the 5 minute break. This was outside of class. Yet the School Supertindent says there is no rule prohibiting SPANISH.

   b. During October when the armband were being worn; he told Lucy Ramirez that she should not write no white paper but on brown paper. He was making fun of our skin tone.

   c. He is constantly putting the students down with remarks such as those mentioned above.

2. Mr. Lopez uses some of the techniques:

   a. In this class during Sept. in front of Cleofas Tamez, he told the students "he wished they were all dead before the age of 21. He stated that it was for their own good because they were too stupid to survive in this world.

   b. Armando de Hoyos was literally kicked out of class by Mr. Lopez. This happened last school year.

   c. A student does not like to attend a class where he is constantly called an idiot.

3. Mrs. Harper is not qualified to teach students because of her RACISM and BIGOTRY.

   A. Ten Years Ago, the Freshman Class of 1958-59. Irma Benavidez was told by Mrs. Harper that it was a previliage to be sitting next to an anglo.

   B. Mario Trevino was told by Mrs. Harper, "You have been acting so dam smart alecky this period." She was angry at the class because she was corrected on one of her mistakes.. She grabed Mario by the arm and told him the above.

Students can not learn with Mrs. Harper. The students do not like her. We can not learn because she has built up a bad and fearful attitude toward her. Since Jr. High most Mexican-American students are warned of the RACISM and BIGOTRY of the Red Headed Ant.

9. Our classes should be smaller in size, say about 20 students to one teacher to insure more effectiveness.

   A. We want parents from the community to be trained as teacher's aides.

   B. We want assurances that a teacher who may disagree politically or philosophically with administrators will not be dismissed or transferred because of it.

   C. Teachers should encourage students to study and should make class more interesting, so that students will look forward to going to class.

10. There should be a manager in charge of janitorial work and maintenance details and the performance of such duties should be restricted to employees hired for that purpose. IN OTHER WORDS NO MORE STUDENTS DOING JANITORIAL WORK.

    EXAMPLE: P.E. Boys should not be made to pick up paper at the football field.

11. RIGHTS—STUDENT RIGHTS

    1. We want a free speech area plus the right to have speakers of our own.

       A. We would like September 16 as a holiday, but if it is not possible we would like an assembly, with speakers of our own.

       We feel it is a great day in the history of the world because it is when Mexico had been under the Spanish rule for about 300 years. The Mexicans were liberated from the harsh rule of Spain. Our ancestors fought in this war and we owe them tribute because we are Mexicans too.

       Yes, you will say that the students from Irish descent will want St. Patricks Day. In Boston and New York where there is a heavy population of

Irish students; they have St. Patricks day as a Holiday.

When we have the Stock Show we have a day or half off too. So we are entitled to September 16.

12. Being civic minded citizens, we want to know what is happening in our community. So, we request the ritht to have access to all types of literature and to be able to carry suffient information. It carries things like the gossip column, which is unnecessary.

13. The dress code should be abolished. We are entitled to wear what we want. This includes Jr. High which the code is very strict there. The girls cannot wear a short dress because they are suspended or are given three (3) licks.

14. We request the buildings open to students at all times.

15. We want Mr. Harbin to resign as Principal of Fly Jr. High School. He openly shows his RACISM and BIG-OTRY.

16. We want a Mexican-American counselor fully qualified in college opportunities.

17. We need more showers in the boys' and girls' dressing rooms. They should be enlarged.

18. No reprisals against students participating in the walk out.

19. That an Advisory board of Mexican-American citizens, chosen by the citizens, to be established in the school board in order to advise the school board on needs and problems of Mexican-Americans.

E. AGREEMENT BETWEEN THE CRYSTAL CITY SCHOOL BOARD AND THE NEGOTIATING COMMITTEE OF STUDENT BOYCOTT SPOKESMEN AND REPRESENTA-TIVE PARENTS

January 4, 1970

The parties to this document agree to the following:

ISSUE: I. CONDITIONS UNDER WHICH STUDENTS ARE TO RETURN TO SCHOOL

ACTION:

A. Grades established before December 9th shall remain intact.

B. Grades missed by students on walk-out during December 9-19 will not be used, with the exception of 3-weeks tests and 6-weeks tests.

C. Students who attended classes may drop an equal number of grades as those missed by students who participated in the boycott. This does not include 3-weeks tests or 6-weeks tests.

D. Students participating in the boycott will be given the opportunity to take the 3-weeks and/or 6 weeks tests during regular class time while non-affected students are given study periods. Teachers will cooperate with walk-out students in providing subject matter covered during December 9-19.

E. The practice of applying a two-point-per-day penalty for unexcused absence will not apply.

F. Time lost in connection with Driver Education classes can be made up, if possible, during regular class periods. Otherwise, students will be allowed to make their own financial and time arrangements with qualified personnel. Cooperation from faculty will be expected in order to reach these alternate objectives.

ISSUE: II. ESTABLISHMENT OF GRIEVANCE PROCEDURE TO FACILITATE EFFECTIVE COMMUNICATION

ACTION:

A ten-member parents' advisory committee will be formed. It will be composed of eight Mexican-Americans and two Anglos to be selected by high school students. The recently formed local "church-men's group", chaired by Dr. Robert Stauber, will prepare a proposal for consideration and approval by both parties to this agreement. In addition, the establishment of an "ombudsman" function to facilitate effective communication between the advisory group and school authorities will be developed and included in said proposal.

The target date for completing and submitting this proposal is January 31, 1970.

ISSUE: III. EXPLORATION OF BI-CULTURAL AND BI-LINGUAL PROGRAMS TO BE IMPLEMENTED IN ACCORDANCE WITH RECOMMENDATIONS FROM COMPETENT EDUCATIONAL AUTHORITIES MUTUALLY AGREED UPON BY THE PARTIES HEREIN NAMED

ACTION:

Contacts with the Texas Education Agency (TEA), already partially initiated by Crystal City school authorities, will be vigorously pursued in order to facilitate the availability of qualified education specialist(s) to help establish an acceptable program, subject to funding availability.

ISSUE: IV. UTILIZATION OF PROFESSIONAL CONSULTANTS TO EVALUATE CERTAIN TESTING PROCEDURES AND TO RECOMMEND CHANGES WHICH WOULD OVERCOME ALLEGED INEQUITIES

ACTION:

The school board acknowledges the probable existence of inequities in the administration of tests designed to measure school-entry readiness. In seeking a remedy to this problem, the TEA will be requested to provide suitable technical assistance. Any specialist(s) assigned to this task will consult with parents and students who represent the original complaint issue. The most competent available resources will be sought and utilized, as recommended by the state agency.

ISSUE: V. IDENTIFY AND APPLY METHODS OF OVERCOMING PATTERNS OF ETHNIC ISOLATION

ACTION:

Contact will be made with the appropriate resource at the University of Texas (TAC) and/or the TEA to seek corrective measures. Problem identification will include attention to the allegation that Anglo children in certain grades are not found in lower achievement sections, contributing to patterns of artificial ethnic separation.

ISSUE: VI. REVISION OF METHODS BY WHICH CERTAIN STUDENT POSITIONS ARE DETERMINED

ACTION:

A. *Most Representative Student*—The designation for this position will be changed to "Faculty Student Representative".

B. *Cheerleaders*—Procedure will be changed to provide for election by student body.

C. *Baseball Sweetheart*—Provide for only one such honoree (instead of two) to be nominated and elected by members of the team.

D. *Prom Servers*—Provide for election by junior class from one list of all sophomore students without regard to ethnic grouping.

E. *Twirlers and Drum Major*—Provide for selection by the CCISD school superintendent four non-resident band directors (or other similarly qualified persons) and four band members (elected by the band) to judge and select candidates by a point system. Mechanics of such a system will be constructed in a manner which will best assure impartial and independent selections.

ISSUE: VII. COMPLAINTS AGAINST CERTAIN SCHOOL PERSONNEL

ACTION:

Specific complaint substance was noted by the board and will be given appropriate consideration at the time of contract renewal. Such related problems, requiring improved sensitivity to cultural diversity, will be included for attention by previously noted consultants.

ISSUE: VIII. CONSIDERATION OF THE NEED FOR ADDITIONAL COUNSELING PERSONNEL

ACTION:

Availability of additional counseling personnel will be

explored. If funds are available, through Title VI, Sec 8910, or otherwise, a qualified bi-lingual candidate will be recruited and employed.

ISSUE: IX. APPROPRIATE SCHOOL-WIDE OBSER-VANCE OF SEPTEMBER 16 (DIEZ Y SEIS)

ACTION:

Observance of this holiday will provide for a suitable assembly program (during the last regular class period of the day for the high school). Students will be permitted to select speakers and/or program content, subject to approval by the school administration. Such assemblies will include participation by the total junior high and senior high student bodies.

ISSUE: X. INEQUITABLE ETHNIC DISTRIBUTION OF STUDENTS REGARDING SIZE OF CLASSES

ACTION:

Superintendent will examine the extent and nature of the problem. Particular attention will be given to alleged disparities in classes in which driver education, civics and English are offered. Such technical assistance as may be indicated will be sought from previously identified resources in order to implement corrective measures. Such remedies as are found to be in order will be applied to take effect not later than September, 1970.

ISSUE: XI. INADEQUACY OF SHOWER FACILITIES

ACTION:

The school board acknowledged the problem as a high priority need among facility improvements under consideration. It was agreed that the stated condition would be carefully evaluated as to costs involved, etc., and that the most feasible action would be taken, within the limitations of available funds.

ISSUE: XII. ACCESS TO SCHOOL FACILITIES DUR-ING OFF-HOURS

ACTION:

Said facilities will be open for student use on Monday, Tuesday and Thursday of each school week, between the hours of 7:30 P.M. and 9:30 P.M. Access areas will include the library, typing room, one or more class-rooms, as needed. Supervision during such hours will be provided by school personnel.

ISSUE: XIII. ALLEGED PRESSURES ON FACULTY MEMBERS DESIGNED TO INHIBIT EXPRES-SION OF VIEWS OR PARTISAN SUPPORT IN CONNECTION WITH CONTROVERSIAL IS-SUES

ACTION:

Both parties agreed that it could be anticipated that this problem would likely be resolved through the establish-ment of an effective grievance procedure as has been set forth under Issue II.

ISSUE: XIV. CRITICISMS OF EXISTING STUDENT NEWSPAPER AND SUGGESTIONS FOR CRITICAL IMPROVEMENTS

ACTION:

The school board will take appropriate action to assure that the student newspaper (The Javelin Herald) reflects the highest possible standards of professional journal-ism, including the regular presentation of divergent viewpoints and generally meaningful content with likely appeal to a wide cross-section of the student population.

ISSUE: XV. REVIEW AND UP-DATING OF DRESS CODES

ACTION:

The student council will be requested by the school administration to examine present student handbook provisions and to recommend to the board suitable revisions in keeping with currently acceptable styles and fashions. Such revisions will apply to both junior and senior high school levels.

ISSUE: XVI. PROVISION OF TRAINING FOR TEACH-ER AIDES

ACTION:

Resolution had already been accomplished, a fact pre-viously unknown to the protest group.

ISSUE: XVII. REVIEW OF PRACTICES IN CONNEC-
TION WITH STUDENTS PERFORMING CUS-
TODIAL DUTIES

ACTION:

Physical Education students will be given an option as
to whether they will participate in the regularly scheduled P.E. activity or choose to assist in clean-up activity
on the athletic field and elsewhere on school property.

appendix four

PROGRAM FOR BILINGUAL
AND BICULTURAL EDUCATION,
CRYSTAL CITY SCHOOL BOARD, 1973

RECOMMENDATION — 1

To promote educational success on the part of the mono-lingual student, through permitting him to learn to speak, to read, to write, and to think in his vernacular (mother tongue) with limited exposure to listening and oral skills in a second language (English).

RECOMMENDATION — 2

The continued development by the mono-lingual student of his own language as he is learning to function successfully in the second language.

RECOMMENDATION — 3

The continued development by the bilingual student in his dominant language for instruction while strengthening his second language through listening and oral activities.

RECOMMENDATION — 4

The increased recognition by the *total community* (parents, teachers, administrators, students) of the importance of bilingualism, both in the process and the product through Community Involvement.

RECOMMENDATION — 5

That the Crystal City Independent School District (CCISD) will provide an environment which is conducive to learning.

   a. Staff
   b. Facilities
   c. Materials

The development of an effective program that will give each student an opportunity to progress toward the stated goals.

RECOMMENDATION — 6

The appraisal of the students' level of development of language, concepts, and experiences (avoiding testing in the student's second language until he has sufficient control of the language so that his true verbal abilities can be measured).

RECOMMENDATION — 7

That the Crystal City Independent School District (CCISD) recognizes the need for the development and implementation of a program which will assist each student in becoming proficient in both Spanish and English.

Subject matter and concepts will be taught in the child's dominant language.

That content areas which are critical to the intellectual and emotional development of the child and which affect his success in the school setting, will be taught, initially, through the use of the child's first language, thereby permitting and encouraging the child to enter immediately into classroom activities, enabling him to meet with early successes. This will insure the development of a positive self image.

RECOMMENDATION — 8

That components in Spanish and English language development must be included beginning the Pre-Kindergarten and continuing through the twelfth grade.

RECOMMENDATION — 9

That a component must be included which deals directly with the student's culture and heritage beginning with Pre-Kindergarten and continuing through the twelfth grade.

That special attention will be given to develop in every child a positive identity with his cultural heritage, self assurance, and confidence.

The historical contributions and cultural characteristics identified with the Mexican American will become an integral part of the total program (Pre-K to 12). This will enable all students to understand and appreciate, in a positive sense, historical contributions and the rich culture of the Mexican and the Mexican American.

RECOMMENDATION — 10

That the basic concepts initiating the child into the school environment will be taught in the dominant language of the child.

All orientation to the classroom behavior and his patterns of social interaction with his peers will be developed by drawing from the child's experiences, concepts, and language which he brings from home.

RECOMMENDATION — 11

That language development will be provided in the child's dominant language.

The sequential development of the four language skills—listening, speaking, reading, and writing—will be continued in

the language for which the child has already learned the
sound system, structure and vocabulary. *This enables the
child to develop skills before having to learn a second language.*

RECOMMENDATION — 12

*That language development will be provided in the child's
second language.*

Teaching the *listening* and *speaking* skills by the use of the
audio-lingual instructional technique prior to teaching the reading and writing skills, enabling every child to *learn* a second
language. Unique in this component is the fact that a child does
not have to re-learn language skills. He will merely have to
transfer those skills which he learned in his first language.

RECOMMENDATION — 13

*That subject matter and concepts will be taught in the second
language of the child.*

Content areas will be taught in the child's second language,
but not until after he has become literate in his own language. The teaching techniques are audio-lingual in order to
insure the development of listening and speaking skills. As
the child's second language ability develops more content and
other skills, reading and writing will be incorporated.

RECOMMENDATION — 14

The acceptance of the position taken by researchers concerning
teaching of reading. "Research has strengthened the position
that children must be taught to read in their mother tongue.
(MacNamara 1967, Modiano 1968, Orata 1953, Pryor 1968,
Richardson 1968)"

RECOMMENDATION — 15

That bilingual children will be taught to read in their dominant
language (stronger language). Only those children whose mas-

tery of both languages is *so strong* that they can fully compre-hend the beginning reading materials can receive instruction in either language, or both.

In either case reading will be introduced in only one language. Reading in the second language will be *delayed* until the child becomes fully literate in his first language. We will not confuse the problems of learning a new language.

RECOMMENDATION — 16

That reading in the second language be delayed until the child has learned to read in the first. The child should be able to read with ease anything placed before him. This will show us that he has internalized all the rules for decoding *his language.* In the case of Spanish we are dealing with phonetically transcribed language, so we expect the child to read easily, smoothly, with no hesitations or halts, and to decode any but highly complex new words.

Because of the vast transcription differences between Spanish and English, a child is faced with learning a whole new set of decoding skills in English.

The better a child can read in his first language, the less trouble he will have learning to read in his second language, and the less he will confuse the decoding rules for the two languages.

RECOMMENDATION — 17

That no recommendation as to grade placement be given at this point since it will vary with each child, with each language, with each class and each school. This will be determined for each child individually.

RECOMMENDATION — 18

That oral English be stressed in order to familiarize the students with the sound of an unknown tongue following the basic order, the development of the listening skills before introducing the child to the development of oral skills.

RECOMMENDATION — 19

That children not be introduced to reading in the second language before they have learned to *read well* in their mother tongue; to do so would only mean that they would be almost as confused as if they were taught to read in English from the *start*.

RECOMMENDATION — 20

That the Crystal City Independent School District (CCISD) accept the Paulo Friere method for teaching reading and writing in Spanish. That a thirty (30) minute period for this instruction be set aside.

RECOMMENDATION — 21

That all curriculum from Pre-Kindergarten to grade twelve be reviewed and that all personnel begin immediately to develop new Spanish oriented curriculum. All materials which will be developed will reflect the Chicano culture and heritage.

RECOMMENDATION — 22

That the Crystal City Independent School District (CCISD) accept Spanish and English on an equal basis as the official languages of the district.

notes

preface

1. A list of those persons I interviewed appears in the Bibliography.
2. Students and others who were particularly helpful to me are mentioned in the Acknowledgments and in the Bibliography.

chapter one: the setting

1. I am aware of the tremendous difficulties of looking at "history" to determine causation. For an excellent study into the limits of historical analysis in providing explanations for political scientists, see David Underhill, "Death at a Later Age: Political Science versus the Columbia Rebellion," in *An End to Political Science*, ed. Marvin Surkin and Alan Wolfe (New York: Basic Books, Inc., 1970). For a general theoretical investigation into the causes of revolts and revolutions, see Harry Eckstein, "On the Etiology of Internal War," *History and Theory* 4, no. 2 (1965): 133-63.
2. See Paul S. Taylor, *An American-Mexican Frontier* (Durham, N.C.: Duke University Press, 1934), for a history of the area. Taylor's works are among the very few that have been done on the area.
3. Ibid., p. 61.
4. Ibid., p. 184. Other historians have seemed to document this charge, made more famous throughout the Southwest now by Reies Tijerina's *Alianza* movement. See F. L. Olmsted, *A Journey through Texas* (New York: Mason Brothers, 1859).

5. R. C. Tate, "History of Zavala County, Texas" (unpublished M.A. thesis, Southwest Texas State College, San Marcos, Texas, 1942), p. 88.

6. See Ernest Holdsworth, Sr., "A History of Zavala County" (mimeographed article, Crystal City, Texas, date unknown), and his account of "King Fisher," a late nineteenth century ranchman.

7. Although the word "colonialism" may seem provocative, conditions in South Texas have been sufficiently similar to those in such areas as Southern Africa to merit use of the word. In Southern Africa, it should be recalled, the English and Afrikaner groups also found a sparsely populated area which the Africans had earlier considered their homeland. In introducing farming and ranching, the Europeans attracted and employed many Africans and thereby also had an inexhaustible supply of cheap labor. For more on the applicability of the colonial analogy, see Joan Moore, "Colonialism: The Case of the Mexican-Americans," *Social Problems* 17, no. 4 (1970): 463-72, and Rodolfo Acuña, *Occupied America* (San Francisco: Canfield Press, 1972).

8. For excellent accounts of Anglo and Mexican attitudes towards each other, see Americo Paredes, *With His Pistol in His Hand* (Austin, Texas: University of Texas Press, 1958); and Ozzie Simmons, "Anglo-Americans and Mexican-Americans in South Texas: A Study in Dominant-Subordinate Group Relations" (Ph.D. dissertation, Harvard University, 1952).

9. James Weeks Tiller, "Some Economic Aspects of Commercial Cool Season Vegetable Production in the Texas Winter Garden" (Ph.D. dissertation, University of Oklahoma, 1969).

10. Taylor, p. 93.

11. Seldon C. Menefee, *Mexican Migratory Workers of South Texas*, prepared by the Federal Works Agency, Works Progress Administration (Washington, D.C.: U.S. Government Printing Office, 1941), p. 52.

12. Tiller, pp. 48-49. County acreage under cultivation increased from 522 acres in 1919 to 11,132 acres in 1929. From 1920 to 1930 the population of Zavala County increased from 3,108 to 10,349. That of Crystal City increased from an estimated 800 to 6,609. (*The Texas Almanac, 1970-71* [Dallas, Texas: A. H. Belo Corporation, 1969], pp. 170, 172.)

13. See Taylor, *American-Mexican Frontier*, regarding this point.

14. The 1930 census showed that Zavala County was composed of the following groups: Native Whites—2,617; Foreign-born Whites—52; Mexicans—7,660; Negroes—19. (William McKinley Pridgen, "A Survey and Proposed Plan of Reorganization of the Public Schools in Zavala County," M.A. thesis, University of Texas, Austin, 1939, p. 7.).

15. Menefee, p. 52. In noting this increasing unemployment, Menefee (p. 18) stated that nonetheless "both growers and contractors desire to see the Mexican colony in Crystal City maintained at its present size, in spite of increasing slackness of employment during the spinach season, as insurance against a possible future labor shortage."

16. Ibid., p. 37.

17. Ibid., p. 13.

18. Ibid., p. xv.

19. Aiding in the prosperity of the town was the federal government's

decision to build an alien internment camp for Japanese and Germans on the outskirts of Crystal City. At its peak the camp contained several thousand aliens. After the war these facilities were turned over to the city for housing, schools, and other much-needed structures. (From interviews with Sam Anderson, Director of Urban Renewal, Crystal City, November 11, 1970; and R. C. Tate, former Superintendent of Schools, Crystal City, December 7, 1970.)

20. Tiller, p. 66.

21. Ibid., p. 195.

22. Emphasizing the seriousness of the problem, the 1970 U.S. Census figures showed that all the counties of the Winter Garden Area lost population between 1960 and 1970, averaging about a ten percent loss. (U.S. Department of Commerce, Bureau of the Census, *1970 Census of Population* [Texas: Advance Report, PC(IV)-45, January, 1971].)

23. Regarding nomenclature, I have tended to use the words "Mexican," "Mexicano," "Mexican American," and "Latin" interchangeably. Where I am talking about Mexicans of Mexico (which is rare), I have tried to make this clear. I have tried to restrict the more recent term "Chicano" to groups which prefer to be known by this name. Because any one term becomes tedious after constant usage, however, I have tried to use numerous terms for people of Mexican heritage.

24. Pridgen, p. 39. By "white scholastic" population Pridgen meant the total Anglo and Mexican school-age population in the county. Negroes in the community have never formed anything but a minuscule minority. Pridgen (p. 18) does note of the Blacks: "These colored children all do field work for a living and spend little time in the school provided for them."

25. Menefee, p. 57, records that of the 535 children between the ages of seven and eighteen in their random sample, the average number of school grades completed was 2.2 years.

26. Dr. Douglas Foley and Walter Smith of the School of Education of the University of Texas at Austin have recently examined the Crystal City Independent School District's school board minutes from 1930 onward. See their unpublished work, "Selected References Pertinent to Chicano and Black Citizens of Cristal," 1972.

27. Paul Taylor, *Mexican Labor in the United States, Dimmit County, Winter Garden District, South Texas*, Vol. VI, No. 5 (Berkeley: University of California Press, 1930), p. 377.

28. Ibid., p. 378.

29. Tate, p. 47. Tate, incidentally, went on to become Superintendent of the Crystal City schools for a time following the war. In 1971 he became head of the privately run Crystal City Community School.

30. R. C. Tate was superintendent at the time of the school integration, and he reported that he and the board were happy to abolish the colored school because with so few children it was a drain on the school budget (Interview on December 7, 1970).

31. Tate, Thesis, p. 25.

32. V. O. Key noted in his *Southern Politics* (New York: Random House, 1949), p. 271, that Mexican-American voters in Texas were "man-

aged." In describing politics in South Texas and the rise of certain machines based upon the Mexican vote, Key observed (p. 273) that "the individual [Mexican] usually becomes qualified to vote at the behest of his *jefe*, who may pay his poll taxes and who often holds the tax receipts until election day to insure discipline and orderly procedure. Economic dependency often makes the control easier, and in south Texas there are large landholdings with whole communities employed on a single ranch. A corollary of such employer-employee relationships is political amenability, which simplifies the role of the political leader, sometimes a Mexican-American himself but often not."

33. In other areas of social life, such as churches, clubs, business associations, etc., there was a great deal of segregation, lasting beyond World War II. Shortly after the war nearly all public accommodations were integrated, however. As late as 1971 most social clubs, such as the Country Club, the Rotarians, most women's club, and most churches were segregated. (From an interview with José Angel Gutiérrez, Crystal City, November 13, 1970.)

34. Calvin Trillin, "U.S. Journal: Crystal City, Texas," *The New Yorker*, April 17, 1971, p. 102.

35. Harley L. Browning and S. Dale McLemore, *A Statistical Profile of the Spanish-Surnamed Population of Texas* (Austin: The University of Texas, Bureau of Business Research, 1964), pp. 69-79. The 1970 census figures showed Zavala County ranking eighth in percentage of Spanish-surnamed and Spanish-speaking inhabitants.

36. The U.S. Census lists 7,301 Spanish-surnamed people in Crystal City out of a total population in 1960 of 9,101. This is approximately eighty percent of the population of the city. ("Special Table PH-6," for Zavala County, Texas, 1960 Census, U.S. Bureau of Census, unpublished table.) The Crystal City Chamber of Commerce estimates that the population of Crystal City is approximately eighty-five percent Spanish-surnamed. By the 1970's the percentage was more likely closer to ninety percent.

37. On this point Ozzie Simmons ("Anglo-Americans and Mexican-Americans in South Texas," Ph.D. dissertation, Harvard University, 1952, p. 164) has written of an old community situated on the border, "the small Anglo minority jointly participates with Mexican-Americans . . . and social interaction is ordered on a class basis rather than an ethnic basis. There exist close friendships between Anglos and Mexicans, home visiting and entertaining, and a much greater amount of intermarriage. Starr County, like Brownsville and Laredo, has a long tradition of intermingling between Anglo and Mexican. . . ."

38. Clearly these other new towns in South Texas should be studied for possible comparisons. Two earlier anthropological studies have focused on McAllen and Weslaco. See the work by Ozzie Simmons and also Arthur Rubel, *Across the Tracks* (Austin: University of Texas Press, 1966).

39. In 1909, when the Cross-S Ranch put out another brochure designed to attract more people, seventy-eight families were listed in its registry of citizens. Not one of them was Spanish-surnamed. See *The*

Zavala County Sentinel, Midcentury Edition, November 1, 1957, Section C, p. 7.

40. Taylor, *Mexican Labor*, p. 374.

41. Menefee, p. 26.

42. From interviews with Ray Shafer, President and Business Manager of Teamsters Union Local 657 (San Antonio, November 6, 1970) and Gilbert Brook, Manager, Del Monte Foods, Inc., (Crystal City, February 11, 1971).

43. The plant and the union seem to be a crucial feature distinguishing Crystal City from the new towns of the Valley mentioned earlier. For the impact of the plant in terms of the introduction of "vertical ties" in the community, see Michael Miller and James Preston, "Vertical Ties and the Redistribution of Power in Crystal City," *Social Science Quarterly*, 53, no. 4 (1973): 772-84.

44. Holsomback maintained that he had wanted to quit. See the *Dallas Morning News*, May 7, 1963, p. 1. Several people, however, suggested that Holsomback found it financially rewarding to be in on the government of the city, and that his banking and land interests prospered. It is worth mentioning that Holsomback was one of the four Anglos who refused to see me.

45. From an interview with June Broadhurst, retired city clerk (Crystal City, November 10, 1970).

46. The general outlines of the scandal were clarified for me in an interview with Jack Giletson of the General Land Office (Austin, January, 1971). For coverage of the scandal, see *The Texas Observer*, Austin, 1954-1955.

47. The details of the land scandal involve more than this. I found people either reluctant to talk about it or no longer clear about what exactly happened. The spring, 1955, issues of the *Zavala County Sentinel* occasionally carried reports on grand jury investigations and the scandal statewide. One issue (May 27, 1955, p. 1.) reported that an Anglo paid Mexican veterans $300 for their signature to papers saying they wanted land.

48. *The Zavala County Sentinel*, January 13, 1961, p. 1, reported that only forty-two percent of the homes in Crystal City had sewage connections.

49. For more on the statistical indices of Crystal City, see the appendices; also see *Model Cities Application to the Department of Housing and Urban Development* (Crystal City: Crystal City Urban Renewal Agency, 1967).

50. From an interview with Sam Anderson, Director of Urban Renewal. Mr. Anderson related that Mayor Holsomback feared that Crystal City was in the process of dying, as smaller towns in the area had done. He was thus, according to Mr. Anderson, afraid to embark on programs which would cost the city money.

51. Sam Anderson related that in the early stages of Urban Renewal most of the opposition came from Mexicans in the community (interview).

52. At least one other Mexican, Abie Guevara, had run for the school

board before 1960. He was never successful, although each time he ran the voter turnout increased dramatically over those times when the Anglo incumbents ran unopposed.

53. From an interview with E. C. Muñoz (Crystal City, February 12, 1971).

54. *The Zavala County Sentinel,* April 8, 1960, p. 1. From the election results themselves I was unable to determine whether or not the votes for the Anglo candidates were cast almost completely by Anglos. Since more than 700 Anglos were registered to vote in the district, all the votes for the incumbents could have been cast by Anglos. But since over 600 Mexican Americans were also eligible to vote, they could also have contributed to the total.

55. The following year, for example, only 127 votes were cast in the school-board election.

56. In 1960 twenty-eight of the forty-six graduates from high school were Spanish-surnamed.

57. This episode is based on an interview with the Arnold López family (San Antonio, November 18, 1970).

58. See *The Zavala County Sentinel,* July 15, and July 22, 1960, p. 1. According to Arnold López the board retaliated by refusing to allow the school bus to pick up children in the Mexico Chico section of town. Since the children were legally too close to the school to be picked up, even though the bus had room for them, the school board decided to discontinue the practice of allowing the children to ride the bus (interview).

59. *The Zavala County Sentinel,* February 9, 1962, p. 1. See also the *Sentinel* for March 2, 1962.

60. Even to the present the program has not been popular with the area's farmers and ranchers. James Weeks Tiller (p. 146) noted that the surplus-commodities program was cited by many farmers and ranchers as one of the chief reasons area labor was no longer as good as it used to be.

61. It was of course rare to have widespread Anglo competition for offices, but I was not able to determine the reasons for all these contests. Perhaps the passage of time has dulled people's memories.

62. José Angel Gutiérrez, in an interview with Professors Lyle Brown and Thomas Charlton of the Baylor University Oral History Project, recalled that he was paid money to work for Cleto López, but that López was not in the race to win. López was only running, according to Gutiérrez, to insure that by taking away Mexican-American votes, someone else (who had paid his filing fee) would win. Gutiérrez argued thus that the López race should not be confused with independent Mexican-American candidates trying to buck Anglo domination. Gutiérrez further argued that local politicians would sometimes pay farm-worker truck drivers, or *contractistas,* to round up people and have them vote a certain way. (For access to this interview, I am grateful to José Angel Gutiérrez, and to Professors Brown and Charlton.)

1. For the best account of the 1963 Crystal City election, see Larry Goodwyn, "Los Cinco Candidatos," *The Texas Observer*, April 18, 1963, pp. 3-9. For another fairly thorough account, see William E. Brown, "Crystal City: Symbol of Hope," *Labor Today*, II (December, 1963—January, 1964): 16-20; or "Crystal City: New City Council Names Teamster Mayor," *The International Teamster*, May 1963: 16-21. For unpublished works, see Robert Cuellar, "A Social and Political History of the Mexican-American Population of Texas, 1929-1963" (M.A. thesis, North Texas State University, Denton, Texas, 1969), Chapter 6; and Charles Chandler, "The Mexican-American Protest Movement in Texas" (Ph.D. dissertation, Tulane University, New Orleans, Louisiana, 1968), Chapter 8. For other works done by students, see Carol Earl, "Crystal City, 1965: The Aftermath" (unpublished paper, University of Texas, Austin, 1965); and Mike Miller, "Political Conflict in a Bifurcated Community: Anglo-Chicano Relations in a Small Texas Town" (mimeographed paper, Texas A & M University, College Station, Texas, 1971), pp. 7-17.

2. From a discussion with Mike Miller, graduate student in Rural Sociology at Texas A & M University (November, 1970); and *The Dallas Morning News*, May 7, 1963, p. 18.

3. From an interview with Ray Shafer on November 6, 1970. It should be re-emphasized that having a union in Crystal City was most unusual for the area. As Charles Chandler (p. 109) has noted, "Attempts at labor union organization among agricultural workers have met, and continue to meet, with massive resistance. The combined impact of highly restrictive labor laws, abundant strikebreakers, conservative judges and state officials, the Texas Rangers, and unfavorable news media work against, and so far have prevented, successful labor organization."

Unions, where they existed at all in South Texas, thus tended to be on very weak foundations. For more on the state of unions in South Texas, see U.S. Senate, Ninety-First Congress, Committee on Labor and Public Welfare, Subcommittee on Migratory Labor, Hearings on "Who is Responsible?" *Migrant and Seasonal Farmworker Powerlessness* (Washington, D.C.: U.S. Government Printing Office, July 21, 1970), Part 8-B.

4. At this time the state of Texas had a poll tax. It cost $1.75 for the right to vote.

5. From interviews with Ray Shafer (San Antonio, November 6, 1970), Henry Muñoz (San Antonio, December 5, 1970) and Carlos Moore (Fort Worth, February 25, 1971).

6. From the files of the Urban Renewal Agency, Crystal City, Texas. For being allowed to use the files, I am grateful to Sam Anderson and Mrs. Clarice Jonsson, both of the Urban Renewal staff.

7. From an interview with a former city employee, Crystal City.

8. From interviews with Ray Shafer, Henry Muñoz, and Carlos Moore. Ray Shafer himself had a background that could hardly have been comforting to Crystal City's ruling Anglos. See *Hearings Before the Select Committee on Improper Activities in the Labor or Management Field*,

85th Congress, Second Session, November 18, 1958 (U.S. Government Printing Office, 1959), pp. 15531-37.

9. For discussions of PASO see dissertations of Robert Cuellar, and Charles Chandler.

10. By February, Andrew Dickens had dropped out of the movement, charging that the Teamsters were masterminding the whole affair.

11. Jesús Maldonado had completed only the sixth grade in Crystal City schools, but while in the army he finished the equivalent of a high-school education.

12. From an interview with Jesús Maldonado (Crystal City, December 7, 1970).

13. From an interview with Arnold López (San Antonio, November 18, 1970).

14. Those counting the absentee ballots also noted that López was drawing votes away from the Anglo candidates and tried to send word of the danger out to the Anglo community.

15. From an interview with Carlos Moore.

16. From interviews with Juan Cornejo (Crystal City, December 11, 1970) and Ray Shafer.

17. For a discussion of the issues raised in the campaign, see the study by Larry Goodwyn, and also Captain Jack Loyall, "Remarks Made by Captain J. A. Loyall to the Uvalde Rotary Club" (mimeographed paper, Crystal City, September 16, 1963).

18. Larry Goodwyn, p. 6.

19. Ibid.

20. For an elaboration on this point, and on discrimination between Anglos and Mexican Americans, see Ozzie Simmons, "Anglo-Americans and Mexican-Americans in South Texas" (Ph.D. dissertation, Harvard University, 1952). Simmons notes, for example (p. 5), that "the Mexican's subordinate status is a continuum defined at one extreme by full caste and at the other by modified caste that permits crossing the line in various strategic respects." Simmons further notes that Anglos recognize "cultural assimilation as a criterion in determining the degree and intensity of caste treatment to which it subjects the individual Mexican."

21. As the notice was stated in the paper, "The Crystal City Lions Club is planning a Boy Scout Troop for Anglo-American boys between the ages of 11 and 18. . . ." (*The Zavala County Sentinel*, February 22, 1963).

22. From an interview with Jesús Maldonado.

23. See the previous chapter for a discussion of this point.

24. See the study by Ozzie Simmons.

25. One city official went so far as to maintain, "We never had any trouble before—or any discrimination." (Goodwyn, p. 6.)

26. On election day reportedly 536 of the 542 Anglos registered had voted, for a turnout in excess of ninety-eight percent. See Mike Miller, "Political Conflict," p. 13.

27. For more on the history of the Texas Rangers, see Walter Prescott Webb, *The Texas Rangers* (New York: Houghton Mifflin Company, 1935); and Americo Paredes, op. cit.; also Ben H. Procter, "The Modern Texas Rangers: A Law Enforcement Dilemma in the Rio Grande Valley," in *The*

Mexican Americans: An Awakening Minority, ed. Manuel Servin (Beverly Hills, California: Glencoe Press, 1970), pp. 212-27. Carey McWilliams also mentions the Rangers in his *North From Mexico* (Philadelphia: J. B. Lippincott Company, 1949), Chapter 6.

28. From an interview with Carlos Moore.

29. Although Anglo intimidation was an important part of the campaign, it is worth mentioning another source of intimidation in the Mexican community. As Charles Chandler has observed, "The Mexican-American is more often intimidated by his own ignorance than by explicit threats from the outside. Conservative Anglos are aware of this fact and do not hesitate to make use of it." (Chandler, p. 76.) It was, of course, only when these internal constraints began to break down that the Anglos needed to act.

30. *The Zavala County Sentinel*, March 29, 1963.

31. Larry Goodwyn, p. 5.

32. Ibid. This is the same José Angel Gutiérrez who will become increasingly important in later years.

33. Ibid.

34. From interviews with Henry Muñoz and with Carlos Moore.

35. From an interview with Ray Shafer.

36. The turnout actually exceeded the number of poll taxes bought in the city. This could happen legally because people over the age of sixty did not need to buy a poll tax. Estimating the number of people over sixty in the community has led some to say the turnout was ninety-five percent of those registered or otherwise qualified to vote.

37. Larry Goodwyn, p. 8.

38. Ibid.

39. From an interview with Jesús Maldonado.

40. *The San Antonio Express*, April 7, 1963.

chapter three: governance, 1963-1965

1. Shortly after the election the town received recognition in *Time*, April 12, 1963, p. 25; *Newsweek*, April 29, 1963, p. 26; *The New York Times*, April 14, 1963, p. 49, and May 5, 1963, p. 83; *The National Observer*, April 22, 1963, p. 1; and *The Los Angeles Times*, May 27, 1963, Part II, p. 1. Within six months events in Crystal City were being reported in *The Wall Street Journal*, September 18, 1963; again in *The New York Times*, September 21, 1963, p. 17; and *Look*, October 8, 1963, pp. 68-72. The prominent Mexican magazine, *Mañana*, ran an article, "Una Revolución de Mexicanos en el Sur de Texas," in their September 14, 1963, issue, pp. 20-33. At the end of the year Texas newspaper editors voted the Crystal City story the second most newsworthy event occurring in Texas during the year. It was second only to the assassination of President Kennedy.

2. *The Corpus Christi Caller-Times*, May 19, 1963, p. 2-B. Other papers noted with obvious horror the possibility that the Crystal City revolt might spread to their own communities. See, for example, the editorial

"Could Valley Become Another Crystal City?" in *The Valley Morning Star*, May 12, 1963.

3. *The Dallas Morning News*, May 7, 1963, p. 1.

4. *The Zavala County Sentinel*, April 19, 1963, p. 4.

5. *The Texas Observer*, April 18, 1963, p. 10.

6. Ibid., May 16, 1963.

7. Cornejo had dropped out of school in the third grade. While in the army during the Korean War, however, he had received the equivalent of an eighth-grade education.

8. *The Dallas Morning News*, April 13, 1963.

9. From interviews with George Ozuna (November 6, 1970) and José Angel Gutiérrez (November 13, 1970). Charles Chandler ("The Mexican-American Protest Movement in Texas," Ph.D. dissertation, Tulane University, New Orleans, Louisiana, 1968, p. 180) says that Hernández broke publicly "because a Zavala County law enforcement official was holding five 'hot checks' signed by the councilman."

10. The city charter of Crystal City required that councilmen be owners of property in the city.

11. *The San Antonio Express*, May 2, 1963, p. 1.

12. Ibid.

13. From an interview with George Ozuna.

14. The most common reasons some Anglos stayed on appear to have been because no other jobs were available for them or because they wanted to stay in to keep tabs on the new government. Sympathy or concern for the new government does not seem to have been an important reason.

15. From interviews with June Broadhurst and with George Ozuna.

16. The obvious example that comes to mind is the departure of the French from Guinea.

17. This and other material mentioned here is gathered from interviews with George Ozuna. For two of the most complete newspaper articles on the city administration, see Clarence La Roche, "Crystal City Shows Progress," *The San Antonio Light*, August 3, 1963, and Gladwin Hill, "Crystal City, Texas Tests Mexican-Americans' Political Role," *The New York Times*, September 21, 1963.

18. *The New York Times*, September 21, 1963.

19. Ibid. One could only wonder, however, about what influence the First of Texas Corporation might have had over the city if they had not felt the city administration was handling affairs in a "conservative" manner.

20. Captain J. A. Loyall, "Remarks Made by Captain J. A. Loyall to the Uvalde Rotary Club," mimeographed paper, Crystal City, September 16, 1963, p. 4.

21. *The San Antonio Express*, May 7, 1963, p. 6-D.

22. Ramon Garces, "Tempers Flare in Crystal City," *The Laredo Times*, April 29, 1963.

23. That Captain Allee was the first cousin of Tom Allee, one of the leaders of the Anglo opposition, only made what was obvious more apparent.

24. Governor Connally said that the Rangers were only in Crystal City to preserve law and order, and added that they would stay there "as long as the situation warrants." (*The San Antonio Express*, April 30, 1963.)

25. *The San Antonio Express*, May 2, 1963, p. 7-D. This incidentally, is another example of the enormous gap between Governor Connally and Senator Yarborough. It should not be forgotten that President Kennedy's ill-fated trip to Texas was primarily to patch up this rivalry.

26. See *The Zavala County Sentinel*, June 21, 1963, and August 9, 1963. See also a newspaper article from the files of George Ozuna, "Deputy's Arrest Called 'Frame,' " by Tom Gowan.

27. *The San Antonio Express*, May 5, 1963, p. 6-A.

28. The original petition was declared invalid because it failed to provide for a runoff, which all offices for four-year terms must do according to state law. This first petition had 502 signatures. Reportedly, only 68 of those signing, or thirteen percent, had Spanish surnames, in spite of the effort of the Anglos to claim that the recall petition was not racially inspired. These 502 signatures added up to less than thirty percent of the total number of voters who had cast ballots in the spring election. Thus clearly the opposition could not have presented a *bona fide* recall petition. The second, and valid, petition for the "charter revision" contained 232 signatures.

29. *The Zavala County Sentinel*, November 8, 1963.

30. Although the Anglos in Crystal City were virtually united in their opposition to Los Cinco, it would be a mistake to think that the Anglo community was completely monolithic. For more on Anglo diversity in the town, see Chapter 4.

31. During these early months of the new regime the Anglos also heartily encouraged "responsible" Mexicans to organize a chapter of the more conservative League of United Latin American Citizens (LULAC). Several Mexican Americans who were outspoken in their opposition to PASO came to Crystal City for this purpose, being escorted into town by the Texas Rangers. (*The Corpus Christi Caller-Times*, June 16, 1963.)

The meeting was chaired by Mario Hernández, the member of the council who had broken with the other four. The Anglos seemed to be especially fond of that part of the LULAC code which stated to its members: "Learn how to discharge your duties before you learn how to assert your rights." (Quoted in *The Zavala County Sentinel*, June 22, 1963, p. 1.)

The LULAC chapter withered quickly, however, mainly because its charter stated that it had to be nonpolitical, and because those Mexicans who might have been expected to join LULAC were invited by Anglos to participate in a new political organization being formed.

32. From an interview with Arnold López.

33. It should be noted that the revolt never had any serious middle-class Mexican support. Since the regime had managed to win election without middle-class support, the new government was not necessarily (if all else remained equal) bringing about its own downfall by rejecting these offers of assistance.

34. The San Antonio papers, for example, were frequently headlining

events taking place in Crystal City. Shafer had also been quoted as saying that the Teamsters were hoping to move into six other communities in South Texas. (*The Dallas Morning News*, May 4, 1963, p. 11.)

35. *The Zavala County Sentinel*, August 2, 1963, p. 1.

36. It is interesting, however, that CASAA never came close to representing the actual population ratio of the two groups in the county, which contained three times as many Mexicans as Anglos.

37. *The Laredo Times*, November 20, 1963, p. 1.

38. At the time the application was turned down, the city had no library and their health building was a 20 x 20 foot structure thirty to forty years old. According to Ozuna, the jail was a dingy six cells that were even older than the health center (interview).

39. *The Zavala County Sentinel*, December 20, 1963, p. 1.

40. As an example of the greater conservatism of the county, that very fall the county had decisively defeated a proposal to repeal the poll tax, although the proposal carried in two of Crystal City's three precincts. (See *The Zavala County Sentinel*, November 8, 1963, p. 1.)

41. Working in the Anglos' favor was the fact that proportionately far fewer of the Mexican populace than the Anglo populace were eligible to vote. A minority of perhaps ten percent of the local Mexican population were still Mexican nationals and thus not able to vote. Also, the Mexican population was much younger than the Anglo population. According to the 1960 census, the median age of the Spanish-surnamed population of the county averaged only seventeen years. (See "Special Table PH-6," for Zavala County, Texas, 1960 Census, U.S. Bureau of the Census, unpublished table.)

42. From an interview with Bill Richey (November 10, 1970). That this type of relationship would dampen the prospects for revolt has been noted by Ozzie Simmons in his study of the Rio Grande Valley ("Anglo-Americans and Mexican-Americans in South Texas," Ph.D. dissertation, Harvard University, 1952), and by Eric Wolf in his more general study, *Peasant Wars of the Twentieth Century* (New York: Harper and Row, 1969).

43. In 1965 the county's best-known absentee landlord became Governor John B. Connally, who bought a several-thousand-acre ranch in Zavala and Dimmit counties. See *The Zavala County Sentinel*, March 26, 1965.

44. For an elaboration of this point, see Robert Cuellar, "A Social and Political History of the Mexican-American Population of Texas, 1929-1963," M.A. thesis, North Texas State University, Denton, Texas, 1969, and Charles Chandler, "The Mexican-American Protest Movement in Texas," Ph.D. dissertation, Tulane University, New Orleans, Louisiana, 1968.

45. On this last point, the same was true in 1963 as in 1964. The Anglos, however, did not realize the seriousness of the Mexican challenge in time to launch an absentee-vote drive on the same scale as in 1964. Carlos Moore did state, however, that had Los Cinco lost in 1963, he was prepared to file suit challenging the legality of many of the absentee votes. (From an interview with Carlos Moore.) Moore claimed that many who voted by absentee vote were neither sick nor going to be out of town on election day.

46. CASAA also encouraged absentee balloting because it allowed them to determine how people had voted much more easily. County authorities could very easily check to see how each absentee voter cast his ballot.

47. *The Zavala County Sentinel*, April 24, 1964, p. 1.

48. *The Kansas City Times*, April 28, 1964; from an article by Robert K. Sanford, "Mexicanos Rule Crystal City, Texas, Well—But Tension Exists."

49. The validity of these charges is difficult to determine. As mentioned earlier, a number of Mexicans in Crystal City were still Mexican nationals, and it does seem probable that some Mexican nationals did vote. Whether they voted for the more radical candidates, however, is another question. One person told me that some Mexican nationals voted for CASAA after being told by Anglos that they would be deported if they did not vote for CASAA. It does seem plausible that Mexican nationals as a group would be more vulnerable to intimidation, having fewer rights and being less sure of what these rights were.

50. *The Zavala County Sentinel*, June 5, 1964, p. 1.

51. For this information I am grateful to Mike Miller.

52. The local PASO activists did have two advantages in 1964 that they had lacked in 1963. First, their people had voted before and had broken the ice in this area of participation. Secondly, the local Mexican population now knew that it was possible to change things in the community through running for office and winning elections.

53. Notice as an indication of county polarization and mobilization that more people actually voted in the race for county sheriff than in any of the statewide races.

54. The sources for the election returns in this table and the previous one are *The Zavala County Sentinel*, May 8, 1964, and June 12, 1964. These were checked against returns kept on record at the county courthouse. Where a discrepancy existed, the county courthouse records were used.

In recognition of the problems involved in making inferences from aggregate data, we also give the precinct returns for the races of county sheriff and U.S. Senator in the hopes that these will give a clearer indication of the similarities in the vote than the countywide totals could:

Office	Absentee	Precincts						Totals
		1	2	4	5	6	7	
U.S. Senate								
McLendon	343	120	44	215	158	413	307	1600
Yarborough	110	55	0	127	287	317	457	1355
Sheriff								
Sweeten	391	158	43	283	196	448	346	1865
Garza	137	86	1	105	300	309	439	1377

Note: Precincts 1, 2, and 4 are from rural areas and other towns in the county. Precincts 5 and 7 represent heavily Mexican areas of Crystal City. Precinct 6 includes the predominantly Anglo section of town and some Mexican-American areas as well.

55. In a discussion with Chuck Caldwell, an assistant to Senator Yarborough, in Austin, Texas, December 3, 1970, Caldwell confirmed that Senator Yarborough's Anglo support had disappeared in the county after 1963. Caldwell noted the polarization in the county and said that "all the campaigning in the world" by Senator Yarborough wouldn't have been able to dent this Anglo opposition.

56. It should also not be forgotten that the 1963 victory by Los Cinco had been by only a narrow margin.

57. From an interview with Henry Muñoz. For a report on Cornejo's Los Angeles speech, see the article by Ruben Salazar, *The Los Angeles Times*, May 27, 1963, Part II, p. 1.

58. *The Zavala County Sentinel*, June 26, 1964, p. 1.

59. Ibid.

60. According to Chandler (p. 198), the split between Cornejo and Ozuna developed when Ozuna awarded a contract to construct the new city hall to a Del Rio firm. Cornejo, according to Chandler, had wanted to use only local labor. Although this would be a slightly different reason for the dispute, it does not conflict with the issues which are said here to have caused the dispute to flare up into the open.

61. Carol Earl ("Crystal City, 1965: The Aftermath," unpublished paper, University of Texas, 1965) also discusses Cornejo from the viewpoint of his trying to build a *patrón* system. For more on the *patrón* system in general, see Clark Knowlton, "Patrón-Peon Patterns Among the Spanish Americans of New Mexico," *Social Forces*, 41, no. 1 (1962): 12-17; Florence Kluckhohn and Fred Strodtbeck, *Variations in Value Orientations* (Elmsford, N.Y.: Row, Peterson, and Co., 1961), Chapter 7; for the patrón pattern as it has worked in Texas, see O. Douglas Weeks, "The Texas-Mexicans and the Politics of South Texas," *The American Political Science Review*, 24, no. 3 (1930): 606-27; and V. O. Key, *Southern Politics* (New York: Random House, 1969), especially pp. 271-274. Chandler also discusses the machine politics of South Texas in his Chapter 3. This machine politics in South Texas has at times had an important influence upon state politics. It should not be forgotten, for instance, that Lyndon Johnson owed his election to the United States Senate in 1948 to "late" returns coming from one of these machine counties.

62. From an interview with George Ozuna; see also *The Laredo Times*, September 2, 1964, p. 1.

63. *The Houston Chronicle*, February 21, 1965, Section 3, p. 8.

64. Chandler (p. 199) has commented on this situation: "Local Anglos—who, of course, would not think of hiring Cornejo—bemoaned the damage an unemployed Mayor would do to their 'image.' "

65. This and the following material from an interview with George Ozuna.

66. From an interview with George Ozuna.

67. From *The Zavala County Sentinel*, March 26, 1965, p. 1.

68. See *The Zavala County Sentinel*, February 19, 1965, p. 1.

69. *The San Antonio Express*, January 14, 1965.

70. Not only were job opportunities opened up for Mexicans that had

never been available before; the city council also appointed the first Negro, Reverend W. L. Green, to the Urban Renewal Commission. The Reverend Green, however, moved out of the community a short time later.

71. One person explained the antagonism that Cornejo was able to arouse in people by noting that after Cornejo became mayor, he was the sort of person who would, upon seeing a worker digging a ditch, "go over and tell him to dig the ditch a little deeper."

72. From an interview with a person involved.

73. Although voting by absentee ballot for this reason is illegal, it is probably something less than fraud.

74. For a similar observation, although in a very different context, see Jan Myrdal, *Report from a Chinese Village* (New York: Pantheon Books, 1965); and his comment, "The Reshaping of Chinese Society," *Contemporary China*, ed. Ruth Adams (New York: Pantheon Books, 1966), pp. 65-91.

chapter 4: the reaction

1. Significantly, at the very moment when the Cornejo slate was losing in Crystal City, in Mathis, another town in South Texas, a slate of Mexican Americans, led however by an Anglo engineer from Ohio, defeated the old Anglo establishment in the town. Like Crystal City, Mathis was overwhelmingly composed of Mexican Americans, and many of these were migrants. The slate won in spite of Anglo charges that if the "radicals" won, Mathis would be turned into another "Crystal City." See Charles Chandler, "The Mexican-American Protest Movement in Texas," Ph.D. dissertation, Tulane University, New Orleans, Louisiana, 1968, and Carol Earl, "Crystal City, 1965: The Aftermath," unpublished paper, University of Texas, Austin, 1965.

2. Carl D. Howard, "Mexican-Americans 'Want to Get on Top,' and They're Gaining," *The National Observer*, April 12, 1965.

3. Mayor Holsomback was not a member of CASAA. Shortly after his defeat, he announced that he was retiring from politics and moved to San Antonio.

4. One elderly Anglo commented that the farmers and ranchers had never been interested in attracting industry to the area because they thought it might compete with their labor supply. For this I am grateful to Mike Miller.

5. Even at the level of state politics, the town and county seem to have been considerably more in sympathy with Republican candidates than was the state as a whole. In his index of Republican strength in Texas, Clifton McClesky found that Zavala County ranked in the upper quartile of all Texas counties. See his *The Government and Politics of Texas* (Boston: Little, Brown and Company, 1963), p. 80.

6. Jack Loyall, "Remarks Made by Captain J. A. Loyall to the Uvalde

Rotary Club," mimeographed paper, Crystal City, September 16, 1963, p.6.

7. It should be noted, however, that the proper sort of Mexican sometimes involved racial categories. An Anglo leader who was to become head of CASAA was quoted confidentially as saying "There is no such thing as a Mexican-American culture. Those Mexicans of German, French, and Scotch ancestry own their own businesses. . . . Culturally the Indians don't have manners. The Spanish do. The more the dilution [of Indian blood], the more American they are. The more Indian, the more they want *from* America."

8. For more on the internal differentiation among Mexican Americans, see Ozzie Simmons, "Anglo-Americans and Mexican-Americans in South Texas," Ph.D. dissertation, Harvard University, 1952. A number of writers have noted that the openings for some qualified Mexicans at the top has produced leadership difficulties for the Mexican masses. This siphoning off of the most talented members of the Mexican community is judged more serious than in the Negro community because of the limited openness of the system to the Mexican. See, for example, James B. Watson and Julian Samora, "Subordinate Leadership in a Bicultural Community: An Analysis," *American Sociological Review*, 19 (August, 1954): 413-21.

9. One Mexican active in CASAA commented that one of the biggest advantages to being in CASAA was that the partisans "got better jobs." These CASAA Mexicans were often as poor as the majority of Mexicans in the community.

10. *The Houston Chronicle*, February 21, 1965, Section 3, p. 8.

11. From an interview with Dale Barker, editor of *The Zavala County Sentinel*, (November 9, 1970).

12. From an interview with one of the CASAA councilmen.

13. *The Zavala County Sentinel*, May 14, 1965, p. 1.

14. From interviews with one of the city personnel beneath him and with one of the city councilmen.

15. *The Zavala County Sentinel*, August 17, 1967, p. 1.

16. From an interview with one of the CASAA councilmen.

17. One Anglo active in CASAA during this period remarked that he did not wish to discuss who the leaders of the movement against Ozuna had been "because some of them are now dead."

18. From an interview with a former Crystal City employee.

19. From an interview with one of the CASAA councilmen.

20. Corroborating this CASAA attitude, one Mexican who came into the government in 1965 reported that he had been able to save a few Mexicans from being fired by telling the city manager that some people couldn't be fired because they were relatives of various CASAA supporters, when in fact they were not relatives at all.

21. See *The San Antonio Light*, September 25, 1965. This episode is gathered from interviews with Mrs. Irma Benavides, sister of Luis and Carlos Avila (Crystal City, February 10, 1971), Mrs. Robert Stauber (Crystal City, November 8, 1970), and Rev. and Mrs. Kenneth Newcomer (Blanco, Texas, October 12, 1970). Note the irony that it was a Negro who prevented the Anglos from killing or more seriously injuring Luis Avila.

22. From an interview with Irma Benavides.

23. From an interview with Jesús Maldonado.

24. *The Zavala County Sentinel,* April 15, 1966, February 2 and February 16, 1967. I did not interview Sheriff Sweeten, but in a letter to Howard Glickstein of the U.S. Commission on Civil Rights, written on August 24, 1970, Sweeten defended his actions as sheriff and gave his general philosophy on things in Crystal City: "I can assure you that I am a contreversial [sic] figure, standing in the way of the criminal type Mexican American but backing the good ones with everything I have and will continue to do so." Sweeten then mentioned several charges that had been brought against him without success, criticized the Commission's report, *Mexican Americans and the Administration of Justice in the Southwest* (Washington, D.C.: U.S. Government Printing Office, 1970), but stated that he recognized and was familiar with most of the problems the report mentioned. He concluded by saying, "Several other problems exist here but I think it can be solved by talking to and working with our good Mexican-American citizens and not with the criminal element. I would like to see America divided in only one way, The good of all races against the bad."

25. These two incidents of physical violence were probably the most important in terms of personalities involved and political ramifications, but there were also fights between Mexicans over politics. These had been occurring since the days of Los Cinco and often took place in taverns. Involving CASAA and PASO people, these brawls would generally see PASO people charging CASAA people with being traitors and Uncle Toms and the CASAA people charging that PASO people were disgracing Mexicans in the eyes of the Anglos.

26. *The Zavala County Sentinel,* July 22, 1966.

27. From an interview with Irma Benavides.

28. Ibid.

29. From an interview with Mrs. Irma Benavides by Mike Miller (November, 1970). For this I am grateful to Mike Miller.

30. In 1966 a half-hearted attempt had been made to take over the county, as had been seriously tried in 1964. Juan Cornejo, again trying for office, ran for county judge. Although he led a field of four in the first primary, he was buried in the runoff, 1,507 to 907 as the votes for his opponents combined. Fewer people voted in these county elections and the challengers lost by greater margins than they had in 1964. The Cornejo organization, PASO, was not seriously revived, as it was difficult to convince the Mexican community that they had a good chance to win the county offices after their defeat in 1964. In November, however, a second attempt by CASAA to change the city charter to create four-year terms for city councilmen and to have them run for staggered terms was narrowly defeated. A rally was held in the Mexican section of town against the change, and its defeat indicated that CASAA had not yet attained complete dominance within the city.

31. From interviews with June Broadhurst (Crystal City, November 13, 1970) and Bill Leonard (Crystal City, December 10, 1970).

32. From an interview with an Anglo leader in CASAA.

33. *The Zavala County Sentinel*, February 16, 1967.

34. From an interview with Bill Leonard (Crystal City, December 10, 1970).

35. Ed Salinas himself said a short time later, "We have had difficult times but we have survived." (*The Zavala County Sentinel*, April 13, 1967.)

36. *The Zavala County Sentinel*, March 23, 1967.

37. Ibid., March 30, 1967.

38. Around four hundred people, again an extraordinary number, voted by absentee ballot in the election. Note that no CASAA candidate would have come close to winning without the absentee votes.

39. *The San Antonio Express*, May 5, 1967.

40. From an interview with Bill Leonard.

41. The possibilities of deals involving various parties to the dispute were suggested by many, but none of this could be confirmed.

42. Texas voting laws are such that there is no complete assurance that one's vote will in fact be secret. Each voter must tear off a stub on his paper ballot, sign his name to the back of the stub, and deposit it in a box separate from the ballots. A number on the stub correlates the stub to the ballot. Although the box of stubs is not supposed to be opened except under court orders, there are often complaints around the state that the boxes of stubs have been opened.

43. One of the CASAA candidates related that they were sorry Falcón had been removed from office instead of Lozano or Roberto Cornejo.

44. From an interview with Jesús Maldonado.

45. From an interview with Eddie Treviño (Crystal City, December 6, 1970).

46. The exception was Irma Benavides' march protesting the school administration's refusal to allow adults to use school facilities in the Adult Migrant Education program. But this didn't lead to any electoral challenge to the board. Instead the Mexicans concentrated their efforts on the city council races. For more on tensions within the schools themselves, see Chapter 5.

47. The use of the words "militant" and "radical" to apply to the non-CASAA Mexicans is meant only in the sense that these Mexicans challenged the basic Anglo superordination in the town. In trying to overthrow Anglo domination and to assert their own independence, these Mexicans threatened the whole economic, social, and political arrangements which had long been operative in the town. For this reason I have occasionally labelled them radicals or militants. This has been done to avoid the excessive use of cumbersome or slightly inaccurate phrases such as "the non-CASAA Mexicans," "PASO," or "the migrants." It does not mean that these Mexicans were violent revolutionaries.

48. Of course, for all the figures the differences between the Anglo population and the Spanish-surnamed population was tremendous, but the median alone was astounding.

49. *Model Cities Application to the Department of Housing and Urban Development* (Crystal City: Crystal City Urban Renewal Agency, 1967), especially Parts II and III.

50. Ibid., letter from Superintendent M. D. Ray, April 13, 1967.

51. Ibid., Part III.

52. Ibid.

53. Ibid., Part II.

54. Ibid., Part III.

55. This should not be taken to mean that all the city leadership was equally concerned about problems of poverty in the city. One Anglo leader expressed a fairly common sentiment when he said, "Here Mexican Americans don't have problems of poverty. Migrants make money in the north and come back here and draw unemployment."

56. From interviews with Sam Anderson (Crystal City, November 11, 1970) and Mrs. Clarice Jonsson, secretary, Urban Renewal Office (Crystal City, December 6, 1970).

57. *The Zavala County Sentinel*, June 8, 1967.

58. From interviews with Mrs. Irma Benavides and Mrs. Enriqueta Palacios (Crystal City, February 10, 1971). Eddie Treviño suggested that he thought the board decided not to keep the Head Start Program because they disliked having to fill out all the governmental forms.

59. *The Zavala County Sentinel*, August 15, 1968.

60. From an interview with Mrs. Irma Benavides, who was on the executive board at the time.

61. *The Zavala County Sentinel*, June 13, 1968, p. 4.

62. Ibid., June 27, 1968, p. 1.

63. Ibid.

64. In actual fact, however, the county was rebuked by Texas Attorney General Crawford Martin, who issued a statement saying the county commissioners court could not serve or appoint another group to serve as administrators of the Community Action Agency. County Judge Taylor said, however, that he didn't care who administered the antipoverty program as long as it was done in a "business-like manner." (*The Zavala County Sentinel*, August 15, 1968, p. 1.)

65. From interviews with Bill Leonard (Crystal City, December 10, 1970), Paulino Mata (Crystal City, December 11, 1970) and John Holdsworth (Crystal City, November 8, 1970).

66. *The Zavala County Sentinel*, January 4, 1968, p. 1.

67. Such views of a "sell-out" were stated forcefully by Mrs. Irma Benavides and Mrs. Enriqueta Palacios.

68. At this same primary election, the Democratic nomination for county commissioner of precinct three was won by F. D. Keller, who beat Natividad Granados (of the Falcón faction) 347 to 265. The seat was then held by Jesús Rodríguez, who, it will be recalled, had chosen not to run for re-election because of the boycott of his store. Rodríguez thus became another example of the difficulty of developing and maintaining moderate Mexican leadership.

69. From an interview with a leader of the anti-CASAA, anti-Cornejo Mexicans.

70. From an interview with Frank Benavides (Crystal City, December 10, 1970).

71. Although Benavides emerged as the top vote-getter on the ticket,

the other members of the "Mata Team" passed over him and elected Mata mayor for another term. This incident is discussed more fully in Chapter 6.

72. From an interview with Sam Anderson. Mr. Anderson related that more money had been spent per capita in Crystal City than had been spent per capita under Mayor Lee in New Haven, Connecticut. Just where and to whom this $14 million had gone was another matter. Many Mexicans charged that the bulk of the money had gone to Anglo landlords, money lenders, and contractors. They said that very little went to the Mexican members of the community. For more on this, see Chapter 6.

73. Unfortunately I have not been able to determine the exact percentage of federal funds the school district has received over this period of time.

74. For a theoretical evaluation of the strategy behind this response to militants, see James Q. Wilson, "The Strategy of Protest: Problems of Negro Civic Action," *Journal of Conflict Resolution*, 5 (September, 1961): 291-303.

chapter five: the second revolt

1. More work needs to be done examining these nearby communities. Although my study is not explicitly comparative, I became increasingly interested in other towns in the area and think that important comparative work could be done here relating to conditions which foster or inhibit political, social, and economic change.

2. Good Neighbor Commission of Texas, *Texas Migrant Labor, Annual Report, 1969* (Austin, 1969), Chapter 8, pp. 1-2. The report estimated the number of workers (not including children) to be 3,400, or approximately one-third of the population of the county. Others have estimated the total to be considerably higher, perhaps because they are including the entire family as migrant workers. Sam Anderson, director of urban renewal in the city, has estimated that "between 5,000 and 7,000 of the city's people are migrant workers. . . ." (*The San Antonio Light*, December 21, 1969, p. 1.)

3. See Chapter I for an elaboration of this point. See also James Weeks Tiller, "Some Economic Aspects of Commercial Cool Season Vegetable Production in the Texas Winter Garden," Ph.D. dissertation, University of Oklahoma, 1969, and annual reports on *Texas Farm Labor* (Austin, Texas: The Texas Employment Commission).

4. See Alexis de Tocqueville, *The Old Régime and the French Revolution*, trans. John Bonner (New York: Harper and Brothers, 1856). De Tocqueville noted, for example, that "Evils which are patiently endured when they seem inevitable become intolerable when once the idea of escape from them is suggested." (p. 214.) For a more recent theoretical exploration into the causes of revolution, see James C. Davies, "Toward a Theory of Revolution," *American Sociological Review*, 27, no. 1 (1962): 5-19; and Harry Eckstein, "On the Etiology of Internal Wars," *History and Theory*, 4, no. 2 (1965): 133-63.

5. Since opinion surveys weren't given to the Mexican-American population of Crystal City to document empirically these attitude changes, I have instead tried to note changes through other factors, mainly through issues raised in campaigns by Mexican Americans running for office. Through an examination of these campaigns, one cannot help but be impressed by the degree of radicalization of the Mexican-American community. How much this radicalism was always there, but was dormant because of the futility of trying to express it, is perhaps impossible to determine conclusively. There is reason to believe, however, that the local government itself, through its own actions and inactions, became an important agent of radicalization. For a general exploration on the role of government as creator (rather than reflector) of attitudes, see Murray Edelman, *The Symbolic Uses of Politics* (Urbana, Illinois: University of Illinois Press, 1964), and his "Research Orientations," in *Frontiers of Democratic Theory*, ed. Henry Kariel (New York: Random House, 1970), pp. 352-70.

6. The word "Chicano" apparently stems from the word "Mexicano" or *Me-Chicano*. In Nahuatl, the language of the Aztecs, the founders of what is now called Mexico City were called Mexicanos. The Nahuatl x is roughly the phonetic equivalent of the sound between the English *sh* and *ch*. "Chicano" is thus a shortened form of the word "Mexicano."

7. For a summary of developments in Mexican-American politics in the 1960's and earlier, see Alfredo Cuellar, "Perspectives on Politics" in Joan W. Moore, *Mexican Americans* (Englewood Cliffs, N.J.: Prentice Hall, 1970), pp. 137-56; and John Martinez, "Leadership and Politics," *La Raza: Forgotten Americans* (Notre Dame, Indiana: University of Notre Dame Press, 1966), pp. 47-62.

8. The word "gringo," of uncertain origin, is a pejorative word for Anglos. José Angel Gutiérrez, while president of MAYO, defined the word to be "a person or an institution that has a certain policy or program or attitudes that reflect bigotry, racism, discord, prejudice and violence." See Appendix 2.

9. In Texas there had been several earlier statewide organizations for Mexican Americans. For a discussion of these, see the dissertations of Robert Cuellar and Charles Chandler.

10. From a MAYO pamphlet, in possession of Dr. Jorge Lara-Braud, Hispanic American Institute, Austin, Texas.

11. The word "Raza" refers to people of Mexican ethnicity and culture. Translated literally it means "race," but those who use the word prefer its translation as "people." For more on the meaning of the word, see, for example, William Madsen, *Mexican-Americans of South Texas* (New York: Holt, Rinehart, and Winston, 1964), Chapter 3.

12. From a MAYO pamphlet.

13. Although not occurring in the big city barrios, the Cesar Chavez efforts at the unionization of farm workers also indicated a rise in dissatisfaction and in protest among Mexican Americans of the Southwest.

14. For more on the role of the family in Mexican-American life, see, for example, Madsen, Chapter 6; and Leo Grebler *et al.*, *The Mexican-American People* (New York: The Free Press, 1970), Chapter 15.

15. For more on the school system as it relates to Mexican Americans, see Thomas Carter, *Mexican Americans in School: A History of Educational Neglect* (New York: College Entrance Examination Board, 1970).

16. From interviews with several Mexican Americans in Crystal City.

17. The subject of José Angel Gutiérrez's master's thesis was, presciently, "The Empirical Conditions for Revolution in Four South Texas Counties," Saint Mary's University, San Antonio, 1969.

18. Figures supplied by Superintendent Angel Gonzales, Crystal City Independent School District, Crystal City. From an interview with Gonzales (Crystal City, November 11, 1970).

19. U.S. Bureau of the Census, 1960, "Special Report PH-6." Mentioned also in Gutiérrez's master's thesis, p. 61. By 1970 the figure had moved up to 3.0 years for males over twenty-five, and 3.1 years for females over twenty-five. The figures thus continued quite low. See U.S. Bureau of the Census, 1970 Census of Population, *General Social and Economic Characteristics: Texas*, Final Report PC(1)-C45 (Washington, D.C.: U.S. Government Printing Office, 1972), p. 1117.

20. In truth these figures for educational improvement in the population twenty-five years old and over do not accurately reflect changes in education in the community. For those Mexicans in the community between the ages of fourteen and twenty-one, the level of educational attainment is much higher than 2.3 years. Because many of these young people tend to leave the community upon graduating from high school, the educational attainment of Mexicans over twenty-five in the community remains depressed, as a residual category. See Joan Moore, *Mexican-Americans: Problems and Prospects* (Madison, Wisconsin: Institute for Research on Poverty, 1966), p. 23.

21. From an unpublished paper by José Angel Gutiérrez, "Aztlán: Chicano Revolt in the Winter Garden Area," Crystal City, 1970, p. 5; and Mike Miller, "Political Conflict in a Bifurcated Community," mimeographed paper, Texas A & M University, 1971, p. 3.

22. Gilbert Conoley and Juan Ibarra, *Inter-Office Memorandum*, Texas Education Agency, December 22, 1969, p. 1. For the 1968-1969 school year the district had a total student enrollment of 2,906. Of these, 2,518 were Mexican Americans, 376 were Anglos, and 12 were Negroes.

23. I say "almost universally recognized" because of an incident described to me by school trustee Eddie Treviño, which will be related later.

24. From interviews with Diana Palacios (Crystal City, February 10, 1971), Mario and Blanca Treviño (Crystal City, December 5, 1970) and Irma Benavides (Crystal City, February 10, 1971).

25. From an interview with Irma Benavides.

26. From an interview with Vice-Principal (and former mayor) Paulino Mata (Crystal City, December 11, 1970).

27. From an interview with Irma Benavides.

28. United States Commission on Civil Rights, *Issue Presentation for Education Conference* (mimeographed paper, Crystal City, Texas, March 7, 1970).

29. Ibid.

30. Calvin Trillin, "U.S. Journal: Crystal City, Texas," *The New Yorker*, April 17, 1971, p. 102.

31. From interviews with Mario and Blanca Treviño, and others.

32. Ibid. Interestingly, the year before, Diana Palacios had also tried out for cheerleader and was not chosen. There were not the Anglo vacancies at that time, however, and another Mexican, Diana Pérez, was chosen in place of Diana Palacios. Nevertheless, a small protest was made by those who thought Diana Palacios should have been selected cheer-leader.

33. The selection of the one Mexican cheerleader seems to have itself been a process under careful control. Diana Pérez was better accepted by the Anglos than was Diana Palacios. According to Diana Palacios, one school teacher told her that they had not selected her as cheerleader because "she didn't get along with Anglos." (From an interview with Diana Palacios)

34. From interviews with Mario and Blanca Treviño, and from Conoley and Ibarra, *Inter-Office Memorandum*, p. 3.

35. *The Zavala Conty Sentinel*, May 1, 1969, p. 1.

36. Although at the time the students thought that Billings had not gone back on his word, I learned from two separate interviews with Anglo townspeople that Billings had apparently told these people confidentially that he was glad that the school board had reversed his policy change.

37. Conoley and Ibarra, p. 3.

38. From interviews with Mario and Blanca Treviño.

39. His time as president of MAYO will be discussed later in this chapter.

40. From interviews with several Anglos in the community. Gutiérrez's own story is an important one. He discusses much of his life in his interview with Professors Lyle Brown and Thomas Charlton for the Baylor University Oral History Project.

41. Trillin, p. 104.

42. From an interview with Irma Benavides.

43. See Larry Goodwyn, "Los Cinco Candidatos," *The Texas Observer*, April 18, 1963, pp. 3-9. Also see Chapter 2 above.

44. From an interview with José Angel Gutiérrez. He also said of his experiences in 1963, ". . . I was kidnapped and coerced or attempted to be coerced . . . by gringo elements." (*The Congressional Record*, April 15, 1969, p. 9059.) Gutiérrez has gone into this episode more deeply in his interview for the Baylor University Oral History Project. There he says that he was taken at gun-point by a Mexican American to a house where several officials were waiting. The men had a tape recorder, and, Gutiérrez recalled, told him to say into the tape that he had been paid by the Teamsters, that he was being trained to be a communist, and that he was an atheist. He was further ordered to say that everything he had said in criticism of the Anglos and CASAA was just lies and that he had been coerced into saying it. Gutiérrez said that he refused to do so, thinking that he was going to die anyway, but that instead he was let go.

45. José Angel Gutiérrez, "Fact or Fiction?" (mimeographed pamphlet, Crystal City, 1964).

46. Among the most common Anglo explanations given are those charging that Gutiérrez's father was a communist who was run out of Mexico, that his mother was a prostitute, and that they both brought him

up to hate Anglos. Why this would account for the *change* is not clear. Many Anglos also assert that he may have been fathered by an Anglo, and thus he is taking his aggressions out on all Anglos. They also relate that Gutiérrez dated a local Anglo who eventually spurned him. Thus, they think he is taking his revenge for this family out on all Anglos. Others simply charge that Gutiérrez "sold out for money."

47. The word "Aztlán" is an Aztec word referring to northwestern Mexico (i.e., the American Southwest). It has gained currency in the Chicano movement to symbolize both their Indian (as opposed to Spanish) origins, and to reassert their historical claim to the Southwest.

48. Gutiérrez, "Aztlán."

49. For more on Saul Alinsky, see for example his *Reveille for Radicals* (Chicago: University of Chicago Press, 1946). It may also be of interest that Saul Alinsky's organizers were involved in the development of the farm-workers union movement in Delano, California.

50. For more on Henry González, see Charles Chandler's dissertation.

51. From interviews with various people active in the Chicano movement in San Antonio and from one labor lawyer in San Antonio.

52. González, *The Congressional Record*, April 3, 1969, p. 8590. He also said, "José Angel Gutiérrez may think himself something of a hero, but he is in fact only a benighted soul if he believes that in the espousal of hatred he will find love." For more on González's attacks, see an article, "Impetuous MAYO Militants Alarming to Rep. González," by William Grieder of *The Washington Post* staff, printed in *The San Antonio Express*, June 6, 1969. See also an article, "The Chicano Revolt: Where Next?" by Leroy Aarons of *The Washington Post* staff, printed in *The San Antonio Express and News*, January 11, 1970, p. 1.

53. From an article by Kemper Diehl, "MAYO Leader Warns of Violence, Rioting," *The San Antonio Express and News*, reprinted in *The Congressional Record*, April 3, 1969, p. 8591. One of the MAYO pamphlets which received the most publicity stated: "The Gringo took your grandfather's land, he took your father's job, and now he's sucking out your soul. There is no such thing as 'mala suerte' [bad luck]; there is only 'malos gringos' [bad gringos]. He's keeping us in slavery now through our jobs, through the lousy education you're getting at school, through everything that affects us." (Reprinted in *The Congressional Record, ibid.*)

54. González charged in *The Congressional Record*, April 16, 1969, p. 9309, that the Ford Foundation "has supported the spewing of hate, and rather than creating a new political unity it has destroyed what little there was, and rather than creating new leadership it is simply financing the ambitions of some men who are greedy and some who are ruthless, and a few who are plainly irresponsible."

55. MAYO's operating budget of $8,527 was financed by Ford Foundation Funds distributed through intermediary organizations. See *The Congressional Record*, April 15, 1969, p. 9059.

56. For an analytical work exploring the need of protest groups to attract publicity in the media, see Michael Lipsky, "Protest as a Political Resource," *American Political Science Review*, 62, no. 4 (1968): 1144-58. This flamboyance also tended to hide a scholarly mind. See, for example, his master's thesis.

57. From an interview with José Angel Gutiérrez (Crystal City, November 13, 1970).

58. *The Zavala County Sentinel*, October 16, 1969.

59. Gutiérrez believed, as perhaps most community organizers do, that the Mexican-American community had never been either satisfied or apathetic. It was rather, he said, that Mexican Americans had refused to bring increased repression and misery on themselves by trying to engage in protest which might fail. Because the costs of failing were likely to include loss of jobs, Mexicans were thus afraid to engage in political activity unless they felt they were likely to win.

60. *The Zavala County Sentinel*, November 20, 1969, p. 1. One of the Anglo girls chosen as "duchess" to the queen was quoted in an interview later as saying that she agreed with the restrictive clause. She said, "After all, not just *anybody* should be eligible!"

61. Conoley and Ibarra, p. 3.

62. From interviews with Mario and Blanca Treviño, and from an interview with Darrell Ray, elementary principal and former superintendent of schools of Crystal City, conducted by the TEA team of Conoley and Ibarra, (p. 1. of their memorandum).

63. One Mexican-American parent maintained that "the students were not only demonstrating against the school, but also against their parents for failure to act in their behalf in dealing with the School Board or the school administration. . . ." (Conoley and Ibarra, p. 2.)

64. *The Zavala County Sentinel*, November 13, 1969, p. 1.

65. With the crisis in the fall, Anglos seem to have been taken by surprise. The work and activities by Gutiérrez and his staff were either not known or were not taken seriously, probably because the Anglos had confidence that their coalition could now withstand any attack. The pastor of the First United Methodist Church of Crystal City, the Reverend Kenneth Newcomer, recorded in his "A Progress Report on the Churchmen's Committee of Crystal City, Texas" (mimeographed paper, Crystal City, 1970), p. 1, that "many [Anglos] were totally unaware of mounting leadership among Mexican-Americans toward alleviating grievances of their people. . . . In addition, there was the feeling that the existing structures of Crystal City would be able to handle any eventuality." Newcomer also recorded (p. 10) that one Anglo member of the school board stated as late as September 29, 1969, "We have no racial tensions in Crystal City."

66. *The Zavala County Sentinel*, November 20, 1969, p. 2.

67. From an interview with the Reverend and Mrs. Kenneth Newcomer.

68. For an examination of ways to deflect protestors, see Michael Lipsky, "Protest as a Political Resource."

69. From interviews in the community.

70. *The Zavala County Sentinel*, December 11, 1969, p. 1.

71. From an article by Leroy Aarons, "The Chicanos Want In," *The Washington Post*, January 11, 1970, Outlook Section.

72. From a paper by Rick Appleton, a graduate student in Education at the University of Texas, "The Crystal City School Boycott: 1969" (unpublished paper, Austin, Texas, 1970), p. 6.

73. Conoley and Ibarra, p. 4.

74. Throughout the boycott there were always more students absent

from classes than either the newspapers or the student boycotters themselves estimated. This apparently happened because many Mexican parents
pulled their children out of school to avoid the confrontation. For Mexicans in the community under severe cross-pressures, this seemed the safest
course of action to take. If the Anglos threatened them, they could always
say that they had taken their children out of school only because they
feared that violence might break out.

75. Kenneth Newcomer, "A Report," p. 9.

76. Ibid., p. 5. Rumors throughout this period and continuing up to the
present have been extremely common and virulent. The nature and uses of
rumors in Crystal City would itself make an interesting study.

77. From an interview with Mario Treviño. The most comprehensive
press coverage of the entire period of the strike was probably in the two
San Antonio newspapers: *The San Antonio News and Express* and *The San
Antonio Light.*

78. For an excellent account of the Churchmen's Committee, its successes and its problems, see Kenneth Newcomer, "A Report," and *The
Alamo Messenger*, San Antonio, January 2 and January 9, 1970.

79. From an interview with Paulino Mata.

80. From an interview with an Anglo.

81. Leroy Aarons, "The Chicanos Want In."

82. For explorations into problems of negotiating, and of whether or
not to negotiate, see *Racial Conflict and Negotiations: Perspectives and
First Case Studies*, ed. Ellison Chalmers and Gerald Cormick (Ann Arbor,
Michigan: Institute of Labor and Industrial Relations, 1971).

83. Commencing Monday, December 22, TEAM began tutoring more
than 500 students who showed up for its first session in the city park. The
first hour was devoted to a lecture on Mexican cultural history. On the
second day the students split up by grade level and subjects and moved to
churches, a theater, dance halls, front porches, and private homes. Attendance throughout the holidays was reported as good, and at the end of the
two weeks of instruction, the students held a rally to honor the fifty
teachers from TEAM. For more accounts on the TEAM experience, see
Rick Appleton's paper and the San Antonio newspapers for this period.

84. A comprehensive report on the Justice Department's experiences in
Crystal City was compiled by Greenwald and Mata for the Department.
Unfortunately, I was not able to see the report because it is considered
confidential.

85. From interviews with an Anglo board member, a Mexican board
member, Chicano students involved in the negotiations, and one of the
Anglo observers at the negotiations, it seems that Greenwald and Mata
came very close to losing their "mediator" status by siding almost completely with the students. At one point one of the negotiators apparently
asked the board what was wrong with the students electing school cheerleaders and favorites, and threatened to pack up and leave the community,
saying the negotiating team had stayed too long already. He then warned
the board that new people would be sent down and that all sorts of
lawmen would need to be called into the community because of the threat
of outside people converging on Crystal City if the strike were not settled

by the end of the holidays. Shortly after this private castigation of the school board, the board gave in.

86. From an interview with Eddie Treviño.

87. From an interview with Kenneth Newcomer and with a parent of one of the Anglo students who attended the meeting.

88. See Kenneth Newcomer, "A Report." Also confirmed by an interview with Dr. and Mrs. Robert Stauber (Crystal City, November 8 and December 11, 1970).

89. More Mexican students than normal, however, did fail at the end of the year.

90. Gutiérrez, "Aztlán," pp. 7-8.

91. *The Zavala County Sentinel,* January 15, 1970, p. 1. According to Mario Obledo of the Mexican American Legal Defense Fund, in an interview in San Antonio, Texas, October 26, 1970, the Anglo authorities had wanted to declare the children juvenile delinquents. Yet, again according to Obledo, the youths could not be declared delinquents under the penal code because they were charged only with a misdemeanor. Since they were not charged with an offense which is punishable by confinement in jail, they could not be declared delinquents.

92. From interviews with Mario Treviño, one of the students arrested, and with José Angel Gutiérrez.

93. Gutiérrez, "Aztlan," p. 13.

94. From interviews with José Angel Gutiérrez and Ventura Gonzales (fired from Del Monte in the winter of 1971). This claim, however, was denied by Ray Shafer, who argued that job security was one of the main goals the union had fought for (interview).

95. *The Zavala County Sentinel,* October 9, 1969, p. 1.

96. From an interview with Juan Cornejo and from a discussion with Mike Miller.

97. From interviews with Ventura Gonzales, José Angel Gutiérrez and Eddie Treviño. The manager of Del Monte, Gilbert Brook, denied in an interview that the company backed the Teamsters union (Crystal City, February 11, 1971). Note also how similar this seems to be with the role of the Teamsters in their struggle with the Chavez United Farm Workers Organization.

98. *The Zavala County Sentinel,* January 29, 1970, p. 1.

99. *The Zavala County Sentinel,* March 19 and March 26, 1970.

100. Ibid., April 9, 1970, p. 1.

101. From interviews with one of the Anglo school trustees and with the new Superintendent, John Briggs (Crystal City, December 6, 1970). Both stated that they tried very hard to implement the reforms.

102. *The Zavala County Sentinel,* April 2, 1970, p. 1.

103. Ibid., p. 2.

104. Ibid., March 26, 1970, p. 9 (and in Spanish, April 2, 1970).

105. The tremendous difficulty of trying to organize labor in South Texas was related to me by Ray Shafer, president and business manager of Teamster local 657 (San Antonio, November 6, 1970) and Franklin Garcia, Meatcutters Union (San Antonio, January, 1971). This was confirmed in an interview by labor economist F. Ray Marshall, Department of

Economics, University of Texas, Austin, Texas, (Austin, Texas, December, 1970).

106. The head manager of the Del Monte plant, Gilbert Brook, in an interview in Crystal City, commented that Del Monte wanted to stay in Crystal City, but he left the impression that La Raza Unida activity might make them feel forced to move. Perhaps an important reason for their wanting to stay in Crystal City relates to their profits. Although Del Monte's profit figures were kept secret, their Crystal City plant reputedly had a higher margin of profit than any of their other plants in the country. This may have been both because they remained untaxed by the city and because their wages, although high by local standards, were below that of their other plants.

107. As Calvin Trillin has noted (p. 104), the Anglos hate Gutiérrez so much that they "are often at a loss for words hideous enough to describe him although they ordinarily make do with 'communist' until one comes to mind." For a more detailed discussion of the campaign and of Gutiérrez's reaction to Anglo charges, see John Ziller, "Field Research in Crystal City" (unpublished paper, University of Texas, Austin, 1970).

108. John Ziller, "Field Research," p. 5.

109. Ibid., pp. 9-10.

110. *The Zavala County Sentinel*, April 9, 1970, p. 1.

chapter six: la raza unida and the first year of rule

1. From an interview with Eddie Treviño. Treviño was a worker at Del Monte.

2. As was mentioned in the preceding chapter, Esquivel was a printer for the conservative editor of the *Zavala County Sentinel* and also ran a cleaners.

3. From an interview with Eddie Treviño.

4. Ibid.

5. *The San Antonio Express*, September 10, 1970, p. 3-A.

6. *The Zavala County Sentinel*, April 16, 1970, p. 1.

7. Interestingly, however, Mike Pérez two years later became the only elected Raza Unida official to break with the party. See Chapter VII.

8. When I asked Paulino Mata about this story, he said rather that he was surprised that the councilmen had voted to re-elect him mayor. He said that upon asking them why they voted for him, they said they did so because he had more experience than Francisco Benavides. (From an interview with Paulino Mata.)

9. From an interview with Bill Richey.

10. *The Zavala County Sentinel*, July 1, 1971, p. 1.

11. From an interview with Gilbert Brook.

12. *The San Antonio Express*, September 4, 10, 12, and 15, 1971. As quoted in the *Express*, September 10, 1971, p. 3-A, "Briggs said he had been asked to serve as a go-between by the three Anglo members following the April board election and added that he saw 'no wrong' in working to bring harmony and solidarity on the board."

13. One other teacher was also fired by the school board at this time. She died during the summer, however, and thus did not file suit.

14. José Angel Gutiérrez, "Aztlan: Chicano Revolt in the Winter Garden Area," unpublished paper, Crystal City, 1970, pp. 15-16. The reasons given by Gutiérrez appear to be very similar to those given by Stokely Carmichael and Charles Hamilton in their book, *Black Power* (New York: Random House, 1967).

15. Perhaps part of the reason the Anglos failed to have any Mexicans on their ticket stemmed from a difficulty in finding candidates. Jesse Rodríquez had run successfully on the CASAA slate for county commissioner in 1964, but he had later dropped out of politics because of the crippling boycott of his business. Thus the Anglos may have encountered serious difficulties in trying to find Mexicans to run with them. Yet this does not seem to have been a problem for them in city and school-board races. When I asked one Anglo why no Mexicans had been selected to run on the ticket, he replied, "Maybe there weren't any qualified."

16. Irl Taylor was also one of the four Anglos who refused to see me.

17. Although Salas brought suit over this, charging that there was a conspiracy to deny him cases, his case was eventually dismissed. See *The Zavala County Sentinel*, April 15, 1971, p. 1.

18. *The San Antonio Express*, May 8, 1970, p. 14-A.

19. I am grateful to two Crystal City citizens for supplying me with this letter.

20. From interviews with numerous Mexicans in the community.

21. It should not be forgotten that many farmers and ranchers are opposed even to surplus commodities and that some counties do not employ either food stamps or surplus commodities. See J. W. Tiller's dissertation, p. 145, and The Texas Advisory Committee on Civil Rights, *Civil Rights in Texas*, February, 1970, pp. 39-44.

22. The county clerk related to me in an interview (Crystal City, December, 1970) that in her opinion no matter what procedures La Raza Unida Party had followed, she would not have felt they could have qualified for the ballot.

23. City Manager Richey succeeded in getting state officials to call the county clerk to inform her of the judicial decision, but she was adamant in refusing to require polling officials to help illiterates vote. (From an interview with Bill Richey.)

24. Both José Angel Gutiérrez and Bill Richey mentioned this incident. It was also reported in *La Verdad*, December 15, 1970, p. 9.

25. The Mexican-American's fear of governmental authority and governmental agencies has been covered in Leo Grebler *et al., The Mexican-American People* (New York: The Free Press, 1970), Chapter 21.

26. By this time the Reverend Kenneth Newcomer, who had played an important role in trying to bring about negotiations between the school board and the Chicano students during the walkout, had been forced to leave the community. A new minister, far more in sympathy with the local Anglos, has since been installed.

27. The situation was in fact so tense that one college-educated woman reported that she was so nervous in voting that after writing in the Raza

Unida candidates she completely forgot to vote in all federal and state races.

28. From interviews with Enriqueta Palacios and Bill Richey. At whose instigation the F.B.I. decided to investigate the voting procedures is unclear. Unfortunately, the F.B.I. has not made public its findings on Crystal City. Thus, what information they uncovered concerning the truth of these charges against Anglo tactics could not be corroborated by them.

29. Even in counting the write-in votes for the Raza Unida candidates, the Anglos refused to honor the Texas election code and count all votes where the intent of the voter was clearly indicated. Thus, whenever a name was misspelled, the Anglos counted that vote as being for a separate candidate. Although this affected several hundred ballots, in no instance were the totals for all the write-in candidates greater than the total for the Anglo candidate listed on the ballot.

30. Zavala County is not among the heavier producing counties in the state, but its production does average close to one thousand barrels a day. See *The Texas Almanac, 1970-1971* (Dallas: A. H. Belo Corporation, 1970), p. 433.

31. From interviews with Bill Richey and José Angel Gutiérrez. This point is mentioned also in Antonio Camejo, "A Report from Aztlan," *La Raza Unida Party in Texas* (New York: Pathfinder Press, 1971), p. 7.

32. The head manager of the plant, Gilbert Brook, stated in an interview that Ventura Gonzales was fired because "mechanization took away his job."

33. *La Verdad*, March 31, 1971, p. 14.

34. From an interview with José Angel Gutiérrez (Madison, Wisconsin, May, 1971).

35. A big incident arose when one of the Spanish teachers had the students circle all the diphthongs in an article which praised the election of Allende as President of Chile. See *The Zavala County Sentinel*, December 24, 1970, p. 7.

36. *La Verdad*, March 18, 1971, p. 5.

37. Ibid., March 4, 1971, p. 1.

38. From an interview with the superintendent, Angel Gonzales (Crystal City, November 11, 1970).

39. *The Zavala County Sentinel*, April 16, 1970, p. 1.

40. Ibid., January 21, 1971, p. 1.

41. The above incidents were related to me by Mrs. Robert Stauber in an interview. The following year several school districts dropped Crystal City from their schedules, charging that Crystal City was injecting politics and hatred into sports.

42. For more on the Uvalde school system, see "Side by Side—And a World Apart—in Uvalde, Texas," *Newsweek*, June 29, 1970, p. 24. The Uvalde strike is also discussed in the following chapter.

43. *The Zavala County Sentinel*, July 30, 1970, p. 1. This list of influences of the Crystal City schools upon other communities in the area is by no means complete.

44. There was one other school district in the state of Texas which was trying to implement many of the same changes in its schools. The Edge-

wood School District of San Antonio, encompassing an area of San Antonio that is overwhelmingly Chicano, has been working in concert with the Crystal City district on several problems, most notably that of bilingual education.

45. From an interview with a citizen of Crystal City.

46. *The Zavala County Sentinel*, January 14, 1971, p. 1.

47. Ibid.

48. Calvin Trillin, "U.S. Journal: Crystal City, Texas," *The New Yorker*, April 17, 1971, p. 107.

49. For more on the tax boycott, see *The Zavala County Sentinel*, December 17, 1970, p. 1; and June 17, 1971, p. 1; and *La Verdad*, March 18, 1971, p. 5.

50. *The Zavala County Sentinel*, December 17, 1970, p. 8.

51. From an interview with Angel Gonzales.

52. According to a report on the school system by Superintendent Gonzales, over three hundred students out of a scholastic population of nearly three thousand were still not attending school.

53. *The Zavala County Sentinel*, October 29, 1970, p. 1; November 5, 1970, p. 4; and December 17, 1970, p. 1.

54. From an interview with an official of the Texas Education Desegregation Technical Assistance Center (Austin, Texas, January, 1971).

55. Ibid.

56. From an interview with John Briggs.

57. For explorations in the uses of social conflict, see Lewis Coser, *The Functions of Social Conflict* (New York: The Free Press, 1956).

58. Gutiérrez, "Aztlan."

59. For more on this problem which faces all groups seeking vast changes, see Robert Tucker, "The De-Radicalization of Marxist Movements," *American Political Science Review*, 61, no. 2 (1967): 343-58.

60. Richey had earlier done graduate work in government at St. Mary's University in San Antonio and at the University of Texas. He and his wife were two of the first members of Gutiérrez's team, and thus Richey had been in Crystal City since before the school strike. During this time he had been working with the Texas Institute for Educational Development (TIED).

61. Juan Ramirez was apparently also the accountant for the Black Panthers in Oakland.

62. *La Verdad*, March 18, 1971, p. 8.

63. *The Zavala County Sentinel*, June 11, 1970, p. 1.

64. Ibid., June 25, 1970, p. 1.

65. Ibid.

66. Ibid. In actual fact, however, it appears that the town of Mathis had passed a similar resolution after the Action Party had gained control of the city government in 1965. The resolution in Mathis seems to have been prompted by the same feelings. See Charles Chandler, "The Mexican-American Protest Movement in Texas," Ph.D. dissertation, Tulane University, New Orleans, Louisiana, 1968.

67. By the spring of 1973 it seemed that the city had lost its case against Del Monte. (See the following chapter for details.)

68. From an interview with Bill Richey. It should not be forgotten that the Texas Rangers were crucial in the defeat of the Farm Workers strike in Starr County in 1967-1968. For more on this, see Ben Procter, "The Modern Texas Rangers: A Law Enforcement Dilemma in the Rio Grande Valley," in *The Mexican Americans: An Awakening Minority*, ed. Manuel Servin (Beverly Hills, California: Glencoe Press, 1970), pp. 212-27.

69. From an interview with Sam Anderson.

70. From interviews with Bill Richey and José Angel Gutiérrez.

71. Sam Anderson remarked that in terms of per capita spending on urban renewal and public housing, Crystal City ranked ahead of New Haven, Connecticut, which has been noted for one of the most comprehensive urban renewal programs in the country.

72. From interviews with Arnold Lopez, George Ozuna, Bill Richey, and José Angel Gutiérrez.

73. From an interview with José Angel Gutiérrez.

74. From an interview with Fidel Rodríguez (Crystal City, February 11, 1971).

75. From an article in *The Zavala County Sentinel*, date unknown.

76. *La Verdad*, March 18, 1971, p. 1.

77. The legal procedure for the appointment of Urban Renewal Commissioners is that the mayor should do the appointing with the consent of the council. Thus the mayor would not appoint the council majority's candidates, and the council majority would not approve the mayor's.

78. Mayor Mata and Santos Nieto walked out of the meeting at which they were deposed, saying it was illegal because proper notice of the meeting had not been given. See *The Zavala County Sentinel*, December 3, 1970, p. 1.

79. *The Zavala County Sentinel*, December 10, 1970, p. 1., and January 21, 1971, p. 1.

80. From an interview with José Angel Gutiérrez in Madison, Wisconsin.

81. The following summer, however, Sam Anderson resigned. See Chapter 7.

82. From an interview with Bill Richey. William D'Antonio and Irwin Press noted a similar desire by Anglos to attract only certain forms of industry in their study of Fabens, Texas. See their unpublished monograph on Fabens, Texas (Notre Dame University, 1970).

83. From an interview with an anti-La Raza Unida Mexican and an Anglo woman in the town who was also very much against La Raza Unida.

84. From interviews with Bill Richey, José Angel Gutiérrez, and also with Viviana Santiago (a member of Gutiérrez's staff who had done considerable work trying to attract jobs to the town) (Crystal City, February 12, 1971).

85. From an interview with Viviana Santiago.

86. From an interview with Bill Richey.

87. *Industrial Employment Potential of the United States-Mexico Border*, United States Department of Commerce, Economic Development Administration, prepared by Robert R. Nathan Associates, Inc. (Washington, D.C.: U.S. Government Printing Office, December 1968), p. 3.

88. Ibid., p. 4.

89. From interviews with José Angel Gutiérrez, Viviana Santiago, and others.

90. *Industrial Employment Potential of the United States-Mexico Border*, p. 9.

91. Ibid., p. 8.

92. Niles Hansen and William Gruben, "The Influence of Relative Wages and Assisted Migration on Locational Preferences: Mexican Americans in South Texas," *The Social Science Quarterly*, 52, no. 1 (1971), p. 103.

93. Ibid., p. 113.

94. See Saul Alinsky, *Reveille for Radicals* (Chicago: University of Chicago Press, 1946), and Miguel David Tirado, "Mexican American Community Political Organization," *Aztlan: Chicano Journal of the Social Sciences and the Arts*, 1, no. 1 (1970): 53-78.

95. From an interview with José Angel Gutiérrez at Madison, Wisconsin.

96. José Serna had made one of the best showings of the Raza Unida candidates, garnering over forty percent of the vote in his losing write-in effort.

97. Miguel David Tirado, p. 75.

98. See, for example, *La Verdad*, March 31, 1971, p. 4.

99. See, for example, William Madsen, *Mexican-Americans of South Texas* (New York: Holt, Rinehart, and Winston, 1964), Arthur Rubel, *Across the Tracks* (Austin: University of Texas Press, 1966), and Julian Samora and James Watson, "Subordinate Leadership in a Bicultural Community: An Analysis," *American Sociological Review*, 19 (August, 1954): 413-21. They have all noted the difficulty of organizing and unifying Mexican-American people into a durable organization.

100. From interviews with José Angel Gutiérrez and Bill Richey.

101. From interviews with Wayne Hamilton (Crystal City, February 10, 1971) and John Briggs.

102. The county campaign of November, 1970, was a notable exception to this, and occurred perhaps mainly because the county represented a slightly different constituency from the city and school district, one which the Mexicans had never been able to control.

103. The Anglos began to refer increasingly to the people of La Raza Unida as "Gutierristas" in order to distinguish them from the "better-thinking" Mexicans of the community.

104. *The Zavala County Sentinel*, September 17, 1970, p. 1.

105. This passage from Mike Miller, "Political Conflict in a Bifurcated Community," mimeographed paper, Texas A & M University, 1971, pp. 47-48.

106. Ibid., p. 49.

107. From interviews with Anglos in the community, including those who considered themselves to be in this new group.

108. The Anglos, in another indication of changed tactics, had begun to patronize Muñoz's grocery much more heavily after the Chicano boycott was announced. Thus they began to be involved in keeping afloat anti-Raza Unida businessmen, whereas in the boycott against Jesús Rodríguez's grocery earlier in the decade, they had done little to help him.

284 NOTES TO CHAPTER SIX

109. Three independents also entered the race for seats on the city council. The first two, Ralph García and his mother, Mariana García, were noted in the community for being strongly opposed to urban renewal. García's home was condemned by the agency, but he had refused to move out. Instead, he had plastered the house with sayings such as "J. Edgar Hoover Must Go," "Chávez Si, Anhel [Gutiérrez] No," etc. The third candidate was Roberto Cornejo, the brother of Juan Cornejo, and a councilman from 1967 to 1969.

110. *La Verdad*, March 18, 1971, p. 12.

111. This Anglo source must remain anonymous.

112. The Raza Unida organization had rather consciously developed machismo into an anti-gringo weapon. Gutiérrez himself had said earlier that machismo "is not to walk around getting three or four women pregnant and to drink a lot of beer. Machismo is to take on the gringo." (William Greider of the *Washington Post* staff, "Impetuous MAYO Militants Alarming to Rep. Gonzalez," reprinted in the *Austin American*, June 6, 1969.) During the campaign, references were thus made to the lack of virility of the "For Better Government" candidates.

113. *La Verdad*, March 18, 1971, p. 2.

114. For more on the problem of Mexican-American teachers feeling trapped in the school system, see Thomas Carter, *Mexican-Americans in School: A History of Educational Neglect* (New York: College Entrance Examination Board, 1970), Chapter 3.

115. *La Verdad*, March 18, 1971, p. 11.

116. But emphasizing that some Mexicans as well as Anglos felt that La Raza Unida were dangerous extremists, one of the anti-Raza Unida Mexican candidates maintained that "I really feel the real leaders [of Raza Unida] are communists who are trying to create a hatred toward the 'gringo,' the system, and America."

117. I was not in the community for interviewing and observation after February of 1971. Thus this description of the last part of the campaign and its aftermath has been taken from newspaper sources, letters from Crystal City residents, letters from observers of the campaign and election, from telephone conversations, and from an interview with José Angel Gutiérrez when he was in Madison, Wisconsin, on a speaking tour in May, 1971.

118. *The Zavala County Sentinel*, April 1, 1971, p. 7.

119. Ibid., March 18, 1971, p. 1; and Calvin Trillin's article in *The New Yorker*, p. 106.

120. *La Verdad* seemed to play on this by caricaturing him. See *La Verdad*, March 18, 1971, p. 12.

121. *La Verdad*, March 18, 1971, p. 3. Altogether, each of forty-three farms in Zavala County, all of them owned by Anglos, received $5,000 or more from agricultural subsidies. The subsidies on these forty-three farms alone totaled nearly one million dollars.

122. *The Zavala County Sentinel*, March 25, 1971, p. 1.

123. *La Verdad*, March 31, 1971, p. 2.

124. *The Zavala County Sentinel*, March 18, 1971, p. 1.

125. Ibid., April 1, 1971, p. 1.

126. *The San Antonio News*, May 21, 1971, p. 15-A.
127. *The San Antonio Express*, April 2, 1971, p. 1.
128. *The San Antonio Light*, April 1, 1971, p. 1.
129. From a letter by Ed Idar to Charles Burns, Legal Council of the TCTA, April 2, 1971. Quoted partially in *The Zavala County Sentinel*, April 8, 1971, p. 1.
130. *The San Antonio Express*, April 3, 1971.
131. For this information concerning the election-eve rally, I am grateful to Victor Emanuel, who attended the rally.
132. That Gutiérrez was in the army reserves was yet another anomaly that confused Crystal City Anglos. It was another factor which made the charge of his being a communist or a wild-eyed revolutionary less credible.
133. *The Zavala County Sentinel*, April 8, 1971, p. 1. Significantly, the number of absentee ballots dropped considerably now that La Raza Unida had control of the city election machinery, and the ballots were not nearly so one-sided. The anti-Raza Unida candidates averaged around 140 absentee votes each, and the Raza Unida candidates averaged around 120 such votes.

chapter seven; chicano control and the future

1. From interviews with several Anglos in Crystal City.
2. *La Verdad*, May 6, 1971, p. 3 (these and other translations are by the author).
3. In order to study an exposition of the pluralist model, see Robert Dahl, *Who Governs?*, New Haven: Yale University Press, 1961. Rather than finding a political system of dispersed powers with checks and balances preventing the domination of any one group, as the pluralist model would describe politics, Crystal City seems to offer examples of the extent to which the system was weighted against Chicanos. The biases of the social, economic, and political system, which were so clearly exposed in the Chicanos' struggle for political power, all seem to argue heavily that the politics in Crystal City before the revolts included the phenomenon of "stable unrepresentation" of the Chicano population. And the breakdown of stable unrepresentation seems to have occurred only when the challenging groups were willing and able to overcome the biased rules of the game which had been set up by those in power. Outside Teamster support and later the school strike both seem to have been tactics crucial to Chicano successes, and both were considered illegitimate by those in power. (For more on the idea of stable unrepresentation and biased rules of the game, see William Gamson, "Stable Unrepresentation in American Society," *The American Behavioral Scientist*, 12 (November/December, 1969): 15-20; and Robert Paul Wolff, *The Poverty of Liberalism*, Boston: Beacon Press, 1968.)
4. From an interview with a Crystal City Anglo who had already left the community.
5. *The Zavala County Sentinel*, July 1 and June 17, 1971. The commu-

nity school has continued to grow, and as of the spring of 1973 it numbered around 100 students, approximately half of whom were Mexican Americans.

6. Ibid., May 6, 1971, p. 1. This legal dispute continued to drag on for years. As of the spring of 1973 it seemed likely that the school district would have to pay Briggs at least part of the $60,000.

7. *The San Antonio News*, May 21, 1971.

8. *The Zavala County Sentinel*, April 12, 1973, p. 1.

9. Ibid., November 9, 1972, p. 1.

10. From an interview with Bill Richey.

11. *The Zavala County Sentinel*, May 20, 1971, p. 1; and from an interview with Eddie Treviño.

12. *The Zavala County Sentinel*, April 22, 1971, p. 1.

13. *La Verdad*, February 18, 1971.

14. From an interview with José Angel Gutiérrez in Madison, Wisconsin.

15. *The Zavala County Sentinel*, July 8, 1971, p. 1.

16. Shortly after taking over, Cotera was shot and wounded by Ralph García, who was adamantly opposed to urban renewal and had been a thorn in the side of Sam Anderson. Although Cotera was not seriously injured, the violence shocked and frightened many. It was significant, if not perhaps ironic, that the only major political shooting during this period of turmoil was by a Mexican American against another Mexican American. The shooting thus served to emphasize that while Anglos had resisted La Raza Unida forcefully, they had not resorted to this sort of ultimate tactic.

17. For the school board, Raza Unida candidates, Alberto Sánchez, who had recently been appointed Chief of Police, and José O. Mata, an employee at the city health department, received 1,727 and 1,707 votes respectively. Far back were the anti-Raza Unida, or "independent," candidates. Julian Saldivar and Emmett Sevilla, both businessmen, received 845 and 840 votes respectively. The incumbents whose school-board seats fell vacant were those of the two remaining Anglos, Wayne Hamilton and Ed Mayer. Both knew they would be defeated in attempts at re-election, and withdrew in favor of anti-Raza Unida Mexicano candidates. (See *The Zavala County Sentinel*, April 6, 1972, p. 1.) In the city council races, Raza Unida candidates Ventura Gonzales and Pablo Puente were both re-elected, receiving 1,745 and 1,741 votes respectively. They defeated independents Hector Ramón and Eusevio Salinas, who received 517 and 522 votes respectively.

18. The party met in San Antonio, elected state executive committee officers (who were mainly from the earlier MAYO chapter), and adopted a platform. Gutiérrez was elected convention chairman by acclamation. He was, however, one of those reluctant to make the move to statewide races, fearing that the party might be spread too thin. (See *The Zavala County Sentinel*, November 4, 1971, p. 1.)

19. This question came into the spotlight when Dr. Jorge Prieto of Chicago charged that he was offered the job of director of the new Health Clinic on condition that he not support McGovern. He charged that La

Raza Unida was working with the Nixon Administration to defeat the
Democrats, and that the bargain involved Crystal City getting funds for the
clinic. His charges were carried by the wire services, and produced a
response in *La Verdad* (October 12, 1973, p. 7), which noted how little
the Democrats had done for them and said, "Gringo bullets and ballots
haven't stopped us yet, so little political schemes designed to promote the
presidential aspiration of a gringo will certainly not get in our way."

State Republicans clearly mellowed toward La Raza Unida as the fall
campaign proceeded, as pronouncements by Republican gubernatorial
candidate Henry Grover indicated. It seems almost certain that Republicans contributed funds, one way or another, to the Raza Unida campaign.

20. Zavala County was one of three counties in the state carried by
Muñiz. Far fewer people voted in the presidential election, with Nixon
narrowly edging out McGovern in the county.

21. They averaged between one and two percent of the vote. Interestingly, even Ramsey Muñiz did considerably less well than Henry González
had done in his Democratic primary race for governor in 1958. At that
time Gonzalez polled over a quarter of a million votes, which was over
twenty percent of the votes cast.

22. An article on this election, written by John Fry and very much in
sympathy with La Raza Unida, has appeared in *Christianity and Crisis*,
November 27, 1973, pp. 253-257. Luz Gutiérrez, the wife of José Angel
Gutiérrez, and several others were arrested on election day while trying to
serve as poll-watchers. The whole day was quite tense.

23. A record turnout saw 4,048 people voting in the county. Rey Pérez
received 1,949 votes, against R. A. Taylor's 1,912. José Serna had 2,005
votes, against C. L. Sweeten's 1,883. Martha Cruz, the Democratic candidate, defeated Armando Bermea 2,026 to 1,871. Besides the two county
posts which Raza Unida won, they also elected Moises García as constable
of precinct three, Elena Díaz as commissioner of precinct three, and
Rodolfo Espino as constable of precinct two. The Anglos, however, filed
suit to contest the elections, and as of the fall of 1973 the suit had not
been resolved.

24. See *The Zavala County Sentinel*, October 19, 1972, p. 1. To
complicate matters, the police chief, Alberto Sánchez, was also on the
school board as a Raza Unida member. This incident strained his relations
with the other Raza Unida members on the board. The former police chief,
Eliseo Sánchez, had been fired earlier in the year. All this indicated that
community-police relations were strained, even with an all-Chicano force.

25. See *The Zavala County Sentinel*, January 25 and February 8, 1973.
One English teacher commented to me that using Spanish to teach English
was essential, because the students would often "read" English without
understanding or comprehending what the words meant.

26. More comprehensive studies of the school system in Crystal City are
being done by Josué Cruz, currently working for the Department of
Health, Education, and Welfare, and by Douglas Foley and Walter Smith,
both of the School of Education of the University of Texas.

27. Raza Unida city-council candidates—José Cuevas, Richard Díaz, and
Rámon Mata—received 1,543, 1,526, and 1,542 votes respectively. The

'candidatos independientes"—Eliseo Sánchez, Roberto Cornejo, and Manuel Garza—received 1,024, 990, and 991 votes respectively. In the school-board races Raza Unida candidates—Ramón Garza, Ernesto Olguin, and Viviana Santiago—received 1,661, 1657, and 1,642 votes respectively. The independents, or anti-Raza Unida candidates—Mike Pérez, Elfego Martinez, and Jóse O. Mata—received 1,223, 1,201, and 1,205 votes respectively. The margins of victory were very similar to La Raza Unida's victories in 1971; however, considering that many Anglos had left the community in order to place their children in other school systems, the results represented a drop in Raza Unida support among the Mexican Americans of the community greater than the vote totals themselves indicated.

28. A rather comprehensive review of events in Crystal City during 1971-1972, "Texas Chicanos Take Over 'Model City' as Power Base," written by Frank Del Olmo, appeared in *The Los Angeles Times*, September 3, 1972, p. 1. Another review of events in Crystal City was a series of three articles by Richard Beene, carried by the Associated Press. The article appeared in *The Del Rio Herald-News*, July 19, 20, and 21, 1972.

29. From interviews with a teacher in the school system and with a parent.

30. Teachers reported that some children, as young as those in elementary school, continued to have to miss days of school to work in the fields.

31. The Court, in *San Antonio School District v. Rodriguez*, voted 5-4 not to strike down the property-tax system for financing public schools. The majority argued that the right to an education is not a "fundamental right" guaranteed to each American citizen by the Constitution.

32. As far back as 1971 this had been the goal, which of course was similar to the way the school system was being organized. (From an interview with Bill Richey.)

33. Warren Wagner, the owner, argued that the quality of spinach was poorer because of a freeze. He lowered wages because he could not get as much as previously for the spinach. (See *La Verdad*, January 24, and February 2, 1972.)

34. This translates roughly as "Respect for the Rights of Others Is True Peace."

35. Even the town's name began to be affected. It was increasingly referred to as "Cristal."

36. Although I am generalizing about the Anglo community, it should be repeated that were perhaps as many as ten local Anglos who supported La Raza Unida out of a total Anglo population of nearly 2,000.

37. This point is made by Sheldon Wolin, "Political Theory as a Vocation," *The American Political Science Review*, 63, no. 4 (December, 1969), pp. 1062-82.

38. *The San Antonio Express*, July 11, 1971.

39. Kenneth Newcomer, "A Progress Report on the Churchmen's Committee of Crystal City, Texas," mimeographed paper, Crystal City, 1970, p. 10.

40. For this quotation I am grateful to Mike Miller.

41. Leroy Aarons, "The Chicanos Want In," *The Washington Post*, January 11, 1970, Outlook Section.

42. From an interview with an Anglo educator.

43. In fact the role of the Nixon Administration was perplexing to many.

44. The best-known study of this sort is that by Samuel Stouffer, *Communism, Conformity, and Civil Liberties* (Garden City, N.Y.: Doubleday, 1955); a penetrating answer to this mode of thought occurs in Michael Rogin, *The Intellectuals and McCarthy* (Cambridge, Mass.: M.I.T. Press, 1967).

45. See Lipset, *Political Man*, Garden City, N.Y.: Doubleday and Company, 1960; Kornhauser, *The Politics of Mass Society*, Glencoe, Ill.: The Free Press, 1959.

46. See Zeitlin, *Revolutionary Politics and the Cuban Working Class*, Princeton: Princeton University Press, 1967.

47. See Simmons, "Anglo-Americans and Mexican-Americans in South Texas," Ph.D. dissertation, Harvard University, 1952, p. 287; and Wolf, *Peasant Wars of the Twentieth Century*, New York: Harper and Row, 1969.

48. Michael Parenti, "Power and Pluralism: A View from the Bottom," *Journal of Politics*, August 1970, p. 521.

49. Ibid.

50. Regarding further analogies between Crystal City and Black politics in America, examination of Crystal City should perhaps lead us to be cautious in assuming that quiescence means satisfaction, or that progress in the direction of greater racial equality will mean a reduction in racial conflict.

These points may be cause for considerable pessimism regarding Black-White relations in America, for if American Whites were to be generally as tolerant of Blacks as Crystal City Anglos were of Mexicans before the 1969 revolt, many might be inclined to view this as a significant step in amelioration of racial tensions in American society. Instead we should probably remember that, as De Tocqueville noted, change itself may allow greater conflicts to surface.

The Crystal City experience should also lead us to caution in assuming that the election of Black officeholders will in itself be a sign of significant progress in race relations. Instead a far more crucial question may be the *kind* of leadership that emerges. Whether (or how much) this leadership is tied to the existing setup of Anglo domination would clearly seem to be more important. Members of minority groups may be selected for office not so much for the purpose of bringing changes as for preventing them.

As for the Black community being able to choose their own leadership and put this leadership in office with the power to bring greater political, social, and economic equality, it seems possible that such developments will occur only under conditions which approximate those factors which seemed crucial to the Chicano success in Crystal City. But this is a subject which clearly needs more study.

51. Since then, boycotts and protests have also occurred in other places in the state. All deserve to be studied.

52. For this information I am grateful to Josué Cruz. For more on the Uvalde school strike, see the San Antonio newspapers for this period, and

Newsweek, "Side by Side—And a World Apart—In Uvalde, Texas," June 29, 1970, p. 24.

53. Although a minority in the town, Mexican Americans constituted a majority of the school population because their median age was considerably younger than that for the Anglo population.

54. It should be emphasized that I did no personal interviewing in Uvalde and that my knowledge of what occurred in the town during the strike is therefore very limited.

55. This report was temporarily made public by Senator Walter Mondale; upon writing for a copy of the HEW report I was told by Mrs. Dorothy Stuck of the Dallas office that their report was considered confidential because negotiations were still going on with the Uvalde district.

56. The long, bitter strike at Farah in El Paso seems likely to equal the struggle of the farm-workers strike in the Valley. At this writing, however, it is not clear how the strike will be resolved.

57. For more on the farm-workers strike in the Valley, see Ben H. Procter, "The Modern Texas Rangers: A Law Enforcement Dilemma in the Rio Grande Valley," in *The Mexican Americans: An Awakening Minority,* ed. Manuel Servin (Beverly Hills, California: Glenco Press, 1970), pp. 212-27, and *The Texas Observer* for the period from 1967 to 1968.

58. From an interview with Franklin García, San Antonio, January, 1971.

59. From interviews with Ray Shafer and with Ray Marshall, University of Texas (Austin, Texas, January, 1971). Shafer in fact mentioned several unsuccessful attempts at Teamster organization in South Texas.

60. See, for example, William Greider of *The Washington Post* staff, "Cotulla Mayor Raps Town, Schools," reprinted in *The San Antonio Express,* August 20, 1970, p. 18-A.

61. From an interview with Albert Peña (San Antonio, November, 1970).

62. For more on the transformation of intellectuals in colonial states, see Edward Shils, "The Intellectuals in the Political Development of the New States," *Political Change in Underdeveloped Countries,* ed. John Kautsky, (New York: John Wiley, 1962), pp. 195-234.

63. This phenomenon of needing to have the most educated and acculturated members of the Mexican community—those who understood the system best—become the backbone of the leadership, has produced a number of ironies. One of the greatest is that the leadership of the Raza Unida movement has itself been far more acculturated, educated, and "Anglicized" than many of the Mexicans who have been supporters of the Anglos. It has also produced the irony of many Chicanos arguing for their "rights" as American rather than Mexican citizens. For a definite segment of the Mexican-American population, their view of themselves as Americans seems itself to have been a radicalizing influence. In noting this, one Raza Unida leader has commented that the Mexican Americans of the border communities are often more conservative in part because they still compare themselves with Mexicans of Mexico. This comparison, he has argued, leads them to feel gratified that they are "better off" than the

Mexicans on the other side of the river rather than to feel angry that they are not as well off as the Anglos.

64. William Keech, *The Impact of Negro Voting* (Chicago: Rand Mc-Nally, 1968), notes a similar phenomenon occurring among Negro voters in the South. In noting that Negroes in Tuskegee, Alabama, were shut out of the city government even when they constituted close to forty-five percent of the registered voters of the community, Keech (p. 94) concludes that "the vote failed the Negro in Tuskegee when it was most needed."

65. See, for example, *The Houston Chronicle*, March 21, 1971, Sec. 4, p. 1.

66. But it should not be forgotten that a significant number of Mexican Americans do not identify with the Chicano movement, its goals, or its tactics.

67. This and the following quotation are from Mexican residents of Crystal City.

68. In an attempt to prevent the possibility of Del Monte leaving the community, one Raza Unida leader indicated that steps had been made to launch a nationwide boycott of Del Monte products should Del Monte leave the community.

69. Leroy Aarons, in his *Washington Post* article "The Chicanos Want In," has maintained that Gutiérrez was forced to tone down his rhetoric because of the reaction from various national foundations.

70. It should not be forgotten that some of La Raza Unida's most bitter struggles were with other Mexican Americans. This became all the more true as the years passed and Anglos realized that their own political opposition could be counterproductive. Ted Muñoz, a prominent Mexican American who had fought and run against La Raza Unida, was quoted as saying of La Raza Unida, "They've actually increased discrimination here. They not only discriminate against Anglos, but they have turned Mexicans against each other. They attack those of us who don't agree with them and pressure our friends into turning against us." (*The Los Angeles Times*, September 3, 1972.)

71. From a speech by José Angel Gutiérrez at the University of Wisconsin (Madison, Wisconsin, May, 1971), attended by the author.

bibliography

books

Acuña, Rudy. *Occupied America: The Chicano Struggle for Liberation.* San Francisco: Canfield Press, 1972.

Browning, Harley, and McLemore, Dale. *A Statistical Profile of the Spanish-Surname Population of Texas.* Austin: Bureau of Business Research, University of Texas, 1964.

Carter, Thomas. *Mexican-Americans in School: A History of Educational Neglect.* New York: College Entrance Examination Board, 1970.

Dahl, Robert. *Who Governs?* New Haven: Yale University Press, 1961.

Galarza, Ernesto; Gallegos, Herman; and Samora, Julian. *Mexican-Americans in the Southwest.* Santa Barbara: McNally and Loftin, 1969.

Keech, William. *The Impact of Negro Voting.* Chicago: Rand McNally, 1968.

Key, V. O. *Southern Politics.* New York: Random House, 1949.

Kornhauser, William. *The Politics of Mass Society.* Glencoe, Ill.: The Free Press, 1959.

Kuper, Leo, and Smith, M. G. *Pluralism in Africa.* Berkeley: University of California Press, 1969.

Lipset, Seymour Martin. *Political Man.* Garden City, N.Y.: Doubleday, 1960.

Taylor, Paul. *An American-Mexican Frontier.* Durham, N.C.: Duke University Press, 1934.

————. *Mexican Labor in the United States, Dimmit County, Winter Garden District, South Texas.* Vol. VI, No. 5. Berkeley: University of California Press, 1930.

U.S. Department of Commerce. Economic Development Administration. *Industrial Employment Potential of the United States-Mexico Border*, prepared by Robert R. Nathan Associates, Inc. Washington, D.C.: Government Printing Office, 1968.

U.S. Works Progress Administration. Federal Works Agency. *Mexican Migratory Workers of South Texas*, by Seldon Menefee. Washington, D.C.: Government Printing Office, 1941.

Wolf, Eric. *Peasant Wars of the Twentieth Century*. New York: Harper and Row, 1969.

Wolff, Robert Paul. *The Poverty of Liberalism*. Boston: Beacon Press, 1968.

Zeitlin, Maurice. *Revolutionary Politics and the Cuban Working Class*. Princeton: Princeton University Press, 1967.

articles

Alinsky, Saul. "A Professional Radical Moves in on Rochester." *Harper's Magazine*, 231 (July, 1965): 52-9.

—————. "The Professional Radical: Conversations with Saul Alinsky." *Harper's Magazine*, 230 (June, 1965): 37-47.

Brown, William E. "Crystal City: Symbol of Hope." *Labor Today*, 2 (December, 1963-January, 1964): 16-20.

"Crystal City: New Council Names Teamster Mayor." *The International Teamster*, May, 1963: 16-21.

Davies, James. "Toward a Theory of Revolution." *American Sociological Review*, 27, no. 1 (1962): 5-19.

Eckstein, Harry. "On the Etiology of Internal Wars." *History and Theory*, 4, no. 2 (1965): 133-63.

Fry, John. "Election Night in Crystal City." *Christianity and Crisis*, November 27, 1972: 253-57.

Gamson, William. "Stable Unrepresentation in American Society." *American Behavorial Scientist*, 12 (November/December, 1969): 15-20.

Goodwyn, Larry. "Los Cinco Candidatos." *The Texas Observer*. April 18, 1963: 3-9.

Hansen, Niles, and Gruben, William. "The Influence of Relative Wages and Assisted Migration on Locational Preferences: Mexican Americans in South Texas." *Social Science Quarterly*, 52, no. 1 (June, 1971).

La Raza Unida Party in Texas. Articles and speeches by Antonio Camejo, Mario Compean, and José Angel Gutiérrez. New York: Pathfinder Press, 1970.

Martínez, John. "Leadership and Politics." *La Raza: Forgotten Americans*. Edited by Julian Samora. Notre Dame, Ind.: University of Notre Dame Press, 1966.

Moore, Joan. "Colonialism: The Case of the Mexican-Americans." *Social Problems*, 17, no. 4 (1970): 463-72.

—————. Alfredo Cuellar, "Perspective on Politics," in *Mexican Americans*. Englewood Cliffs, N.J.: Prentice-Hall, 1970.

Parenti, Michael. "Power and Pluralism: A View from the Bottom." *Journal of Politics*, August, 1970: 501-30.

"Side by Side—And a World Apart—In Uvalde, Texas." *Newsweek*, June 29, 1970, p. 24.
Tirado, Miguel. "Mexican American Community Political Organization." *Aztlan: Chicano Journal of the Social Sciences and the Arts*, 1, no. 1 (1970): 53-78.
Trillin, Calvin. "U.S. Journal: Crystal City, Texas." *The New Yorker*, April 17, 1971: 102-7.
"Una Revolución de Mexicanos en el Sur de Texas." *Mañana*, September 14, 1963: 20-33.
U.S. Congress. Speeches and Inserts by Henry Gonzáles. *The Congressional Record*, April 3, 1969: 8590-2; and April 16, 1969, p. 9309.
Watson, James, and Samora, Julian. "Subordinate Leadership in a Bicultural Community: An Analysis." *American Sociological Review*, 19 (1954): 413-21.
Weeks, O. Douglas. "The Texas-Mexicans and the Politics of South Texas." *American Political Science Review*, 24, no. 3 (1930): 606-27.
Wilson, James Q. "The Strategy of Protest: Problems of Negro Civic Action." *Journal of Conflict Resolution*, 5 (1961): 291-303.

newspaper sources

Aarons, Leroy. "The Chicanos Want In." *The Washington Post*, January 11, 1970, Outlook Section. Reprinted in *The San Antonio News and Express*, January 11, 1970, p. 1.
Alamo Messenger (San Antonio, Texas). January 2, 1970; January 9, 1970.
Beene, Richard. Three-part article on Crystal City. *The Del Rio Herald-News*, July 19, 20, and 21, 1972.
Dallas Morning News. April-May, 1963.
Del Olmo, Frank. "Texas Chicanos Take Over 'Model City' as Power Base." *The Los Angeles Times*, September 3, 1972, p. 1.
Greider, William, of the *Washington Post* staff. "Impetuous MAYO Militants Alarming to Rep. Gonzalez." Reprinted in *The San Antonio Express*, June 6, 1969.
————. "Cotulla Mayor Raps Town, Schools." Reprinted in *The San Antonio Express*, August 20, 1970, p. 18-A.
Hill, Gladwin. "Crystal City, Texas Tests Mexican-Americans' Political Role." *The New York Times*, September 21, 1963, p. 17.
Houston Chronicle. February 25, 1965, Section 3, p. 8.
La Roche, Clarence. "Crystal City Shows Progress." *The San Antonio Light*, August 3, 1963.
San Antonio Express. April-May, 1963; December, 1969-January, 1970; May 10, 1970; September, 1970; July 11, 1971.
San Antonio Light. December, 1969-January, 1970.
La Verdad (Crystal City, Texas). Issues from 1969-1973.
Zavala County Sentinel. Mid-Century Edition, November 1, 1957. Issues from 1960-1973.

unpublished materials

Appleton, Rick. "The Crystal City School Boycott." Unpublished paper, University of Texas, 1970.

Chandler, Charles. "The Mexican-American Protest Movement in Texas." Ph. D. dissertation, Tulane University, 1968.

Conoley, Gilbert, and Ibarra, Juan. "Inter-Office Memorandum." Memorandum, December 22, 1969.

Cuellar, Robert. "A Social and Political History of the Mexican-American Population of Texas, 1929-1963." M.A. thesis, North Texas State University, 1969.

Earl, Carol. "Crystal City, 1965: The Aftermath." Unpublished paper, University of Texas, 1965.

Foley, Douglas, and Smith, Walter. "Selected References Pertinent to Chicano and Black Citizens of Cristal." Mimeographed paper, University of Texas at Austin, 1972.

Good Neighbor Commission of Texas. *Texas Migrant Labor, Annual Report, 1969.* Austin, Texas, 1969.

Gutiérrez, José Angel. "Aztlán: Chicano Revolt in the Winter Garden Area." Unpublished paper, Crystal City, 1970.

—————. "The Empirical Conditions for Revolution in Four South Texas Counties." M.A. thesis, Saint Mary's University, 1969.

—————. "Fact or Fiction?" Mimeographed pamphlet, Crystal City, Texas, 1964.

—————. Interview with Professors Lyle Brown and Thomas Charlton of the Baylor University Oral History Project, July 8-9, 1971. Baylor University Archives, Waco, Texas.

Holdsworth, Ernest. "A History of Zavala County." Mimeographed article, Crystal City, Texas, date unknown.

Loyall, Jack. "Remarks Made by Captain J. A. Loyall to the Uvalde Rotary Club." Mimeographed paper, Crystal City, Texas, September 16, 1963.

Miller, Mike. "Political Conflict in a Bifurcated Community: Anglo-Chicano Relations in a Small Texas Town." Mimeographed paper, Texas A & M University, 1971.

Newcomer, Kenneth. "A Progress Report on the Churchmen's Committee of Crystal City, Texas." Mimeographed paper, Crystal City, 1970.

Pridgen, William McKinley. "A Survey and Proposed Plan of Reorganization of the Public Schools in Zavala County." M.A. thesis, University of Texas, 1939.

Simmons, Ozzie. "Anglo-Americans and Mexican-Americans in South Texas: A Study in Dominant-Subordinate Group Relations." Ph.D. dissertation, Harvard University, 1952.

Tate, R. C. "History of Zavala County, Texas." M.A. thesis, Southwest Texas State University, 1942.

Tiller, James Weeks. "Some Economic Aspects of Commercial Cool Season Vegetable Production in the Texas Winter Garden." Ph.D. dissertation, University of Oklahoma, 1969.

United States Commission on Civil Rights. "Issue Presentation for Educa-

tion Conference." Mimeographed paper, Crystal City, Texas, March 7, 1970.
United States Department of Commerce. Bureau of the Census. "Special Table PH-6" for Zavala County, Texas, 1960. Unpublished table.
Urban Renewal Staff of Crystal City. "Application to the Department of Health, Education, and Welfare for Model Cities Funds." Crystal City, Texas, 1967.
Ziller, John. "Field Research in Crystal City." Unpublished paper, University of Texas, 1970.

interviews: outside crystal city

Caldwell, Chuck. Administrative Aide to Senator Ralph Yarborough. Austin, Texas, December 3, 1970.
Conoley, Gilbert. Official of the Texas Education Agency. Austin, Texas, November 3, 1970.
Cortés, Ernie. Mexican-American Unity Council. San Antonio, Texas, Fall and Winter, 1970-1971.
Cotera, Juan. Newly-Appointed Urban Renewal Director for Crystal City. Austin, Texas, January, 1971.
Cruz, Josué. Graduate Student in Educational Administration at the University of Wisconsin. Madison, Wisconsin, Spring, 1971.
Emanuel, Victor. Graduate Student in Government at Harvard University. Austin, Texas, Winter and Spring, 1971.
Gámez, Jesse. Attorney. San Antonio, Texas, January 20, 1971.
García, Franklin. Meat-Cutters Union. San Antonio, Texas, January, 1971.
Garza, David. Professor of Government, University of Texas. Austin, Texas, Fall, 1970.
Giletson, Jack. General Land Office of the State of Texas. Austin, Texas, January, 1971.
Gochman, Arthur. Attorney and Former City Attorney of Crystal City. San Antonio, Texas, December 4, 1970.
Guerrero, Andre. Southwest Educational Development Lab. Austin, Texas, January, 1971.
Harp, Reed. Former Resident of Crystal City. Austin, Texas, November 20, 1970.
Havens, Murray. Professor of Government, University of Texas. Austin, Texas, Fall and Winter, 1970-1971.
Lara-Braud, Jorge. Hispanic-American Institute. Austin, Texas, Fall and Winter, 1970-1971.
López, Arnold. Former Resident and Minister in Crystal City, San Antonio, Texas, November 20, 1970.
Loveless, Mr. and Mrs. Marvin. Former Residents of Crystal City. Denton, Texas. October, 1970.
McCleskey, Clifton. Professor of Government, University of Texas. Austin, Texas, April, 1970, and Winter, 1971.

Marshall, Ray. Professor of Economics, University of Texas. Austin, Texas, December, 1970.
Miller, Mike. Graduate Student in Rural Sociology at Texas A & M University. Fall and Winter, 1970-1971.
Moore, Carlos. Teamsters Union Official. Fort Worth, Texas, February 25, 1971.
Muñoz, Henry. Labor Official. San Antonio, Texas, December 5, 1970.
Obledo, Mario. Mexican-American Legal Defense Fund. San Antonio, Texas, October, 1970.
Official, Texas Educational Desegregation Technical Assistance Center. Austin, Texas, January, 1971.
Ozuna, George. Engineer, Former City Manager of Crystal City. San Antonio, Texas, Fall and Winter, 1970-1971.
Patlán, Juan. Mexican-American Youth Organization, Mexican-American Unity Council. San Antonio, Texas, February, 1971.
Peña, Albert. Bexar County Commissioner. San Antonio, Texas, October 29, 1970.
Ragsdale, Crystal. Former Resident of Winter Garden Area. Austin, Texas, Fall, 1970.
Salter, Bill. *San Antonio Express* Newsman. San Antonio, Texas, October 29, 1970.
Shafer, Ray. President and Business Manager, Teamsters Union. San Antonio, Texas, November 6, 1970.
Shapiro, David. Former Assistant to City Manager George Ozuna. Austin, Texas, October, 1970.
Taylor, Joe. Southwestern University Student from Crystal City. Georgetown, Texas, November 3, 1970.
Williams, Reverend Prescott. Austin Presbyterian Seminary. Austin, Texas, November, 1970.
Ziller, John. Student at the University of Texas and Saint Mary's University. Austin, Texas, January, 1971.
NOTE: Several people are not included here because they did not wish their identity revealed.

interviews: crystal city

Anderson, Sam. Director, Urban Renewal Program. November 11, 1970.
Andrade, Erasmo. Director, Title IV Program, Crystal City Schools. November 12, 1970.
Barker, Dale. Editor, *The Zavala County Sentinel.* November 9, 1970.
Benavides, Frank. Councilman, Mayor, Crystal City. December 10,1970.
Benavides, Irma. Secretary, Crystal City Schools. February 10, 1971.
Blanco, Sam. Minister, Swindall Methodist Church. February 8, 1971.
Briggs, John. Former Superintendent, Crystal City Schools. Fall and Winter, 1970-1971.
Broadhurst, June. Former City Clerk. November 10, 1970.
Brook, Gilbert. Manager, Del Monte Foods. February 11, 1971.

Cornejo, Juan. Former Mayor. December 11, 1970.

Gonzales, Angel. Superintendent, Crystal City Schools. November 11, 1970.

Gonzales, Ventura. Councilman, Crystal City. February 10, 1971.

Gutiérrez, José Angel. President, Crystal City School Board, Founder of La Raza Unida Party. Fall, Winter, Spring, 1970-1971.

Hamilton, Wayne. School-Board Member. February 10, 1971.

Holdsworth, John. Resident and Meterologist. Fall and Winter, 1970-1971.

Kone, Minda. Counselor, Crystal City Schools. December 9, 1970.

Leonard, Bill. Former City Councilman. December 10, 1970.

Maldonado, Jesús. Former School-Board Candidate. December 7, 1970.

Mata, Paul. Schoolteacher and Former Mayor, Crystal City. December 11, 1970.

Muñoz, E. C. Former School-Board Candidate. February 12, 1971.

Palacios, Diana. Crystal City High-School Cheerleader. February 10, 1971.

Palacios, Enriqueta. La Raza Unida Activist, Former Member of PASO. February 10, 1971.

Peña, Moses. Pharmacist. December 6, 1970.

Price, Georgia. County Clerk. December, 1970.

Richey, Bill. Former City Manager. Fall and Winter, 1970-1971.

Rodríguez, Fidel. Former Official, Urban Renewal Agency. February 11, 1971.

Santiago, Viviana. Robert F. Kennedy Foundation Fellow. February 12, 1971.

Stauber, Dr. and Mrs. Robert. Medical Doctor. Fall and Winter, 1970-1971.

Tate, R. C. Former School Superintendent. December 7, 1970.

Treviño, Eddie. School-Board Member. December 6, 1970.

Treviño, Mario and Blanca. Students, Crystal City High School. December 5, 1970.

NOTE: In addition, several people are not included here because they did not wish to be identified.

index